Praise for *Accounts Demystified*

'An excellent primer on accounting, this book explains in simple language how to understand balance sheets, profit and loss accounts and cash flow statements. It also has useful chapters covering important subjects like return on capital employed, gearing and book values.'

Jim Slater, investment guru and best-selling author of The Zulu Principle

'I didn't think a book like this could be compulsive reading, but after the first section on balance sheets, the lights truly started to go on. I can't tell you how refreshing it is to read a book on this type of subject that doesn't assume you are George Soros. Thanks a lot; you've really helped me. I have to go finish the book now.'

Tim Peppiatt, Chief Executive, Paperhat Group

'Trust me – no other book makes the subject as simple and clear.'

Jamie Reeve, Chairman, The Great Little Trading Company

'It's like a fog has been lifted ... I suddenly get it and I'm only at page ten.'

Paul Sanett, Development Director, Europe and Africa, Hilton Worldwide

'This is a great book – it does what it says on the can!'

John Bates, Fellow of Strategy and Entrepreneurship, London Business School

'Accounts Demystified is compulsory reading. It has ensured that all of our non-financially trained managers have a common understanding and language.'

Mike Squires, Chairman, Sports Recruitment International

'If making the complex simple is genius, then that is what this book is! It's all you need for sight reading accounts.'

Matthew Peacock, Managing Partner, Hanover Investors

ACCOUNTS DEMYSTIFIED

Accounts
Demystified

The astonishingly simple guide to accounting

Seventh edition

Anthony Rice

PEARSON

Harlow, England • London • New York • Boston • San Francisco • Toronto • Sydney • Auckland • Singapore • Hong Kong
Tokyo • Seoul • Taipei • New Delhi • Cape Town • São Paulo • Mexico City • Madrid • Amsterdam • Munich • Paris • Milan

PEARSON EDUCATION LIMITED
Edinburgh Gate
Harlow CM20 2JE
Tel: +44 (0)1279 623623
Fax: +44 (0)1279 431059
Web: www.pearson.com/uk

First edition published in 1993 (print)
Fifth edition published in 2008 (print and electronic)
Sixth edition published in 2011 (print and electronic)
Seventh edition published 2015 (print and electronic)

ISBN: 978-1-292-08484-8 (print)
   978-1-292-08486-2 (PDF)
   978-1-292-08485-5 (eText)
   978-1-292-08487-9 (ePub)

British Library Cataloguing-in-Publication Data
A catalogue record for this book is available from the British Library

Library of Congress Cataloging-in-Publication Data
Rice, Anthony, author.
Accounts demystified: the astonishingly simple guide to accounting / Anthony Rice. — Seventh edition.
pages cm
Includes index.
ISBN 978-1-292-08484-8
1. Accounting. 2. Corporations—Accounting. 3. Corporations—Great Britain—Accounting. 4. Financial statements. I. Title.
HF5636.R53 2015
657--dc23
2015024607

10 9 8 7 6 5 4 3 2
19 18 17 16 15

Print edition typeset in 9.5pt ITC Giovanni by 71
Printed by Ashford Colour Press Ltd, Gosport

NOTE THAT ANY PAGE CROSS-REFERENCES REFER TO THE PRINT EDITION

This book is dedicated to Charlotte

Contents

About the author

Anthony Rice is not an accountant. He learned accounting the hard way – by keeping the accounts for his own company. It wasn't until the fifth consecutive weekend in the office struggling with the accounting system that he realised, quite suddenly, how simple it all is. From that day, accounting lost its mystery.

Over the next couple of years, he also found that, by focusing on the balance sheet and using diagrams, he could quickly demystify fellow sufferers. Having subsequently spent much of his time analysing companies, first as a strategy consultant and more recently when looking at investment opportunities, he also has some valuable insights into financial analysis.

Preface

A glance at the accounts of most of Britain's larger companies could lead you to conclude that accounting is a very complex and technical subject.

While it can be both of these things, accounting is actually based on an incredibly simple principle that was devised more than 500 years ago and has remained unchanged ever since. The apparent complexity of many companies' accounts results from the rules and terminology that have developed around this fundamental principle to accommodate modern business practices.

I believe that, once you really understand the fundamental principle and how it is applied, you will find that most of the rules and terminology follow logically and easily. This view determines the arrangement of the chapters in *Accounts Demystified* and it is important, therefore, to read them chronologically. You can, however, skip much of Chapter 5, which is primarily for readers who want to actually keep their own accounts. You should, however, read the sections on VAT (if you have any doubt about how VAT works) and the sections from Accrued expenses to Deferred expenses inclusive (pages 82 to 85).

May I also suggest that, before you reach Chapter 6, you photocopy the key parts of Wingate Foods' accounts (pages 271 to 279). From Chapter 6 onwards, the text refers to these pages frequently and you will find it much easier with copies in front of you. You may want to do the same with Listco's accounts (pages 280 to 286) when you get to Chapter 11.

Alternatively, go to **www.accountsdemystified.com**, from where you can print these pages directly. The website also features, among other things, a step-by-step presentation of Chapter 2, an interactive quiz and somewhat more detailed explanations of some of the subjects covered in the book – the availability of which is indicated in the book by this icon:

WWW

If you have any comments or questions, you are very welcome to post them in the forum on the website or email me at **ar@accountsdemystified.com**.

Anthony Rice

Acknowledgements

A number of people have contributed to this book since it was first published more than 20 years ago.

I am especially grateful to Jonathan Munday and Alex Macpherson of accountants Rees Pollock. Jonathan and Alex have reviewed the last several editions of the book in detail and Alex in particular has helped to update this edition with the chapters on listed company accounts. In some cases, I have decided to live with technical errors and omissions in the interests of clarity and/or brevity. For such decisions I am solely responsible.

I would also like to thank the following who volunteered to read the very first edition of this book and all of whom made valuable comments and suggestions: Michael Gaston, Debbie Hastings-Henry, Steve Holt, Alex Johnstone, Keith Murray, Jamie Reeve, Brian Rice, Clive Richardson, David Tredrea, Martin Whittle and Charlie Wrench.

Anthony Rice

Prologue

Sarah

Sarah is the owner and sole employee of a company called Silk Bloomers Limited (known as SBL). Just over a year ago, she went on a business trip to the Far East where, by chance, she came across a company producing silk plants and flowers of unusual quality. On her return to the UK she immediately quit her job and set up SBL (with £10,000 of her own money) to import and distribute these silk plants.

Sarah is a natural entrepreneur and the prospects for her business look extremely good. However, her company has just finished its first year and she has to produce the annual accounts. She has kept good records of all the transactions the company made during the year and has subscribed to a cloud-based accounting system. She's been looking at the system and has worked out some of the things she's meant to *do* but she doesn't *understand* what she's doing or how it will all get translated into a set of accounts, which makes her very uncomfortable.

Tom

Tom has two problems.

The first relates to his employer, Wingate Foods, where he is sales manager. Wingate manufactures confectionery and chocolate biscuits, mostly for the big supermarkets to sell under their own names. Four years ago, the company appointed a new managing director who immediately embarked on an aggressive expansion programme.

Tom's concern is that the managing director seems to want to win orders at almost any cost. Simultaneously, the company is spending a lot of money on new offices and machinery. The managing director is brimming with confidence and continually refers to the steady rise in sales, profits and dividends. Nonetheless, Tom has the nagging suspicion that something is badly wrong. He just can't put his finger on it.

Tom's other 'problem' is that he has some spare cash, which is currently on deposit at the bank. Tom doesn't have Sarah's entrepreneurial spirit and there's no chance of him risking his money on starting a business. He feels, though, that he should perhaps risk a small amount on the stock market. He has been given a couple of 'tips' but would like to check them out for himself.

Tom has therefore decided it is time to learn how to read company accounts so he can form his own opinion of both Wingate and his prospective investments.

Chris

Chris is a financial journalist for a national newspaper who, although not an accountant, can read and analyse company accounts with confidence.

This was not always the case. Chris used to be one of the thousands of people who understand a profit and loss account but find the balance sheet a total mystery. A few years ago, however, a friend explained the fundamental principle of accounting to him and showed him how everything else follows logically from it. Within hours, his understanding of balance sheets and everything else to do with company accounts was transformed.

Recently, Tom and Sarah mentioned their respective accounting problems to Chris. Chris began enthusing about the approach he had been taught and how easy it all was once you really understood the basics. Sarah, never one to miss an opportunity, immediately demanded that Chris should give up his weekend to share the 'secret' with Tom and herself.

Introduction

Wingate's annual report

OK, before we do anything, I think we should have a quick look at Wingate's most recent **annual report and accounts** (which is what we really mean by the phrase 'annual report'). We are going to be referring to this a lot and I think you'll find it helpful to get to know your way around it now. It will also give you an idea of what we're trying to achieve. By the end of this weekend, you should not only understand everything in this annual report, you should also be able to analyse it in detail.

The other thing I should do is give you a brief outline of how I plan to structure the weekend in order to achieve that objective. After that, we might as well go straight into the first session.

Wingate's annual report for year five [reproduced on pages 265 to 279] is a somewhat simplified but otherwise typical annual report for a small to medium-sized private company. As you can see, it consists of eight items:

- ▶ Strategic report
- ▶ Directors' report
- ▶ Auditors' report
- ▶ Profit & loss account
- ▶ Balance sheet
- ▶ Cash flow statement
- ▶ Net debt statement
- ▶ Notes to the accounts

The **strategic report** is an overview by the directors of the company, its business and performance. As such, it should be interesting and worth reading before getting stuck into the numbers.

The **directors' report** and the **auditors' report** often don't tell us a great deal, but it is important to read these reports – we will see why later.

The **profit & loss account** (the 'P&L', for short), the **balance sheet** and the **cash flow statement** are the real heart of an annual report. Everything we're going to talk about is really geared towards helping you to understand and analyse these three 'statements'.

The **net debt statement** is just a useful addendum to the cash flow statement. The **notes to the accounts** are a lot more than just footnotes. They contain many extremely valuable details which supplement the information in the three main statements. You can't do any meaningful analysis of a company without them.

You do realise, Chris, that I hardly understand a word of what I'm looking at here?

Structure outline

That's fine. I'm going to assume you know absolutely nothing and take it very slowly. What we're going to do is to break the weekend up into 12 separate sessions which fall into three distinct parts:

1. The basics of accounting
2. Interpretation and analysis of accounts
3. Listed company accounts

1 The basics of accounting

The basics will take up our first five sessions.

- ▶ In the **first session**, I will explain what a balance sheet is and how it relates to the fundamental principle of accounting.
- ▶ **Session 2** will be spent actually drawing up the balance sheet for your company, Sarah. I know you're not interested in creating accounts, Tom, but this session is important to understanding how the fundamental principle is applied.
- ▶ In **session 3**, I will explain, briefly as it's very straightforward, what a P&L and cash flow statement are and how they are related to the balance sheet.
- ▶ Then in **session 4**, we will actually draw up the P&L and cash flow statement for SBL.
- ▶ Finally, in **session 5**, we'll talk a bit about how the accounting is done in practice.

Why are you starting with the balance sheet, Chris? In Wingate's annual report, the P&L comes first and that's the bit I vaguely understand. Shouldn't we start there?

No, we should not. The balance sheet really ought to come before the P&L; you'll see why later.

2 Interpretation and analysis of accounts

At the end of **session 5**, you should understand the basics of accounting and you may well find that you can look at Wingate's accounts and understand a lot of what's in there.

To be sure we've covered everything, though, in **session 6**, we will work our way through Wingate's accounts, after which I hope you will really feel like you know what's going on.

However, it's all very well to know what a company's accounts mean, but it doesn't actually give you any *insight* into the company. That's why you have to know how to *analyse* accounts. I will start, in **session 7**, by introducing the whole subject of financial analysis to make sure we are all clear about what companies are trying to achieve and explain how, for the purposes of analysis, we separate a company into two components – the 'enterprise' and the 'funding structure'.

In **sessions 8 and 9** respectively we will then analyse the enterprise and the funding structure of Wingate Foods.

Up to this point, all our analysis will have been about understanding the financial performance of companies. We will not have related any of it to the value of the company, which is what potential investors are interested in. I do not plan to go into detailed investment analysis but I will, in **session 10**, explain how most investors relate the performance of a company to its valuation.

3 Listed company accounts

Hopefully, by the time we are done with all of that, you will feel like going off to put some of this stuff in to practice. Before you do, though, or at least before you go off to start looking at the accounts of these stock market companies you want to invest in, Tom, there are some things you need to know about their accounts that we won't have encountered with Wingate.

► In **session 11**, I will introduce you to listed company accounts. (I use 'listed' to mean a company whose shares are available to buy and sell on a stock market.)

► In **session 12**, we will talk, in simple terms, about some of the most common things you will see in listed companies' accounts that didn't come up with Wingate.

After that, you're on your own, although don't forget I've got a website with more detailed explanations of a lot of what we're going to talk about.

PART 1

The basics of accounting

CHAPTER ONE

The balance sheet and the fundamental principle

- ▶ Assets, liabilities and balance sheets
- ▶ Sarah's 'personal' balance sheet
- ▶ The balance sheet of a company
- ▶ The balance sheet chart
- ▶ Summary

What I'm going to do first is explain what assets and liabilities are, which may seem trivial but it's important there are no misunderstandings. Next, I will explain what a balance sheet is and show you how to draw up your own personal balance sheet. We will then relate this to a company's balance sheet.

At that point, I will, finally, explain what I mean by the fundamental principle of accounting and you will see that the balance sheet is just the principle put into practice. I will also show you how we can represent the balance sheet in chart form, which I think you will find a lot easier to handle than tables full of numbers.

Then we'll take a break before we actually set about building up SBL's balance sheet.

Assets, liabilities and balance sheets

Typically, individuals and companies both have assets and liabilities.

An **asset** can be one of two things. It is either:

- ▶ something you own; for example, money, land, buildings, goods, brand names, shares in other companies, etc., or

▶ something you are owed by someone else, i.e. something which is technically yours, but is currently in someone else's possession. More often than not, it's money you are owed, but it could be anything.

A **liability** is anything you owe to someone else and expect to have to hand over in due course. Liabilities are usually money, but they can be anything.

A **balance sheet** is just a table, listing all of someone's assets and liabilities, along with the value of each of those assets and liabilities at a particular point in time.

Sarah's 'personal' balance sheet

You can't say that's a difficult concept, can you? Let's see how it works by writing down on a single sheet of paper all Sarah's assets and liabilities. We will then have effectively drawn up her **personal balance sheet**. I think you'll find it pretty interesting [see Table 1.1].

The top part of this is fine, Chris. We've just got a simple list of all my main assets and their values. We've also got a list of the amounts that I owe to other people.

There are several things here, though, that I don't understand. Why are the liabilities in brackets and what do you mean by 'Net assets' – I'm never sure what people are talking about when they use the word 'net'.

'Net' just means the value of something after having deducted something else. The reason you're never sure what people mean is that they don't explain what it is they're deducting.

In this case, we add up all your assets, which total £113,500. These are your **gross assets**, although we usually leave out the 'gross' and just call them your 'assets'. We then deduct all your liabilities from these assets. The brackets are common notation in the accounting world to indicate negative numbers, because minus signs can be mistaken for dashes. Your liabilities total £62,500 so when we deduct this figure from your gross assets we are left with £51,000. These are your **net assets**.

Your net assets are what you would have left if you sold all your assets for the amounts shown and paid off all your liabilities. In other words, your net assets are what you are worth.

Table 1.1 Sarah's personal balance sheet

SARAH'S PERSONAL BALANCE SHEET		
As at today		
	£	£
Assets		
House/contents	100,000	
Investment in SBL	10,000	
Pension scheme	2,000	
Jewellery	1,000	
Loan to brother	500	
Total		113,500
Liabilities		
Mortgage	(60,000)	
Credit card	(500)	
Overdraft at bank	(1,500)	
Phone bill outstanding	(500)	
Total		(62,500)
Net assets		**51,000**
Net worth		
Inheritance	30,000	
Savings	21,000	
Total		51,000

Note: Brackets are used to signify negative numbers.

OK, so we've listed my assets and liabilities and shown what the net value of them is. That seems to fit your description of a balance sheet. So what's this whole bit at the bottom headed 'Net worth'?

A fair question. My description of a balance sheet wasn't entirely accurate. As well as listing your assets and liabilities and showing that you are worth £51,000, your balance sheet also shows how you came to be worth that much.

So how could you have come to be worth £51,000? There are only two ways:

1. You could have been given some of your assets. In your case you inherited £30,000. This is effectively what you 'started' out in life with; you didn't have to earn it.

5

2. You could have saved some of your earnings since you first started work. I don't just mean savings in the form of cash in a bank account or under your bed. I also include savings in the form of any asset that you could sell and turn into cash, such as your house, jewellery, etc. In other words, your savings means all your earnings that you haven't spent on things like food, drink and holidays, which are gone for ever.

In your case, you have saved a total of £21,000 in your life so far. To emphasise the point, notice that your balance sheet does not show £21,000 in cash; your £21,000 savings are in the form of various assets.

Naturally, what you have been given plus what you have saved must be what you are worth today, i.e. it must equal your net assets. This is what we call the **balance sheet equation**:

$$\text{Net worth} = \text{Assets} - \text{Liabilities}$$
$$\text{(gross)}$$

Fine. That all seems pretty simple. What's it got to do with company accounts?

Everything. A company's balance sheet is exactly the same thing.

The balance sheet of a company

Let me just summarise Wingate's balance sheet for you and you'll see what I mean. A company can have all sorts of assets and liabilities which I'll come on to later (if you're still with me). For the moment, I'll group them into a few simple categories [see Table 1.2].

We're going to come across these categories a lot so you ought to know right away what they are:

▶ **Fixed assets** are any assets which a company uses on a long-term continuing basis (as opposed to assets which are bought to be sold on to customers); e.g. buildings, machinery, vehicles, computers.

▶ **Current assets** are assets you expect to sell or turn into cash within one year; e.g. stocks, amounts owed to you by customers.

▶ **Current liabilities** are liabilities that you expect to pay within the next year; e.g. amounts owed to suppliers.

Table 1.2 Wingate's summary balance sheet

WINGATE FOODS LTD		
Balance sheet at 31 December, year five		
		£'000
Assets		
Fixed assets	5,326	
Current assets	3,482	
Total assets		8,808
Liabilities		
Current liabilities	(2,906)	
Long-term liabilities	(3,055)	
Total liabilities		(5,961)
Net assets		**2,847**
Shareholders' equity		
Capital invested	325	
Retained profit	2,522	
Total shareholders' equity		2,847

▶ **Long-term liabilities** are liabilities you expect to have to pay, but not within the next year; e.g. loans from banks.

Just as we did for your personal balance sheet, Sarah, we can add up all the assets and deduct all the liabilities to get the company's net assets:

$$£8,808k - £5,961k = £2,847k$$

I use the letter 'k' to represent thousands, just as we use the letter 'm' to represent millions. So £8,808k is equivalent to £8,808,000 or £8.808m. It's a convenient shorthand, which I will use from now on.

Now look at the section labelled **shareholders' equity**. This is exactly the same as the section on your personal balance sheet labelled 'net worth' – it's just another phrase for it. As with your personal balance sheet, it shows how the net assets of the company were arrived at.

Capital invested is the amount of money put into the company by the shareholders (i.e. the owners). In other words, it is what the company 'starts with'. It is the equivalent of 'inheritance' on your personal balance sheet.

Although I say it's what the company 'starts with', I don't mean just money invested when the company first starts up. I include money invested by the shareholders at any time, in the same way as you might get an inheritance at any point in your life. The point is that it is money the company has not had to earn.

Retained profit is what the company has earned or 'saved'. A company sells products or services for which the customers pay. The company, of course, has to pay various **expenses** (to buy materials, pay staff, etc.).

Hopefully, what the company earns from its customers is more than the expenses and thus the company has made a profit.

The company then pays out *some* of these profits to the taxman and to the shareholders. What is left over is known as retained profit. This is equivalent to the 'savings' on your personal balance sheet.

When we said you had savings of £21,000, Sarah, I emphasised that this did not mean that you had £21,000 sitting in a bank account somewhere. Similarly, retained profit is very rarely all money; usually it is made up of all sorts of different assets.

So presumably your balance sheet equation applies in just the same way?

Yes, it looks like this:

$$\text{Shareholders' equity} = \text{Assets} - \text{Liabilities}$$
$$2{,}847 = 8{,}808 - 5{,}961$$

The balance sheet equation rearranged

So, if I understand you correctly, Chris, the net assets are what would be left over if all the assets were sold and the liabilities paid off. This amount would belong to the shareholders; hence the term 'shareholders' equity' which is just another phrase, really, for the net assets. Is that right?

Yes.

*So the company doesn't **ultimately** own anything. I mean, it's got all these assets, but if it sold them, it would have to pay off its liabilities and then give the rest of the proceeds to the shareholders.*

Yes, that's right. After all, a company is just a legal framework for a group of investors (i.e. the shareholders) to organise their investment. Ultimately, *people* own things, not companies. This way of looking at a company's balance sheet leads us to write the balance sheet equation slightly differently:

Assets	=	Shareholders' equity	+	Liabilities
8,808	=	2,847	+	5,961

This is what your maths teacher at school used to call 'rearranging the equation'. What it's saying is that the assets must add up exactly to the liabilities plus the shareholders' equity.

We can simplify the balance sheet equation even more if we want. As you just said, all the company's assets are effectively owed to someone, whether it be employees, suppliers, banks or shareholders. *Someone* has a claim over each and every one of the assets. Thus we can say that the assets must equal the **claims** on the assets:

$$\text{Assets} = \text{Claims}$$

This equation is the **fundamental principle of accounting**: at all times the assets of a company must equal the claims over those assets. As you can see, the balance sheet is just the principle put into practice. By the time we have finished, you will see how everything to do with company accounts hinges on this principle.

One of the benefits of looking at a balance sheet in this simple way is that we can display it as a chart, which will make it a lot easier to see what's going on when we start building up SBL's balance sheet.

The balance sheet chart

The **balance sheet chart** [Figure 1.1] consists of two **bars**, each of which consists of a number of **boxes**. These should be interpreted as follows:

▶ The height of each box is the value of the relevant asset or liability.

▶ The **assets bar** (the left-hand bar) has all the assets of the company stacked on top of one another. The height of the bar thus shows the total (i.e. gross) value of all the assets of the company.

> ▶ If you compare this chart with Wingate's summary balance sheet [Table 1.2] you will see that we have a fixed assets box with a height of £5,326k and a current assets box with a height of £3,482k. The height of the bar is £8,808k, which is the total value of all Wingate's assets.

> ▶ The **claims bar** (the right-hand bar) shows all the claims over the assets of the company. At the top we show the liabilities to third parties which the company must pay at some point. At the bottom we show the claims of the shareholders (the shareholders' equity) which the shareholders would get if all the assets were sold off.

Again, we can compare this bar to Wingate's summary balance sheet [page 7] and see how the heights of the boxes match the individual items. As you would expect, the height of the bar is the sum of the liabilities and the shareholders' equity.

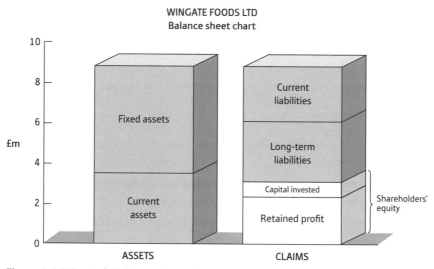

Figure 1.1 Wingate's balance sheet chart

The most important thing about this diagram is that the two bars are the same height. This must be true by definition of our balance sheet equation.

When a company is in business (i.e. 'trading'), all the different items that make up its balance sheet will be continually changing. On our balance sheet chart this means that both the heights of the bars and the heights of the boxes will change. Whatever happens, though, the height of the assets bar will *always* be the same as the height of the claims bar.

As you explain it here, Chris, I think I get it. In fact, it all looks fairly straightforward. I'm pretty sure, though, that I couldn't go away and draw up SBL's balance sheet on my own.

Maybe not, but in a couple of hours' time you will be able to, I promise. You'll be amazed how easy it is. Before we get on to that, though, let's just summarise what we've covered so far.

Summary

- An asset is something a company either owns or is owed by someone else.
- A liability is something a company owes to someone else.
- A company's balance sheet consists of two things:
  1. A list of the company's assets and liabilities, their value at a particular moment in time and therefore what the company's net assets are; this is the value 'due' to the shareholders.
  2. An explanation of how the net assets came to be what they are. There are only two ways:
     (a) The shareholders invested money in the company.
     (b) The company made a profit, a proportion of which it retained (rather than paying it out to the shareholders).
- Someone, either a third party or the shareholders, has a claim over each and every asset of the company.
- Thus, whatever happens, the assets must always equal the claims over the assets. This is the fundamental principle of accounting.

11

Creating a balance sheet

- ▶ Procedure for creating a balance sheet
- ▶ SBL's balance sheet
- ▶ The different forms of balance sheet
- ▶ Basic concepts of accounting
- ▶ Summary

Now you know what a balance sheet is and how to look at one as a chart, we're ready to set about actually creating one. First, I'll briefly describe the procedure and then we'll build up SBL's balance sheet step by step.

Procedure for creating a balance sheet

We create a balance sheet at a particular date by entering all the **transactions** the company has ever made up to that date and then making various adjustments:

- ▶ A transaction is anything that the company does which affects its financial position. This includes raising money from shareholders and banks, buying materials, paying staff, selling products, etc.
- ▶ Naturally, large companies make many thousands of transactions each year which is why they have computers and large accounts departments. The accounting principle, however, is exactly the same, whatever the size of the company.
- ▶ As you will see, even when we have entered all the transactions up to our balance sheet date, we need to make various adjustments if the balance sheet is going to reflect the true financial position of the company.

Bear in mind always that a balance sheet is only a snapshot at a particular moment – a few seconds later it will be different, even if only slightly.

SBL's balance sheet

SBL made well over a hundred transactions in its first year. Rather than go through every one of them, I have summarised them so we have a manageable number. I have also identified the three adjustments we need to make [Table 2.1].

Don't worry for the time being if you don't understand some of the things on this list – I will explain them as we go along.

What we are going to do is look at the effect each of these transactions and adjustments has on SBL's balance sheet. We will do this using the balance sheet chart as follows:

- ▶ We will draw one chart for each transaction or adjustment.
- ▶ Each chart will show two balance sheets – the balance sheet immediately before the transaction/adjustment and the balance sheet immediately after the transaction/adjustment.
- ▶ I will shade in the boxes that change due to each transaction or adjustment.

Table 2.1 Summary of SBL's first-year transactions and adjustments

SILK BLOOMERS LIMITED

First-year transactions and adjustments

1 Issue shares for £10,000.

2 Borrow £10,000 from Sarah's parents.

3 Buy a car for £9,000.

4 Buy £8,000 worth of stock (cash on delivery).

5 Buy £20,000 worth of stock on credit.

6 Sell £6,000 worth of stock for £12,000 cash.

7 Sell £12,000 worth of stock for £30,000 on credit.

8 Rent equipment and buy stationery for £2,000 on credit.

9 Pay car running costs of £4,000.

10 Pay interest on loan of £1,000.

11 Collect £15,000 cash from debtors.

12 Pay creditors £10,000.

13 Make a prepayment of £8,000 on account of stock.

14 Pay a dividend of £3,000.

15 Adjust for £2,000 of telephone expenses not yet billed.

16 Adjust for depreciation of fixed assets of £3,000.

17 Adjust for £4,000 expected tax liability.

[To see a step-by-step presentation of the accounting for these transactions, please go to **www.accountsdemystified.com**]

Transaction 1 – pay £10,000 cash into SBL's bank account as starting capital (share capital)

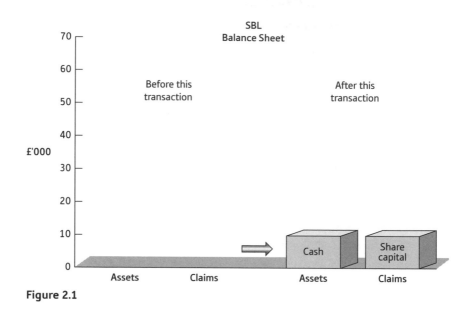

Figure 2.1

Before this transaction, SBL had no assets and therefore no claims over those (non-existent) assets.

The first thing Sarah did was to pay £10,000 of her own money into the company's bank account so that the company could commence operations. In return she received a certificate saying she owned 10,000 £1 shares in the company. Thus the company acknowledges that she has a claim over any net assets the company might have.

Since the company has no other assets or liabilities yet, the whole £10,000 must be 'owed' to the shareholders. Sarah, as the only shareholder, would claim it all.

To account for this transaction, we create a box on the assets bar called **cash** with a height of £10,000 and another box on the claims bar called **share capital**, also with a height of £10,000. This is SBL's balance sheet immediately after completion of this transaction.

Transaction 2 – SBL borrows £10,000 from Sarah's parents

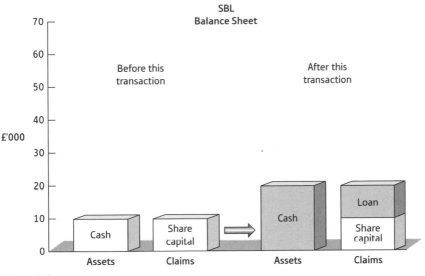

Figure 2.2

SBL needed more cash than Sarah could afford to invest herself, so she persuaded her parents to lend the company £10,000.

Immediately *before* this transaction, the balance sheet looks as it did immediately after the last transaction (with £10,000 of cash and £10,000 of share capital).

As a result of this transaction, the company has more cash in its bank account. Hence the cash box gets bigger by £10,000.

At the same time, however, a liability has been created. At some point the company will have to repay Sarah's parents the £10,000. They have said they will not ask for repayment for at least three years, so this is a **long-term loan**.

Notice two things:

▶ The two bars remain the same height.

▶ Sarah, as the shareholder, has not been made richer or poorer by this transaction – she still has a claim over £10,000 worth of the company's assets.

Transaction 3 – buy £9,000 of fixed assets (car)

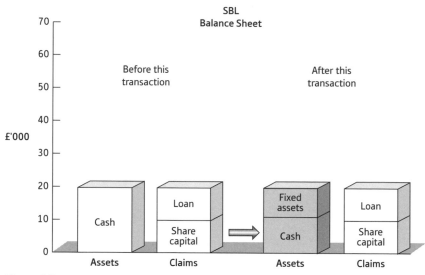

Figure 2.3

Before Sarah could start business, she needed a car to visit potential customers and deliver stock. This car cost SBL £9,000.

Since Sarah paid for the car in cash, the cash box must go down by £9,000. At the same time, SBL has acquired assets worth exactly £9,000. Hence, the company's total assets have not changed and the assets bar remains the same height.

No claim over the company's assets has been created or changed by this transaction, so the claims bar stays the same height as well. As always, the balance sheet remains in balance.

I didn't pay cash, actually, Chris; I paid with a cheque.

Yes, but, to an accountant, paying cash simply means paying at the time, as distinct from paying in, say, 30 days' time which many suppliers agree to. Paying by cheque or banker's draft means that the cash goes out of your bank account almost immediately, so we call that a cash payment.

Transaction 4 – buy £8,000 of stock (cash on delivery)

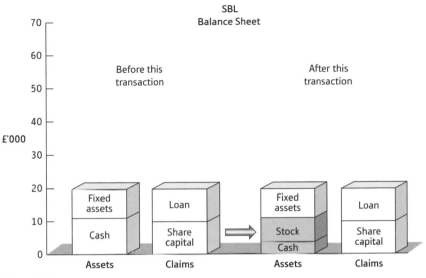

Figure 2.4

The first stock of silk flowers that Sarah bought had to be paid for at the time of purchase, as the supplier was nervous about SBL's ability to pay. This transaction is very similar to the previous one. The cash box goes down by another £8,000, but SBL has acquired another asset, stock, which is worth £8,000. Thus we create another box on the assets bar called stock with a height of £8,000. The bars therefore remain the same height.

Notice that we have made two entries on the balance sheet for every transaction so far. Obviously, if we change one box we must change another one to make the bars remain the same height.

If you have ever heard the term **double-entry book-keeping**, and wondered what it meant, you now know. It's exactly what we're doing when we change two boxes to enter a transaction. As you can see, there is nothing very difficult about it. The 'double entry' of transactions on a balance sheet is the way we apply the fundamental principle that the assets must always equal the claims.

Transaction 5 – buy £20,000 of stock (on credit)

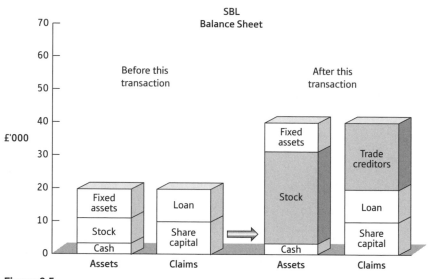

Figure 2.5

Sarah subsequently persuaded her supplier to agree that SBL need not pay until 60 days after delivery of the stock. This gave her time to sell some of the stock and get some cash into the company's bank account (otherwise she would not have had enough money to pay for the stock).

The stock bar therefore goes up by the amount of new stock (£20,000). This time, however, the cash box does not change. Instead, we have created a liability to the supplier. The supplier has a claim over some of the assets of the company. Liabilities to suppliers are called **trade creditors**. Thus we create a new box on the claims bar called trade creditors with a height of £20,000.

Notice that, despite the transactions to date, nothing has been done which has made Sarah, as the shareholder, richer or poorer. Her claim over the company's assets is still what she put in as share capital, i.e. £10,000.

Transaction 6 – sell £6,000 of stock for £12,000 (cash on delivery)

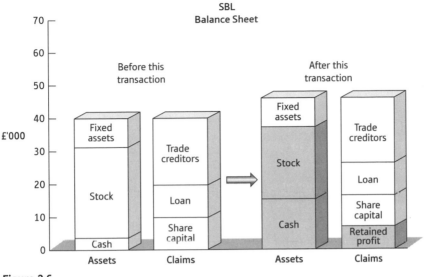

Figure 2.6

SBL sold, for £12,000 paid cash on delivery, stock which had only cost SBL £6,000. The £6,000 profit is not owed to anyone else, so it must belong to the shareholders. This, therefore, *is* a transaction which affects the shareholders' wealth.

The cash box goes up by £12,000 (since this is how much cash SBL received) and the stock box goes down by £6,000 (since this is the value of the stock sold). Hence the assets bar goes up by a net £6,000.

We create a new box on the claims bar called **retained profit** and give it a height of £6,000. This means the claims bar goes up by £6,000 and the balance sheet remains in balance.

You will remember that the claims of the shareholders ('shareholders' equity') are made up of the capital invested plus the retained profit. Shareholders' equity is therefore the £10,000 share capital Sarah put in plus the £6,000 retained profit from this transaction. SBL has done what companies exist to do: make their shareholders richer.

Transaction 7 – sell £12,000 of stock for £30,000 on credit

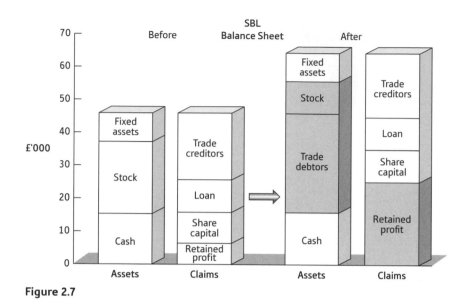

Figure 2.7

SBL subsequently sold £12,000 worth of stock for £30,000. The difference between this transaction and the last is that Sarah agreed that her customers need not pay immediately. Instead, she sent them invoices for later settlement.

In addition to the fundamental principle, there are two basic concepts that we apply when drawing up a set of accounts. One of these is known as the **accruals basis**. This means that any sales and purchases that a company makes are deemed to have taken place (i.e. are **recognised**) when the goods are handed over (or the services performed), not when the payment is made. Thus, as soon as SBL delivered the stock, we would say the sale had been made and enter it on the balance sheet, even though the customer had not yet paid.

I'm not sure I see why this matters, Chris.

It's a question of when we say the profit was made. It may be clearer with a simple example. Assume that on Monday you buy two tickets to a concert for £40. On Tuesday you sell them to a friend of yours for £50. You actually hand over the tickets to your friend on the Tuesday, but you agree that she need not pay you until Wednesday. On which of the three days would you say you had made the £10 profit?

Tuesday, I suppose.

Exactly, the day you handed over the goods. We use the same principle with companies to decide into which year the profit of a particular transaction goes.

Let's get back to SBL and see how we enter this transaction. We have to create a new box on the assets bar which we call **trade debtors**. This is what SBL is owed by the customers, so the box has a height of £30,000. The stock box must go down by £12,000, since this is the amount of stock that has been sold. The net impact is that the assets bar has gone up by £18,000, which is the profit on the transaction.

This £18,000 of profit (or extra assets) belongs to the shareholders, not to anyone else. Hence we increase retained profit by £18,000 and the two bars balance again.

Transaction 8 – rent equipment and buy stationery for £2,000 on credit

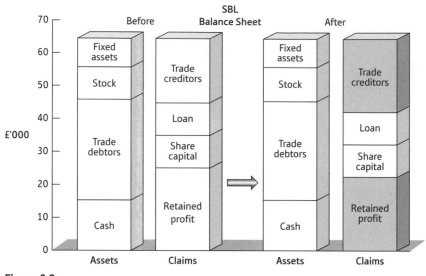

Figure 2.8

Sarah decided to rent the office equipment (word processor, fax, etc.) that she needed. She got all these things, as well as stationery, etc. from a friend in the office supply business, who sent her a bill for £2,000 but agreed she could pay whenever she could afford it.

Since SBL didn't pay at the time of the transaction, its liabilities must have gone up by £2,000. Thus we increase the height of the trade creditors box by £2,000.

What, though, is the other balance sheet entry? We haven't actually bought the equipment so we can't call it a fixed asset and the stationery is more or less used up during the year.

These items are what we call the expenses of running the business. They reduce the profits made by selling stock and thus reduce the shareholders' wealth.

Our 'double entry' is therefore to reduce the retained profit box by £2,000, which makes our bars balance again.

Transaction 9 – pay car running costs of £4,000 in cash

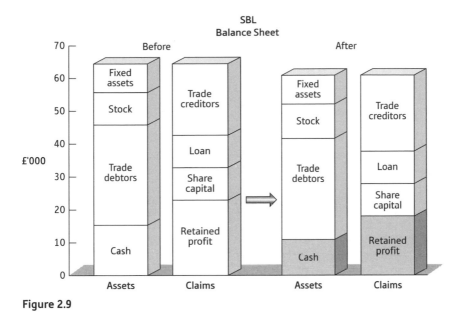

Figure 2.9

Sarah had to pay for petrol, servicing, etc. on the car. These were all paid in cash.

Clearly, as a result of this transaction, the cash box must go down by £4,000. This money is gone for ever. This transaction therefore represents another expense of the business. Consequently, the shareholders are poorer and we reduce retained profit by £4,000.

Transaction 10 – pay £1,000 interest on long-term loan

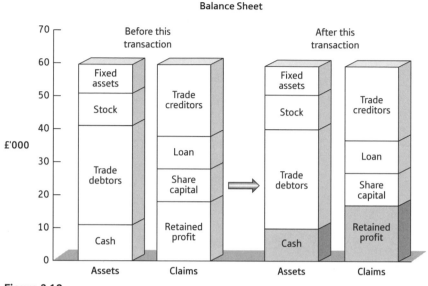

Figure 2.10

Sarah's parents generously said they would not ask SBL to repay their loan for at least three years. They do, however, want some **interest**. Sarah agreed that SBL would pay them 10 per cent per year. Thus SBL paid £1,000 in interest at the end of the year.

This was paid in cash so the cash box goes down again by £1,000, and once again it is the poor old shareholder who suffers: retained profit goes down by £1,000.

Transaction 11 – collect £15,000 cash from debtors

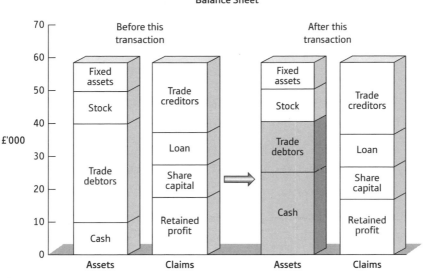

Figure 2.11

As we have already seen, in the course of the year, Sarah sold stock for £30,000 to be paid for at a later date. We accounted for this in Transaction 7. Later in the year, she actually collected £15,000 of the £30,000 owed by her customers.

The entries for this transaction are very straightforward. The cash box goes up by £15,000 and the trade debtors box down by £15,000.

Notice that retained profit is not affected by this transaction. We recognised the profit on the sale of these goods when the goods were delivered (Transaction 7). In this transaction we have merely collected some of the cash from that transaction.

Transaction 12 – pay £10,000 cash to creditors

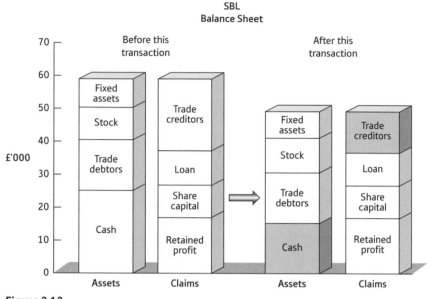

Figure 2.12

In the same way that Sarah sold stock on credit, she also bought £22,000 of stock and other goods on credit. Obviously, these things have to be paid for eventually and, during the first year, £10,000 was paid out to creditors.

The cash box goes down by £10,000 and the trade creditors box goes down by £10,000 since the company now owes less than before.

As with collecting cash from trade debtors, this transaction has no impact on profit.

Transaction 13 – make a prepayment of £8,000 for stock

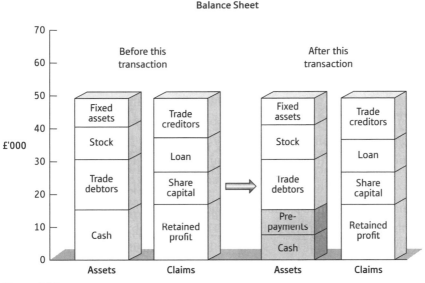

Figure 2.13

Towards the end of the year, Sarah paid a new supplier in advance for some stock. This stock had not been delivered by the balance sheet date.

Clearly, the cash box goes down again by £8,000 since SBL actually paid out this much cash. What, though, is the other entry?

Are the shareholders richer or poorer as a result of this transaction? The answer is no, because, although SBL has paid out £8,000 in cash, the company is owed £8,000 worth of stock. This is an asset to SBL.

Thus we create a new box on the assets bar called **prepayments** with a height of £8,000. This says that the company is owed goods with a value of £8,000. We use the term 'prepayments' as shorthand for 'goods and services the company has paid for but not yet received'.

Once again, the balance sheet balances.

Transaction 14 – pay a dividend of £3,000

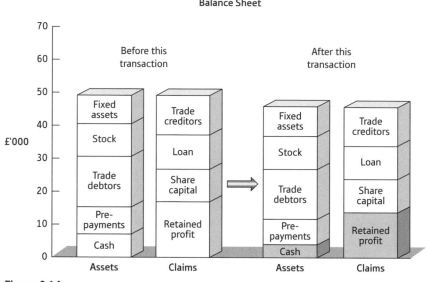

Figure 2.14

Just before the end of the year, although she had not drawn up proper accounts, Sarah knew that she had made a small profit. As the company had some cash in the bank, she therefore decided, as a shareholder, that the company should pay a dividend.

Since the company has paid out cash, the cash box must go down by £3,000. A dividend is simply the shareholders taking out of the company some of the profits that the company has made. Thus retained profit must also go down by £3,000.

So the box you have been calling 'retained profit' all this time is really all the profit the company has made less what is paid out to the shareholders. Hence the term 'retained' profit?

Correct.

Adjustment 15 – adjust for £2,000 telephone expenses not yet billed

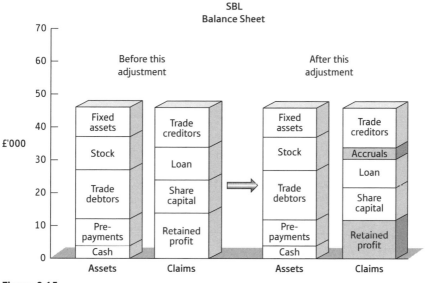

Figure 2.15

Thanks to a mix-up in administration, SBL has not received a bill for its telephone and fax usage for the year. We know, however, that a bill will appear sooner or later and Sarah estimates that it will be for around £2,000.

We included sales in our balance sheet even when they were not paid for at the time of delivery. This is what I called the 'accruals basis' of accounting. This applies equally to expenses. SBL has incurred the telephone and fax expenses even though it hasn't received the bill, let alone paid for them.

We therefore reduce retained profit by £2,000 and create a box on the claims bar called **accruals** with a height of £2,000.

Accruals are any expenses you haven't been billed for, but know you have incurred and will have to pay.

Adjustment 16 – adjust for £3,000 depreciation of fixed assets

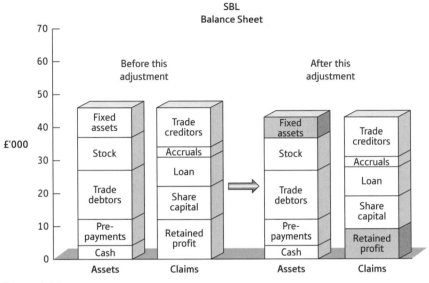

Figure 2.16

When Sarah bought the car, we put it on the balance sheet at the price she paid for it. Since Sarah has been using the car to visit customers during the year, its value will have declined, i.e. it will have **depreciated**. This effectively means that the shareholders have become poorer because, if all the assets were sold off, there would be less cash for the shareholders.

In other words, there is a cost to the shareholders of Sarah using the car and we therefore need to allow for this cost in the accounts.

The way we do this is as follows:

▶ We put the asset on the balance sheet initially at the price the company paid for it (as we did in Transaction 3).

▶ We then decide what we think the useful life of the asset is.

▶ We then gradually reduce the value of the asset over that period (i.e. we depreciate it).

In SBL's case, assume the car has a useful life of three years. If we also assume that it will lose its value steadily over that period, then at the end of one year it will have lost a third of its value, i.e. it will have gone down from £9,000 to £6,000.

We therefore reduce the fixed assets box by this amount. If an asset has lost some value, the shareholders must have become poorer, so again we reduce the retained profit by £3,000.

The value of an asset on a balance sheet is known as the **net book value**.

Note that this is not necessarily what you could get for the asset if you sold it: it is the cost of the asset less the total depreciation on the asset to date.

Adjustment 17 – adjust for £4,000 expected tax liability

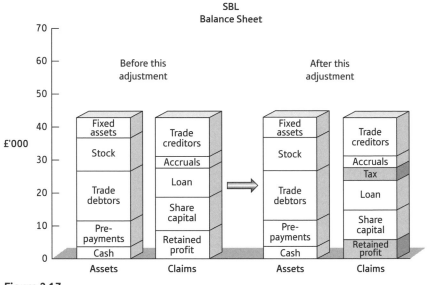

Figure 2.17

Unfortunately, SBL is going to have to pay some corporation tax, which is the tax payable on companies' profits. Tax is not easy to calculate accurately, because the taxman has complicated rules. We can make an estimate, though, and I would think that £4,000 will be fairly close. This tax will be payable about nine months after SBL's financial year end.

We thus create a box called **tax** (more accurate, perhaps, would be **corporation tax liability**) with a height of £4,000.

The other entry is again retained profit, since the £4,000 would otherwise have belonged to the shareholders. Paying tax makes the shareholders poorer.

And that, you will be glad to hear, is it. That's our last balance sheet entry done. The final balance sheet [Figure 2.17] is SBL's balance sheet at the end of the year.

The different forms of balance sheet

OK, so we've got the balance sheet chart. How do I turn that into something I can show my accountants?

There are two common layouts of a balance sheet, although they are both essentially the same.

The 'American' balance sheet

As you will recall, our balance sheet chart is based on the balance sheet equation:

$$\text{Assets} = \text{Claims}$$
$$= \text{Liabilities} + \text{Shareholders' equity}$$

We can simply lay out our balance sheet according to this equation [Table 2.2]. This is literally just the 'numbers version' of our balance sheet chart. We list all the assets and total them up. Below that we list all the claims. The only difference between this and the balance sheet chart is that I have listed the assets and claims under the category headings that I talked about when we first looked at Wingate's balance sheet. This format is used by virtually all American companies.

Table 2.2 SBL's balance sheet: American style

SILK BLOOMERS LIMITED

Final balance sheet – American style

	£'000	
Assets		
Fixed assets		6.0
Current assets		
Stock	10.0	
Prepayments	8.0	
Trade debtors	15.0	
Cash	4.0	
Total current assets		37.0
Total assets		**43.0**
Claims		
Current liabilities		
Trade creditors	12.0	
Accruals	2.0	
Tax payable	4.0	
Total current liabilities		18.0
Long-term liabilities		10.0
Shareholders' equity		
Share capital	10.0	
Retained profit	5.0	
Total shareholders' equity		15.0
Total claims		**43.0**

The 'British' balance sheet

As you will remember, we can rearrange the balance sheet equation to look like this:

$$\text{Assets } - \text{ Liabilities } = \text{ Shareholders' equity}$$

This equation is the basis of British and many European balance sheets. The attraction of this layout is that it displays more clearly the net assets of the company and how those net assets were attained [Table 2.3]. Of course, none of the individual assets or liabilities has changed.

The other thing you would normally do is to put the previous year's balance sheet alongside the current year's so they can be compared. Since SBL didn't exist last year, there's no balance sheet to show. If you look at Wingate's balance sheet on page 272, however, you will see that it is laid out in the British style and has the previous year's figures alongside this year's.

Basic concepts of accounting

As I mentioned earlier, in addition to the fundamental principle, there are two basic concepts that we always apply when drawing up a set of accounts. These concepts are:

- ► The accruals basis
- ► The going concern assumption

Table 2.3 SBL's balance sheet: British style

SILK BLOOMERS LIMITED

Final balance sheet – British style

		£'000
Net assets		
Fixed assets		6.0
Current assets		
Stock	10.0	
Prepayments	8.0	
Trade debtors	15.0	
Cash	4.0	
Total current assets		37.0
Current liabilities		
Trade creditors	(12.0)	
Accruals	(2.0)	
Tax payable	(4.0)	
Total current liabilities		(18.0)
Long-term liabilities		(10.0)
Net assets		**15.0**
Shareholders' equity		
Share capital	10.0	
Retained profit	5.0	
Total		**15.0**

The accruals basis

We discussed this when looking at SBL. To summarise it:

- ▶ Revenue is recognised when it is earned, not when cash is received.
- ▶ Expenses are recognised when they are incurred, not when cash is paid.

The going concern assumption

Go back to when we first started discussing balance sheets. We agreed that shareholders' equity is what the shareholders of a company would get if the company sold all the assets and paid off all its liabilities.

This is a nice, simple way of looking at a balance sheet to understand what it is saying. In practice, however, if a company were to stop trading and try to sell its assets, it may not get as much for some of them as their value on the balance sheet. For example:

▶ When a company stops trading, it can be very hard to persuade debtors to pay.

▶ Fixed assets may not have the same value to anyone else as they do to the company.

Accounts are therefore drawn up on the basis that the company is a going concern, i.e. that it is not about to cease trading.

Let's now recap quickly before going on to look at the P&L and cash flow statement.

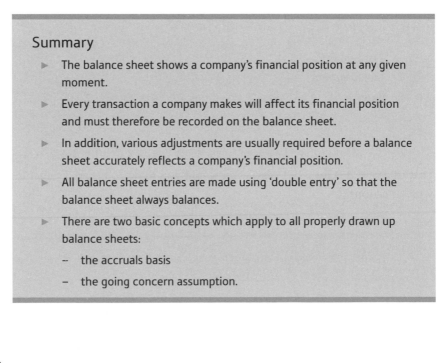

Summary

▶ The balance sheet shows a company's financial position at any given moment.

▶ Every transaction a company makes will affect its financial position and must therefore be recorded on the balance sheet.

▶ In addition, various adjustments are usually required before a balance sheet accurately reflects a company's financial position.

▶ All balance sheet entries are made using 'double entry' so that the balance sheet always balances.

▶ There are two basic concepts which apply to all properly drawn up balance sheets:

  – the accruals basis

  – the going concern assumption.

CHAPTER THREE

The profit & loss account and cash flow statement

- ► The profit & loss account
- ► The cash flow statement
- ► 'Definitive' vs 'descriptive' statements
- ► Summary

Now we know what a balance sheet is and how to construct one, we can move on to the P&L and cash flow statement. In this session, all I am going to do is explain what the P&L and cash flow statement are. We'll see how to construct them in our next session.

The profit & loss account

Let's start by looking at a hypothetical situation relating to an individual's P&L. Assume you're a fortune-hunter, Tom, after Sarah for her money. What would you want to know before asking her to marry you?

How rich she is or, as you would say, what her net worth is.

So if I told you that her net worth today is £25,000, and added that it was only £20,000 this time last year, what would you think of her as a target for your 'affections'?

Not a great deal.

Which could just be one of your bigger mistakes, Tom. We know Sarah's net worth has gone up by £5,000 over the last year. There are many ways that could have happened. Here are two very different ones:

► It could be that Sarah earned a total of £15,000 during the year and spent £10,000 of this on food, drink, holidays, tax, etc. The remaining £5,000 she saved, either by spending it on real assets or by putting it in her bank deposit account. Add these savings to the £20,000 net worth she had at the start of the year and you get her net worth today of £25,000.

► An alternative scenario is that, a year ago, Sarah landed an extremely well-paid job, earning £500,000 a year. She's quite extravagant, but in a normal year could only have spent (including a lot of tax) £245,000 of this income on herself. She should, therefore, have saved £255,000. Unfortunately, during the year she had to pay an American hospital for a series of operations for her brother. He's better now, but the operations cost her a total of £250,000. As a result, she only saved £5,000 during the year.

What would you feel about Sarah in each of those situations, Tom?

I'd obviously write her off in the first case. In the second, I'd be more than a little interested, provided she didn't have any more sick relatives.

Exactly. My point is that, as well as knowing what Sarah's net worth is and by how much it has changed since last year, an explanation of *why* she only got £5,000 richer during the year can be very important. If we're going to make a sensible judgement about a company's future performance, we need a similar explanation. This is what a P&L gives you.

If you look at the bottom of Wingate's balance sheet on page 272, you will see that the company's retained profit (its 'savings') rose by £279k during the year from £2,243k to £2,522k. If you look on page 271, you will see Wingate's P&L, the penultimate line of which shows retained profit in year five of £279k. This is not a coincidence! The P&L is just giving you more detail about how and why the retained profit item on the balance sheet changed over the last year. That's all there is to it.

The cash flow statement

Let's now go back to your fortune hunting for a moment, Tom. Suppose you have discovered that Sarah's current net worth is actually £10m, having risen from £9m this time last year. You have seen the equivalent of her P&L which shows that this rise in her net wealth is due to all the interest on money in various deposit accounts. In short, you expect this increase in her already vast wealth to continue. How would you feel about her?

I'd be down to the jewellers in a flash, although I have the feeling you're going to tell me that would be a mistake.

I'm afraid so. Let me give you some more information about Sarah. Most of her money is tied up in a 'trust' set up for her by her wealthy grandparents. All the interest on this money is kept in the trust as well. Although Sarah is the beneficiary of the trust and therefore effectively owns all the assets in it, she is not allowed access to them for another 10 years. Meanwhile, she's more or less out of ready cash and is going to be penniless for those 10 years.

How would you feel if you married her and *then* learned about this situation, Tom?

Sick as a parrot, I imagine.

Precisely. My point this time is that an individual or a company can be rich and getting richer, but at the same time the cash they have to spend in the short term can be running out. However rich you are, you can't survive without cash to spend.

I take the point, but I don't quite see how this would happen to a company.

Take SBL as an example. In Transaction 7, SBL sold stock for £30,000 but agreed that the customers need not pay for a while. As we saw, this made the shareholders richer, but did not immediately bring in any cash. Later, in Transaction 11, some of this cash was collected. If it hadn't been, though, and SBL had still been obliged to pay its suppliers, SBL would have run out of cash completely.

Far more small companies go out of business through running out of cash than by being inherently unprofitable.

If we look at a company's balance sheets, we can see how the cash balance changed over the period between the balance sheet dates. The cash flow statement merely explains how and why the cash changed as it did.

I hear what you say, Chris, but look at Wingate's cash flow statement on page 273. This shows a reduction in cash during the year of £317k. But the balance sheet on page 272 shows cash going down by only £5k from £17k to £12k.

What you say is right, but there is a simple explanation. In accounting terms, an overdraft is like a negative amount of cash. It's no different from your own current account really. You either have a positive balance or you are in overdraft, i.e. you have a negative amount of cash. As it happens, Wingate had two bank accounts. One had a positive balance in it, the other was in overdraft. You can see the overdraft detailed in Note 11 of the accounts on page 278. The cash flow statement shows the total cash change of both of these, so what you have is as follows:

- ► At the end of year four, Wingate had cash of £17k and an overdraft of £621k, making a net overdraft of £604k.

- ► At the end of year five, Wingate had cash of £12k and an overdraft of £933k, making a net overdraft of £921k.

- ► The difference between these net overdraft figures is £317k, which is what the cash flow statement shows cash going down by.

'Definitive' vs 'descriptive' statements

Let's just summarise what we know about the three key statements in a set of accounts.

- ► The balance sheet tells us what the assets and liabilities of a company are at a point in time.

- ► The P&L tells us how and why the retained profit of the company changed over the course of the last year.

- ► The cash flow statement tells us how and why the cash/overdraft of the company changed over the last year.

The balance sheet is thus the **definitive** statement of a company's financial position. It tells us absolutely where a company stands at any given moment. The P&L and cash flow statement provide extremely important information but, nonetheless, they are only **descriptive** statements: they describe how certain balance sheet items changed during the year.

We could easily draw up statements to show how other balance sheet items changed, if we wanted to. In fact, the notes to Wingate's accounts do this. Look, for example, at the balance sheet on page 272. This shows that fixed assets went up from £4,445k at the end of year four to £5,326k at the end of year five. If you look at Note 8 on page 277, you will see that it consists of a table, the bottom right-hand corner of which shows these two figures.

This table is merely a descriptive statement of how and why the fixed assets figure has changed over the last year. The only reason the P&L and cash flow statement are given such prominence in the annual report is because they are so important.

All of this presumably explains why you insisted on starting with the balance sheet.

Yes. As I said earlier, the balance sheet is the fundamental principle of accounting put into practice. The balance sheet's role as the core of the accounting system is the single most important thing to understand about accounting. In fact, if you really understand a balance sheet and double entry, everything else about accounting suddenly becomes very simple.

If you ever find yourself confused about how to account for a transaction, the first thing you should do is look at the impact on the balance sheet. Then, if the transaction affects retained profit, you know it affects the P&L; if it affects cash, you know it affects the cash flow statement.

What you need to know now is how we draw up the P&L and cash flow statement. Before doing that though, let's just pause for another summary.

Summary

- ► The balance sheet is the definitive statement of a company's financial position. It tells you what a company's assets and liabilities are at a point in time and hence what the company's net assets are. It also tells you how the company came by those net assets.

- ► The P&L is a descriptive statement. It tells you how and why the retained profit item on the balance sheet changed over the course of the last year.

- ► The cash flow statement is also a descriptive statement. It tells you how and why the cash/overdraft as shown on the balance sheet changed over the course of the last year.

- ► You can draw up descriptive statements for any other item on the balance sheet. The only reason that the P&L and cash flow statement are given such prominence in an annual report is because they describe the most important aspects of a business.

CHAPTER FOUR

Creating the profit & loss account and cash flow statement

- ► Creating the profit & loss account
- ► Creating the cash flow statement
- ► Summary

Now we're clear about what the P&L and cash flow statement are, we need to see how they are created. First we'll look at the P&L. I'll start by showing you the P&L at its most simplistic and then we'll modify it slightly to make it more useful. We'll then repeat the same exercise for the cash flow statement.

Creating the profit & loss account

The P&L as a list

Of the 17 entries processed to get the balance sheet of SBL, only nine affected the retained profit of the company. These nine entries are shown in Table 4.1. Against each entry I have put the amount by which it affected retained profit. Entries that decrease retained profit are in brackets. As you can see the net effect on retained profit of all nine entries is £5,000.

From the balance sheet we know that the retained profit of SBL rose from zero to £5,000 in the course of the year. As we saw in the last session, a P&L merely shows how the retained profit changed over a period of time. The list in Table 4.1 shows exactly that: this is your P&L. What could be simpler than that?

Not a lot, I agree, but this doesn't look anything like Wingate's P&L.

You're right, it doesn't. That's because this P&L has two contradictory problems. On the one hand, it is too detailed. Most companies have hundreds or thousands of transactions in a year. It would be totally impracticable to list them all and very few people would have the time or inclination to read such a list anyway. What we do, therefore, is to group the transactions into a few simple categories to present a summary picture.

On the other hand, the P&L in Table 4.1 is not detailed enough. It shows that SBL made a profit of £24,000 on selling stock (Transactions 6 and 7). What it does not show is how much stock SBL had to sell to make that profit. For all we know, SBL might have sold £500,000 worth of stock for £524,000, or, alternatively, £6,000 worth of stock for £30,000. The impact on retained profit would be exactly the same.

If you look back at Transactions 6 and 7 [pages 21–23] you will see that, in fact, SBL sold a total of £18,000 worth of stock for £42,000.

Table 4.1 Entries which affected SBL's retained profit

SILK BLOOMERS LIMITED

Entries affecting retained profit during first year

Entry number	Transaction/Adjustment	Impact on retained profit £'000
6	Sell stock (for cash)	6.0
7	Sell stock (invoiced)	18.0
8	Equipment rental, etc.	(2.0)
9	Pay car expenses	(4.0)
10	Interest on loan	(1.0)
14	Pay dividend	(3.0)
15	Telephone expenses accrued	(2.0)
16	Depreciation of fixed assets	(3.0)
17	Accrue corporation tax	(4.0)
	Total	5.0

Note: The numbers in brackets are negative, i.e. they reduce retained profit.

A more useful P&L

We therefore re-write the above P&L as shown in Table 4.2.

Notice the following things about it:

- ▶ We show the total value of sales during the year (£42,000) as well as the total cost of the products sold (£18,000). The difference between these two (£24,000) we call **gross profit**. Gross profit is the amount by which the sales of products affect the retained profit.
- ▶ We then take all the **operating expenses** and group them into categories. By operating expenses we mean any expenses related to the operations of the company which are not already included in cost of goods sold. We exclude anything to do with the funding of the company. Thus interest, tax and dividends, which all depend on the way the company is funded, are non-operating items. In SBL's case, the operating expense categories are 'Selling & distribution' (made up of car expenses and depreciation) and 'Administration' (made up of equipment rental, stationery and telephone expenses).
- ▶ The profit after these operating expenses we therefore call **operating profit**, which in SBL's case is £13,000.
- ▶ Sarah's parents then take their interest (£1,000), leaving **profit before tax** ('PBT') of £12,000.
- ▶ Profit before tax is effectively all the profit that is left over for the shareholders after paying the interest to the lenders (Sarah's parents, in this case). As with individuals' income, however, the taxman wants his share of a company's profits before the shareholders get anything. We thus deduct tax of £4,000.
- ▶ This leaves **profit after tax** ('PAT') which is all due to the shareholders. Some of this is paid out to the shareholders as dividends (£3,000). What is then left (£5,000) is the retained profit.

Isn't the term 'profit & loss account' slightly misleading, Chris? As I see it, the P&L shows the profit the company has made for the shareholders, which is the profit after tax. Then some of that profit is distributed to the shareholders as a dividend; the dividend is nothing to do with the profit or loss of the company.

Table 4.2 SBL's profit & loss account in first year of trading

SILK BLOOMERS LIMITED		
First year profit & loss account		
		£'000
Sales		42.0
Cost of goods sold		(18.0)
Gross profit		24.0
Operating expenses		
Selling & distribution	(7.0)	
Administration	(4.0)	
Total		(11.0)
Operating profit		**13.0**
Interest payable		(1.0)
Profit before tax		12.0
Tax payable		(4.0)
Profit after tax		**8.0**
Dividend paid		(3.0)
Retained profit		**5.0**

You are 100 per cent correct and it *is* very misleading, particularly for new-comers to accounting. It would be better to call it something like 'Explanation of the change in retained profit'. As it happens, the accounting standards authorities decided some time ago to address this issue in a different way. I will come back to it when we talk about Wingate.

Creating the cash flow statement

The cash flow statement as a list

Of the 17 entries we made on SBL's balance sheet, 11 affected the amount of cash the company had at the end of the year. These are shown in Table 4.3. Four of these entries increased the amount of cash the company had; the other seven (shown in brackets again) decreased the cash balance. The net effect of these 11 entries was to increase cash between the start and end of the year by £4,000.

From the balance sheet, we know that the cash in the company rose from zero to £4,000 during the year. The statement in Table 4.3 just shows how this happened. This is your cash flow statement.

Table 4.3 Entries which affected SBL's cash flow

SILK BLOOMERS LIMITED

Entries affecting cash during first year

Entry number	Transaction/Adjustment	Impact on cash £'000
1	Issue shares	10.0
2	Borrow from parents	10.0
3	Buy fixed assets for cash	(9.0)
4	Buy stock for cash	(8.0)
6	Sell stock for cash	12.0
9	Pay car expenses	(4.0)
10	Interest on loan	(1.0)
11	Collect cash from debtors	15.0
12	Pay creditors	(10.0)
13	Pay for stock in advance	(8.0)
14	Pay dividend	(3.0)
	Total	4.0

Note: As with the P&L, the numbers in brackets are negative, i.e. they reduce the amount of cash that the company has.

As with the P&L, this list would become very long and not very informative for companies of significant size. Again, we can improve the situation by grouping the entries under six different headings, as shown in Table 4.4.

- ▶ **Operating activities** consist of all items that relate to the company's operations. In SBL's case this included buying and selling stock, paying expenses, collecting cash in from debtors and paying cash out both to creditors, and as a prepayment for stock.

- ▶ **Capital expenditure** includes all buying and selling of fixed assets which enable the operating activities to take place. In SBL's case, this was just the purchase of a car.

- ▶ **Returns on investments and servicing of finance** means the interest paid on loans and any dividends or interest received on investments or cash that the company has on deposit. In SBL's case, we have just the £1,000 interest payment on the loan from Sarah's parents.

- ▶ **Taxation** is the tax on the profits of the company. In SBL's case, the tax was accrued but had not actually been paid. Hence there is no impact on cash.

- ▶ **Equity dividends paid** is the dividends paid out to shareholders. In SBL's case, this was the £3,000 paid to the sole shareholder, Sarah.

- ▶ **Financing** consists of all transactions relating to the raising of funds to operate the business. In SBL's case, this meant issuing some shares to Sarah in return for cash and borrowing more cash from her parents.

Drawing up a cash flow statement under these headings does make it easier to understand quickly where the cash in the business has come from and gone to. The operating activities section, however, is normally written in a different way. To understand this, we have to consider the relationship between profit and cash flow.

Table 4.4 SBL's cash flow statement in first year of trading

SILK BLOOMERS LIMITED

Cash flow statement for first year

		£'000
Operating activities		
Buy stock for cash	(8.0)	
Sell stock for cash	12.0	
Pay car expenses	(4.0)	
Collect cash from debtors	15.0	
Pay creditors	(10.0)	
Pay for stock In advance	(8.0)	
		(3.0)
Capital expenditure		
Purchase of fixed assets		(9.0)
Returns on investments and servicing of finance		
Interest payable on loan		(1.0)
Taxation		
Corporation tax		0.0
Equity dividends paid		
Interim dividend		(3.0)
Financing		
Shares issued	10.0	
Loan from Sarah's parents	10.0	
		20.0
Net change in cash balance		**4.0**

Profit and cash flow

Let's suppose you decide to sell flowers (real ones this time) from a stall on the pavement. You'd go down to the market at the crack of dawn and pay cash there and then for your flowers. You would then set up your stall on the pavement and sell the flowers for cash to any passing customers. If, on one particular day, you bought £100 worth of flowers at the market and sold them for a total of £150, you would have made a profit on the day of £50. Your cash flow on the day would also be £50, as you would have £50 more cash at the end of the day than you had at the start.

Now consider a completely different situation. Assume that on Monday you buy a £2 phone card. On Tuesday a friend asks you to make an urgent phone call for him and promises to give you £1 more than you spend (but says he can't give it to you until Wednesday). You use up all the units on the card, so your friend owes you £3. Your friend duly gives you the £3 on Wednesday.

Let's now look at your profit and cash flow on each of the three days:

[£]	Monday	Tuesday	Wednesday	Total
Profit	0	1	0	1
Cash flow	(2)	0	3	1

On Monday you have to pay out £2 to buy the card, but it is still an asset worth £2 so you haven't made a profit or a loss. At the end of Monday, therefore, your cash is down by £2, but your profit is zero.

On Tuesday, you provide a service to your friend for £3. The cost of providing this service is the depreciation in value of the phone card, which goes from being worth £2 to zero. Your profit on the day is therefore £1. Your cash flow, however, is zero, because you neither paid out nor received any cash.

On Wednesday, you receive the promised £3, so your cash flow is £3, although your profit is zero.

There are two things you should notice about this:

> ► **Profit and cash flow on any one day are not the same.** Similarly, with most businesses, profit and cash flow are not the same in any particular year (or month, etc.).

> ► **Over the three days, profit and cash flow *are* the same.** Similarly, with businesses, total profit and total cash flow will be the same in the long run. The difference between them is just a matter of timing.

These observations form the basis of a different cash flow statement. What we do is start out by saying that cash flow *should* equal profit and then adjust the figure to show why it didn't.

This version of the SBL cash flow statement is shown in Table 4.5. All the sections of this cash flow statement are identical to the previous one except 'Operating activities'. The first line of this section, as you can see, is operating profit. The rest of the section consists of the adjustments we have to make to operating profit to get the cash flow due to the operating activities. Let's look at each of these adjustments in turn.

Impact of depreciation on cash flow

The first adjustment is £3k of depreciation which we included in our balance sheet to allow for the fact that the fixed assets had been 'used up' during the year. Depreciation therefore affects operating profit. It does not, however, affect cash. Hence, if all the sales and costs which give rise to the £13k operating profit were cash transactions except the depreciation, then the cash flow during the year would be £3k higher than the operating profit. Hence we **add back** depreciation, as shown in Table 4.5.

Table 4.5 SBL's cash flow statement re-stated

SILK BLOOMERS LIMITED

Cash flow statement for first year (re-stated)

		£'000
Operating activities		
Operating profit	13.0	
Depreciation	3.0	
Increase in trade debtors	(15.0)	
Increase in stock	(10.0)	
Increase in prepayments	(8.0)	
Increase in trade creditors	12.0	
Increase in accruals	2.0	
		(3.0)
Capital expenditure		
Purchase of fixed assets		(9.0)
Returns on investments and servicing of finance		
Interest payable on loan		(1.0)
Taxation		
Corporation tax		0.0
Equity dividends paid		
Interim dividend		(3.0)
Financing		
Shares issued	10.0	
Loan from Sarah's parents	10.0	
		20.0
Net change in cash balance		**4.0**

Impact of trade debtors on cash flow

As it happens, there were other transactions that did not involve cash. £30k worth of sales were made on credit, although, in the course of the year, some of this money was collected. At the end of the year, £15k was still due from customers. The effect of this £15k is that sales that actually became cash in the year were lower than the sales recognised in calculating operating profit.

This has the effect of making cash flow lower than operating profit. Thus we subtract £15k from the operating profit.

Impact of stock on cash flow

At the end of the year, SBL had some stock it had not sold. This stock was treated as an asset of the company and was not included in the calculation of operating profit for the year. Nonetheless, buying stock requires cash to be spent. The effect of this stock is to make cash flow lower than operating profit. Once again, therefore, we make an adjustment on our cash flow statement.

But that's not necessarily true is it, Chris? Most of the stock was bought on credit and some of it hasn't been paid for yet.

That's a good point, but what we do is to separate the stock from the method of payment. In other words, we assume that the stock was all paid for in cash. If in fact it wasn't, then the balance sheet will show us owing money to the supplier under trade creditors. As you will see in a minute, we adjust the cash flow statement to take account of any trade creditors at the year end.

Impact of prepayments on cash flow

Just as with stock, we have paid out cash which is not included as an expense in our operating profit calculation. Again, this will tend to make cash flow lower than operating profit and we have to make an adjustment downwards.

Impact of trade creditors/accruals on cash flow

Some of the expenses we recognised in calculating our operating profit and some of the stock we have at the year end have not actually been paid for. Our cash flow statement so far assumes that they have, however. We must therefore adjust the cash flow upwards to take account of the creditors and accruals at the year end.

Interpretation of the cash flow statement

Having made these adjustments, the operating activities section of the cash flow statement is now much more useful. We can see at a glance that operating cash flow (negative £3k) was substantially worse than operating profit (positive £13k) and we can see that this was caused by making sales on credit, building up stock and making a prepayment for some stock. This was offset to some extent by not paying suppliers immediately and by the fact that some of the operating expense was depreciation, which doesn't affect cash.

The effect of a previous year's transactions

I'm looking at Wingate's cash flow statement on page 273, which shows an increase in debtors reducing cash by £643k in year five. According to Wingate's balance sheet on page 272, debtors at the year end were £2,239k. Why aren't these two figures the same?

This is an extremely important point which I was just about to come on to. What you have to remember is that, at the start of the year, most companies will have some debtors left over from the previous year. These debtors will be collected during the current year. Thus you have to allow for the cash you collect from these debtors in your cash flow calculation. The effect of this is that the cash flow adjustment due to debtors is the *change* in debtors from the start of the year to the end.

It sounds plausible, Chris, but I don't think I'm really with you. Can you give us an example with numbers?

Of course. Assume you run a company which has been going for a few years. Your sales for this year are £100k and your expenses are £80k, giving you an operating profit of £20k. As we said before, if all your sales and expenses are paid in cash at the time, your cash flow must also be £20k.

Now assume that *last* year some of your customers did *not* pay in cash, so that at the end of that year (i.e. the beginning of this year) you were owed £15k. Those customers paid up during *this* year so that, on top of receiving the cash from this year's sales, you also received an extra £15k in cash. Your cash flow for the year would be:

	£'000
Operating profit	20
Last year's debtors collected	15
Total	35

If we now assume that, in fact, some of *this* year's sales were made on credit and that at the end of this year you are still owed £30k by customers, the cash flow would be £30k lower:

	£'000
Operating profit	20
Last year's debtors collected	15
This year's debtors not collected	(30)
Total	5

As you can see, what we are actually doing is adjusting operating profit downwards by the increase in debtors (i.e. 30 – 15) between the start and end of the year.

So with SBL it just happened that the debtors at the start of the year were zero, so the increase in debtors was the same as the year-end debtors' figure, since $15 - 0 = 15$?

Exactly. You will notice that I wrote 'Increase in trade debtors' on SBL's cash flow statement. All the other adjustments are identical to this, in that we have to allow for any amounts at the start of the year and thus our adjustments are all based on the increases in the items.

If, for example, trade debtors went down during the year rather than up, what would happen?

Just what the arithmetic would tell you. You would end up getting more cash in than you would have done if all your sales were for cash. Thus your adjustment to operating profit would be upwards rather than downwards.

Summary

- The P&L for a particular period is, at its most simplistic, a list of all the balance sheet entries made during that period which affect retained profit.

- In practice, we summarise these entries and show different 'levels' of profit (gross profit, operating profit, profit before tax, profit after tax).

- The cash flow statement at its most simplistic is a list of all the balance sheet entries for the relevant period which affect cash.

- In practice, we summarise these entries into a number of categories.

- Profit and cash flow from operations are not usually the same during any given period. In the long run, however, they must be the same.

- The usual form of cash flow statement therefore starts with the operating profit for the period and shows why the cash flow during that period was different.

CHAPTER FIVE

Accounting in practice

- ▶ More essential concepts
- ▶ Setting up your software
- ▶ Accounting in a simple world
- ▶ Accounting in the real world
- ▶ 'Proving' your balance sheet
- ▶ Summary

Those first four sessions were really useful, Chris. I think I do now understand what a balance sheet is and how the P&L and cash flow statement relate to it. And I also understand the theory of double entry. But I still don't really understand how that relates to what's going on in my accounting system, so I still don't think I'm going to be able to go home and use it with any confidence.

Understood. What we've been talking about is most of what you need to know. I just need to join a few more dots. Now, there are lots of different accounting systems out there and they're all a bit different from each other. I can't therefore talk you through step by step how to go about using your particular system. However, the core of all accounting systems is identical, because in the end they all have to do what we have just been doing manually for SBL. So what I'm going to do is talk about the basic things you have to do to produce a set of accounts and explain what is going on in the accounting system when you do those things.

In other words, this is about *understanding* what you are doing. I hope you *will* then be able to go home and start doing your accounts with renewed confidence. Tom, even if you never want to actually do this yourself, it's worth your time, because I'm going to introduce a couple of new subjects you need to know about and as for everything else, it can't do you any harm to understand what the accountants at work are talking about. You can, if you really want, switch off when we talk about 'debits and credits', as you can understand and analyse accounts without understanding this, but it's not hard, so I recommend you stay with us.

Is this now book-keeping we're doing here, Chris, or is it accounting?

Well, **book-keeping** is usually described as the process of recording all the daily transactions of the company. **Accounting** is the process of taking the book-keeper's work and turning it into a set of accounts. Frankly, the distinction doesn't matter that much to us. We just want to get a set of accounts done.

Before we get into the process, we need to cover a few more concepts. Although Sarah was prompted into this weekend by having to get her annual accounts done, I'm going to assume that we are trying to produce monthly accounts. I really recommend *everyone* to do their accounts at least quarterly and preferably monthly. The more you do it, the easier it gets. The principles, of course, are the same, whatever frequency you choose.

More essential concepts

Nominal ledger and nominal accounts

Each of the items that make up the balance sheet (i.e. each of the boxes on our balance sheet chart) is actually called a **nominal account**. So, if we look at SBL's final balance sheet [page 39], we can see that SBL's nominal accounts would be:

Fixed assets	Trade creditors
Stock	Accruals
Trade debtors	Tax payable
Prepayments	Loan
Cash	Share capital
	Retained profit

The word 'account' seems to be everywhere! It's a bit confusing.

You're not kidding and we are about to see yet more uses of it. I am going to try to be very precise with my language and never use the word 'account' without something before it that tells you what type of account I'm talking about. And you should do the same until you have got some experience and confidence with all this stuff.

Now, in practice, accountants like to keep a lot of detail at their finger-tips. They do this by having many more nominal accounts than those listed above.

For example, instead of just one nominal account called fixed assets, they would typically have a nominal account for each different type of fixed asset (e.g. freehold properties, leasehold properties, plant and equipment, cars, etc.). The sum of all these nominal accounts would add up to the total fixed assets. In terms of our balance sheet chart, this just means the fixed assets box is in fact several boxes, but the height of all those boxes combined is the same as the height of the single fixed asset box I showed.

Similarly, there would not be one nominal account called retained profit but a separate nominal account for each different type of income and expense that together make up retained profit. Thus, SBL would have:

- ▶ Sales
- ▶ Cost of goods sold
- ▶ Car expenses
- ▶ Car depreciation
- ▶ Equipment rental
- ▶ Stationery
- ▶ Telephone expenses
- ▶ Interest payable
- ▶ Tax payable
- ▶ Dividends paid

This makes it easy to derive the P&L from the balance sheet as we did in our last session. A large company may have hundreds of nominal accounts to help track its revenues and expenses. The principles remain the same, of course.

You say that, Chris, but a lot of these entries in retained profit made retained profit lower. So if they have their own boxes on the balance sheet chart, they're going to have to have a 'negative' height, aren't they?

Correct. This is a problem if you are trying to draw them on the balance sheet chart, although I could of course draw them going downwards from the horizontal axis. It's not a problem to an accounting system, because it just adds and subtracts numbers.

All the nominal accounts make up the **nominal ledger**. In the past, the nominal ledger was exactly what its name implies – a large book in which details of each of the nominal accounts were kept. Today, of course, the nominal ledger is part of your computerised accounting system.

Sales and purchase ledgers

Most companies have dozens of suppliers, if not hundreds or even thousands. It is obviously very important to keep detailed records of all transactions with suppliers, so accounting systems have a separate 'ledger' for this purpose. Such **purchase ledgers** are linked to the nominal ledger so that whenever a change is made to the purchase ledger, the relevant nominal accounts in the nominal ledger (e.g. trade creditors, cash, retained profit) are automatically updated.

Likewise, companies can have many customers and it is essential to keep a record of all transactions with them. This is done in the **sales ledger**.

Let's be clear about something here. Lots of books you could read about book-keeping and/or accounting talk about the sales ledger and the purchase ledger in the same breath as the nominal ledger, as if these three ledgers are all 'equal' parts of your accounting system. This is *wrong*. It's as wrong as talking about the P&L, balance sheet and cash flow statement as if they are three equal parts of a set of accounts, which, as you now know, is not correct. The balance sheet is the backbone of the accounts.

Similarly, the nominal ledger is the backbone of your accounting system. It is the equivalent of the balance sheet. It contains the nominal accounts that make up your balance sheet. The sales and purchase ledgers are very, very *useful*, just as the P&L and cash flow statements are very useful. But they are *not* the *essence* of the accounting system.

Source documents

If you buy goods from a supplier, there might be a lot of documents, including perhaps the following:

- ▶ A **purchase order**. This records the fact that the goods have been ordered.

- ▶ A **delivery note**. This is enclosed with the goods to say what is included in the delivery.

- ▶ An **invoice**. This lists, at a minimum, the goods purchased, the 'tax point' date (which is the official date of the sale and purchase for VAT purposes), the amount charged for the goods and any applicable VAT.

- ▶ One or more **statements**. The supplier will issue statements to its customers every so often, itemising all the invoices that are still unpaid.

For our purposes, the only document that matters is the **invoice**. This is the official record of the transaction to buy the goods and is what we use to make the entries into the accounting system (**the source document**). Of course, if you buy something in a shop, you might just be given a till receipt. While possibly not quite matching an invoice for amount of information, it is still the source document for that purchase.

Likewise, all your sales should have source documents. Usually, this will be sales invoices that you issue, but if you are a shop, it might be the information from your electronic till, or it might just be handwritten receipts.

Journal entry

A **journal entry** is a change you make to the balance sheet that is made directly to the nominal ledger (i.e. to two or more nominal accounts). It is often an end of period adjustment such as we saw with SBL. This distinguishes it from, say, entering a sales invoice, which you enter into the sales ledger and let the accounting system make any relevant entries into the nominal ledger.

The debit and credit convention

The debit and credit convention is a very simple but very clever concept.

Unfortunately, it *appears* to totally contradict something you've taken for granted since you first got a bank account.

Let's start with what you take for granted. If you had £100 on deposit at your bank, you would say you were £100 in credit. If you then paid an extra £50 into your account, your bank would say they had credited your account with £50. Similarly, if you withdrew £50, the bank would say they had debited your account. Hence, we associate crediting with getting bigger or better and debiting with getting smaller or worse. Is that fair?

Perfectly. You're not going to tell us it's wrong?

Not wrong, just not the whole story. What I need you to do now is forget that you associate 'credit' with positive balances and good things and that you associate 'debit' with negative balances and bad things. Can you do that for a few minutes?

Yes, but I'm already nervous this is about to get confusing.

Don't worry, it's not. Look at this diagram [Figure 5.1]. This shows a much simplified balance sheet chart with some of the most common boxes (i.e. nominal accounts) that a small company might have. As always, we list all the assets on the left-hand bar and all the claims on the right-hand bar.

Now comes the leap of faith:

> ▶ All the nominal accounts on the assets bar are **debit** balances. When you increase one of these boxes, you are **debiting** the account. When you decrease one, you are **crediting** it.

> ▶ All the nominal accounts on the claims bar have **credit** balances. When you increase one of these boxes, you are **crediting** the account. When you decrease one, you are **debiting** it.

I'm afraid this leap of faith looks like a no-jump, Chris. You're telling me that if I have cash in the bank, that would be a debit balance. That must be wrong, surely.

Trust me, it's not. The statements and letters that the bank sends you are looking at your bank account from the point of view of *its* balance sheet. If you deposit money with your bank, it owes you that money. You have a claim over their assets. Thus, from *its* point of view, your bank account appears on the claims side of its balance sheet and is thus a credit balance. This shouldn't surprise you really. Banks are hardly famous for looking at things from their customers' point of view.

On *your* balance sheet, that cash is an asset and is thus a debit balance. Both are consistent with the convention – you just have to be clear whose balance sheet you are talking about.

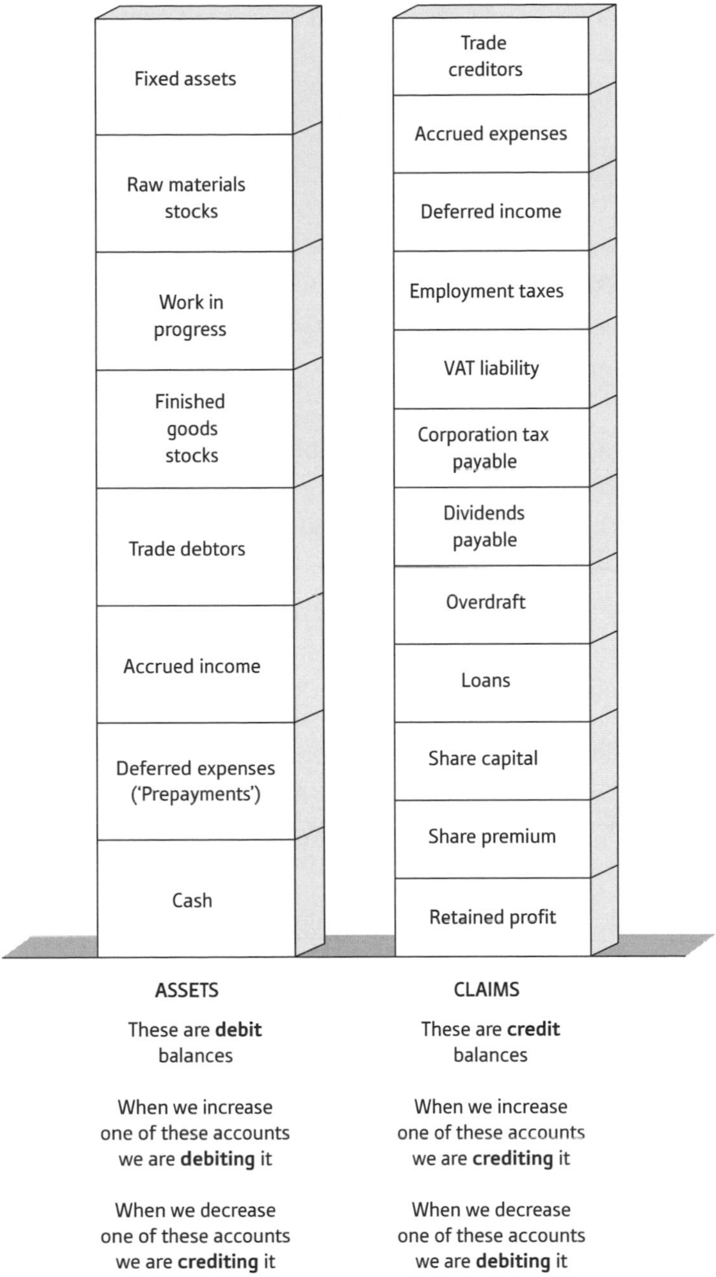
Fixed assets
Raw materials stocks
Work in progress
Finished goods stocks
Trade debtors
Accrued income
Deferred expenses ('Prepayments')
Cash
Trade creditors
Accrued expenses
Deferred income
Employment taxes
VAT liability
Corporation tax payable
Dividends payable
Overdraft
Loans
Share capital
Share premium
Retained profit
ASSETS
These are **debit** balances
When we increase one of these accounts we are **debiting** it
When we decrease one of these accounts we are **crediting** it
CLAIMS
These are **credit** balances
When we increase one of these accounts we are **crediting** it
When we decrease one of these accounts we are **debiting** it

Figure 5.1 Model balance sheet chart

I think I can see that in principle but I don't see why this convention is so clever or why it helps me.

The clever bit is that, for any transaction, you must always credit one nominal account and debit another. This has to be true if you think about it:

- ► If you *increase* a nominal account on the assets bar, you are debiting the account. To make the balance sheet balance, you must do one of two things. Either you reduce another asset account, which would be crediting that account, or you increase an account on the claims bar, which would also be crediting the account. Thus, you have one debit and one credit whatever.

- ► If you *decrease* a nominal account on the assets bar, you are crediting the account. To make the balance sheet balance, you either increase another asset account, which would be debiting that account, or you decrease an account on the claims bar, which would also be debiting the account. Once again, you have got one credit and one debit.

- ► If we run through some of SBL's transactions, you will see how the convention works in practice.

Let's start with the first transaction we posted for SBL [page 16]. Sarah invested £10,000 cash into SBL in return for shares in the company. This resulted in the cash nominal account going up by £10,000 and the share capital nominal account going up by £10,000.

We would describe this transaction as follows:

Debit **Cash**	£10,000
Credit **Share capital**	£10,000

After this transaction we would say the cash account has a debit balance of £10,000 and the share capital account has a credit balance of £10,000.

Let's now look at Transaction 3 [page 18]. SBL bought a car for £9,000 in cash. The car became a fixed asset of the company. Thus the cash nominal account went down by £9,000 and the fixed assets nominal account went up by £9,000. We would therefore say:

Credit **Cash**	£9,000
Debit **Fixed assets**	£9,000

Transaction 9 was paying your car expenses of £4,000. This resulted in cash going down by £4,000 and retained profit going down by £4,000. Thus:

Credit **Cash**	£4,000
Debit **Retained profit**	£4,000

What about something like Transaction 6 where I sold some stock? In that transaction, three nominal accounts changed – stock, cash and retained profit.

That's no problem. What I said earlier about having one debit and one credit wasn't exactly true. You must have *at least* one debit and *at least* one credit but you can have more than one of each, *provided that the total debits add up to the total credits for any transaction.* If that weren't the case, the balance sheet wouldn't balance.

In Transaction 6, SBL sold £6,000 worth of stock for £12,000 cash. Hence, cash went up by £12,000, stock down by £6,000, retained profit up by £6,000. We can thus say:

Debit **Cash**	£12,000
Credit **Stock**	£6,000
Credit **Retained profit**	£6,000

As it happens, accountants take the convention one step further and put the debits in one column and the credits in another as follows:

	Debit	Credit
Increase **Cash**	£12,000	
Decrease **Stock**		£6,000
Increase **Retained profit**		£6,000
	£12,000	**£12,000**

The debits are always in the left-hand column. As you will notice, this is consistent with my balance sheet chart, which has the assets bar on the left. Accountants don't usually include the 'Increase' and 'Decrease' because they can tell immediately from whether it's a debit or a credit, but I think it helps when you are new to it.

Just to make sure I get this right. Earlier you said that we should think of the nominal accounts that represent expenses, like Cost of goods sold, Stationery or whatever, as boxes of negative height that reduce the size of the overall retained profit box. In terms of debits and credits, these boxes will have 'debit' balances. Is that right?

It is exactly right. What I want you to do now is run through all 17 of SBL's transactions and write down the debits and credits that relate to each. Lay them out as I did the last transaction; i.e. with the debits in a column on the left and the credits on the right. Then check your answers against my list [Table 5.1].

Table 5.1 Debits and credits relating to SBL's transactions (1—9)

TRANSACTION	DEBIT	CREDIT
1 Issue shares		
Increase **Cash**	10,000	
Increase **Share capital**		10,000
2 Loan from parents		
Increase **Cash**	10,000	
Increase **Long-term loans**		10,000
3 Buy car		
Decrease **Cash**		9,000
Increase **Fixed assets**	9,000	
4 Buy stock for cash		
Decrease **Cash**		8,000
Increase **Stock**	8,000	
5 Buy stock on credit		
Increase **Stock**	20,000	
Increase **Trade creditors**		20,000
6 Sell stock for cash		
Increase **Cash**	12,000	
Decrease **Stock**		6,000
Increase **Retained profit**		6,000
7 Sell stock on credit		
Decrease **Stock**		12,000
Increase **Trade debtors**	30,000	
Increase **Retained profit**		18,000
8 Equipment rental, etc.		
Increase **Trade creditors**		2,000
Decrease **Retained profit**	2,000	
9 Car expenses		
Decrease **Cash**		4,000
Decrease **Retained profit**	4,000	

Table 5.1 Continued (Transactions 10–17)

TRANSACTION	DEBIT	CREDIT
10 Loan interest		
Decrease **Cash**		1,000
Decrease **Retained profit**	1,000	
11 Collect cash from debtors		
Increase **Cash**	15,000	
Decrease **Trade debtors**		15,000
12 Pay creditors		
Decrease **Cash**		10,000
Decrease **Trade creditors**	10,000	
13 Prepayment		
Decrease **Cash**		8,000
Increase **Prepayments**	8,000	
14 Pay dividend		
Decrease **Cash**		3,000
Decrease **Retained profit**	3,000	
15 Telephone accrual		
Increase **Accruals**		2,000
Decrease **Retained profit**	2,000	
16 Depreciation		
Decrease **Fixed assets**		3,000
Decrease **Retained profit**	3,000	
17 Accrue tax liability		
Increase **Tax liability**		4,000
Decrease **Retained profit**	4,000	

Trial balance

The **trial balance** (or **TB** for short) is just a list of all the nominal accounts in the nominal ledger showing the balance in each (i.e. the height of the box) at a point in time. For the avoidance of doubt, each balance takes into account *every* transaction and adjustment the company has *ever* made up to that point in time that affects that nominal account. In other words, it is like a very detailed balance sheet, albeit laid out differently.

The TB is actually a major milestone in the accounting process, in that:

> ▶ It is the end of the process of getting all our transactions and adjustments into the accounting system.

> ▶ It is the starting point for the process of producing our balance sheet, P&L etc., all of which are derived from the TB.

Which brings us to the chart of accounts or layout of accounts.

Chart of accounts (layout of accounts)

The **chart of accounts** is little more than a template. It determines how each nominal account should be treated for the purposes of producing the balance sheet and the P&L. So it identifies:

> ▶ which of the nominal accounts are part of retained profit, so the software can add them together to get net retained profit for the balance sheet;

> ▶ which nominal accounts should be listed under each of the categories on the balance sheet, such as fixed assets, current assets, current liabilities, shareholders equity, etc.;

> ▶ which of the nominal accounts that make up retained profit should be listed under which category on the P&L, such as sales, cost of sales, **overheads**, etc.

You can usually set up more than one chart of accounts that will produce balance sheets and P&Ls that are laid out differently, but which are based on the same underlying TB. For example, you might want a very detailed balance sheet and/or P&L for your own checking purposes, but less detailed ones for presentation to your fellow directors. A chart of accounts allows you to summarise your data by grouping nominal accounts together and presenting them as just one figure. As ever, it's just simple arithmetic.

OK, so the nominal account balances are the cumulative effect of every transaction that's ever been carried out by the company. That means, for example, that the sales nominal account will show all the sales ever made by the company. But don't I want to see the sales for the most recent month or the financial year up to date?

You do, of course. But this is easily done. If your year end is, say, 31 March and you are doing your accounts for, say, August, the accounting system simply has to take the balance of the sales nominal account at the end of August and subtract the balance in that nominal account as it was at the end of July. The difference *must* be the sum of the entries made in August, which is therefore your August sales. Likewise, the system can subtract the balances at the end of March from the end of August balances to get the financial year to date.

Audit trail

An **audit trail** is a listing kept by most accounting systems of everything you do on the system. Even if you reverse (i.e. cancel) a transaction, the audit trail will not actually delete the cancelled transaction. It will instead maintain the original transaction and add an additional transaction that exactly cancels out the original one. This means you can always track what has been done (and by whom, if you have different users with different logins to the system).

VAT (Value Added Tax)

Sadly, we can't talk about accounting without understanding a bit about VAT.

Before you go into VAT, can you tell me what 'value added' means?

Yes. A company buys in raw materials, equipment, services; these are the company's **inputs**. The company's employees then do things to or with these inputs in order to make products or provide services. The products and/ or services are then sold; these are the company's **outputs**. **Value added** is the difference between the outputs and the inputs; in other words, it's the amount of value that the employees add to the inputs.

So what is VAT?

VAT is exactly what it says: a tax on the value added in products and services. The rules can be very complex but, in general terms, it works as follows.

Most products and services are subject to VAT, although some are classified as **exempt** or **zero-rated**, in which case VAT is not charged. Companies fall into one of two groups as far as VAT is concerned: those that are **VAT registered** and those that aren't. You register for VAT if your annual sales are more than a certain figure (the figure changes every year, but it is of the order of £80,000). If you are registered, you have to add VAT to the amount you charge for your products or services (your outputs) and then pass that VAT on to Her Majesty's Revenue and Customs ('HMRC'). Thus a company that is registered for VAT does not actually *pay* any VAT, it merely collects it for HMRC. You can, however, if you are registered, reclaim from HMRC the VAT you pay on most of your purchases (your inputs). The net amount that HMRC gets in from you is therefore the VAT on the difference between your inputs and your outputs, which is therefore VAT on the value added. Hence the name.

So who does pay the tax?

You, me and the other 60 million people in the country. We are charged VAT by the shops when we buy things. Since we are not VAT registered, we cannot reclaim the VAT.

So how does this work with your double-entry system?

Very neatly, as it happens. Let's look at a simple example. The rate of VAT is changed every once in a while (and can be different rates on different categories of products or services), but we will assume it is 20 per cent. Let's say you sell some consulting work that you want £1,000 for. You would have to add 20 per cent VAT to that, making a total charge to the customer of £1,200. The accounting entries would be as follows:

	Which bar?	Debit	Credit
Increase **Debtors**	Assets bar	1,200	
Increase **VAT liability**	Claims bar		200
Increase **Retained profit**	Claims bar		1,000

As you can see, the VAT does not affect retained profit at all. The customer owes you the VAT, but you immediately increase the liability to HMRC on your balance sheet by the amount of the VAT.

When you make purchases, you will be charged VAT. The VAT element of each purchase *reduces* your liability to HMRC and does not affect retained profit.

Every three months (or every month if you are a big company), the balance in the 'VAT liability' box is paid to HMRC. If, as happens in a number of circumstances, the VAT on your purchases is greater than the VAT on your sales, then HMRC will pay you instead.

The last point to note is that, while the sales figure that appears on a company's P&L (the £1,000) doesn't include the VAT, the debtors figure on the balance sheet (the £1,200) does. We have to remember this when we come to analyse the accounts later.

Setting up your software

When you first start using your accounting system, there are *lots* of set-up tasks you *could* do and the system may encourage you to do. There are only two you *really* need to do, at least in principle, before you can get going. The rest of them you can do as you go along or when you are more familiar with the system.

Financial year

You have to tell your accounting system the start and end dates of your financial year. This is so it knows how to calculate your year to date figures. Normally you would specify simply the start or end date of your financial year and the system would assume your year is 12 months long.

Opening balances

This is the only thing that really requires any explanation. As we now know, the balance sheet is the definitive statement of a company's situation at any point in time. It has to reflect *every* transaction the company has *ever* made up to that point in time. If your company has been trading for a while before you start using an accounting system (or if you are swapping from one system to another) and you are not planning to enter every individual transaction since the company started, then somehow you have to allow for this fact.

We deal with this by entering 'opening balances'. What this means is taking the balance sheet of the company (perhaps from your accountant) at midnight on the day before the day from which you want to start entering transactions and entering the relevant balance for every nominal account that makes up that balance sheet. When you start entering your transactions, they will 'add' to the historic balances, so your TB and hence your balance sheet in the accounting system will reflect the balances from every transaction the company has ever made. So:

- ▶ Let's suppose your year end is 31 March.
- ▶ However, you want to start entering transactions with effect from 1 July.

> ► You need somehow to get the balances for each of your nominal accounts as at 30 June and enter them as 'opening balances' in the system (all dated 30 June).

Other set-up tasks

As I said, you can do pretty much everything else as you go along. However, there are a few things worth mentioning:

> ► **Nominal accounts.** You can set up all your nominal accounts yourself if you want. However, there are lots that are the same for every company – e.g. share capital, bank account, trade debtors. Most accounting systems therefore offer you a choice from several standard sets of nominal accounts (appropriate to different types of companies), which you can then add to as and when you want. This just saves you some time, but it can be irritating if you pick an inappropriate set, so do think about it.

> ► **VAT rate.** If you are VAT registered, you might want to set the 'default' rate of VAT in the system, because the rate at any given time is the same for *most* goods and services (but not all, so you do need to check the rate for your particular products and services). The default means that, whenever you enter a sales or purchase invoice into the system, it will assume the VAT rate is the default rate and thus enter that figure and calculate the VAT amount, saving you time. It will let you over-ride both the percentage and the amount if you need to.

Accounting in a simple world

But before we go any further, Sarah, let me give you the most useful piece of advice I've got to give about this entire subject . . .

Until you are really confident you know what you are doing with any particular task on your accounting system, print out the TB or balance sheet before you make the entry and compare it with the TB or balance sheet immediately after you make the entry. Then think about what's changed in terms of the balance sheet chart. Have the right boxes gone up or down? This is the best way to make sure you understand what the system is doing and once you've got that, you'll find the whole thing dead easy.

Let's start by taking a really simple situation. Afterwards, we will look at why the world isn't that simple and how we deal with the complications. So let's assume the following:

► You have an invoice or receipt from the supplier for each of your purchases – and the date on each document corresponds to the month in which you want the purchase to appear in your accounts.

► Likewise, you have issued a sales invoice for each of your sales – and the date on each document corresponds to the month in which you want the sale to appear in your accounts.

► The only payments you have received or made were in respect of some or all of those invoices and they were all made online, so they appeared on your bank statements immediately.

Purchase invoices/receipts

Your accounting software will have a button you click to enter purchase invoices. For each invoice, you simply have to:

► Choose the right supplier account (and, if it doesn't yet exist in your system, create it first).

► Enter the relevant details of the invoice.

► Choose the nominal account in which you want the expense to appear – e.g. travel costs or stationery or whatever.

► Check the VAT has been calculated properly by the system.

► Make sure you mark the physical invoice when you've entered it, so you know you've done it and don't enter it twice.

When you click 'save' (or whatever) after entering the invoice details, the accounting system will:

► Save all those details in the supplier account in the purchase ledger.

► Enter the following in the nominal ledger:
  – Increase (credit) **Trade creditors**.
  – Decrease (debit) **VAT liability** (if you are VAT registered and can reclaim the VAT).
  – Decrease (debit) **Retained profit (Travel expenses)**.

► Record the transaction in the audit trail.

Note how I've described the third entry in the nominal ledger. I'm assuming this purchase invoice was in respect of travel expenses. I've written the entry as I have (i.e. mentioning retained profit) because I want you to remember that the nominal account you are amending is one of the many nominal accounts that together make up the retained profit 'box' on the balance sheet.

Sales invoices

Entering all your sales invoices is exactly analagous to entering the purchase invoices, except that it is the sales ledger that records the details of each invoice and the entries it makes on the nominal ledger will be:

- ► Increase (debit) **Trade debtors**.
- ► Increase (credit) **VAT liability**.
- ► Increase (credit) **Retained profit (Internet sales)**.

So when you've done this for every sales and purchase invoice, then, in our simple world, you've actually worked out what your total profit to date is, because every transaction that affects retained profit has now been entered.

Your balance sheet is still wrong in places, however, because it currently says you are still owed all the money for all your sales and you still owe your creditors for all your purchases, whereas in practice you will have paid some suppliers and received some money from customers.

Dealing with cash payments and receipts

This is equally simple. Somewhere in your accounting system is a button that allows you to enter payments received from customers. You then simply choose the right customer account, enter the amount of the **remittance** and then tell the system which invoice(s) the remittance is paying (because you may have several invoices to any given customer waiting to be paid).

When you click save, the accounting system will:

- ► Record the details of the payment in the relevant customer account in the sales ledger.

- ▶ Enter the following on the nominal ledger:
  - – Increase (debit) **Cash**.
  - – Decrease (credit) **Trade debtors**.
- ▶ Record the transaction in the audit trail.

And of course, when you enter payments made to suppliers, which you do in exactly the same way, the accounting system will:

- ▶ Record all the details of the payment in the relevant supplier account in the purchase ledger.
- ▶ Enter the following on the nominal ledger:
  - – Decrease (credit) **Cash**.
  - – Decrease (debit) **Trade creditors**.
- ▶ Record the transaction in the audit trail.

At this point, in our very simple world, your TB would be done. Assuming you've got your chart of accounts set up, you could click the relevant buttons to get your actual balance sheet and P&L.

What about the cash flow statement?

Well, most of the accounting systems for smaller businesses don't produce a cash flow statement for you. This has to be done manually, following the methodology we talked about earlier.

Accounting in the real world

I hope you can see that the accounting system is providing functionality that is useful to you (i.e. the sales and purchase ledgers) and, at the same time, doing the double entry onto the nominal ledger, so every transaction is being properly recorded on the balance sheet.

Of course, the real world is not as simple as this. There are lots of 'exceptions' that we have to deal with. Believe me when I say that none of these exceptions is hard to understand. You just need to deal with them one at a time. Let's now look at the most common ones.

Accrued expenses ('Accruals')

As we saw with SBL, sometimes we know we have incurred a cost in a month, but have not yet received an invoice, let alone paid the supplier. We need to allow for the cost in this month. This is done by way of a **journal entry**. So you click the button on your accounting system for journal entries and simply tell the system which nominal accounts you want to adjust and by how much, and enter a date so the system knows which month the entry belongs in (most people just use the month end date). So this journal will make the following entries:

- ▶ Increase (credit) **Accrued expenses** (usually shortened to just 'accruals').

- ▶ Decrease (debit) **Retained profit (stationery)**.

We also have to make accrued expenses entries when we *have* received an invoice from the supplier but it has a date that is *after* the month in which the expense belongs. This is because most accounting systems work off the date of the relevant source document. If you enter an invoice dated March, the cost will appear in retained profit in March. If you want that cost to appear in February, you have to make an accrual with a February date. You must not just 'change' the date on a source document to suit yourself, because you will get in trouble with the VAT inspector.

OK, but what happens when you do the March accounts? You're going to have to enter the invoice because of the VAT, aren't you? Which means you're going to record the cost twice in your accounts.

Yes, you must enter the invoice, so you are right. The answer to the problem is that you 'reverse the accrual'. In other words, you make the journal entries you made except the other way around so they cancel each other out. And you give the second journal a March date, so that the entries are recorded in March. Take a look at Table 5.2.

- ▶ Column 0 shows an imaginary, much simplified balance sheet at the end of February but before we have made the accrual.

- ▶ In column 1, I show the two entries that make up the journal entry for the accrual, which I am assuming is for £350 before VAT. Note that when we accrue for costs in this way, we don't allow for the VAT,

Table 5.2

	0 Balance sheet before accrual	1 Accrue cost	2 Balance sheet at end of Feb	3 Post the invoice	4 Reverse the accrual	5 Balance sheet at end of March
Total assets	10,000		10,000			10,000
Claims						
Trade creditors	6,000		6,000	420		6,420
VAT liability	1,000		1,000	(70)		930
Accruals	0	350	350		(350)	0
Share capital	1,000		1,000			1,000
Retained profit	2,000	(350)	1,650	(350)	350	1,650
Total	10,000	0	10,000	0	0	10,000

because VAT is driven solely by the dates on invoices. The accrual thus has no effect on VAT.

▶ This then gives us the balance sheet at the end of February in column 2. You can see that retained profit has gone down in February by £350, as we wanted.

▶ Then column 3 shows the three entries that the accounting system makes for you when you enter the invoice dated March. As you say, the £350 cost is now being deducted from retained profit twice. And you can see that the VAT is now entered into the balance sheet and reduces the amount of VAT payable.

▶ Column 4 shows the second journal entry (dated March) that cancels out the February journal entry.

▶ And so, assuming for these simplistic purposes that there were no other transactions for the company in March, column 5 gives us the balance sheet at the end of March. As you can see, this correctly reflects:

  – the trade creditors figure;

  – the VAT liability;

  – the retained profit.

Accrued income

If you make a sale that belongs in February, but the invoice you issue, for whatever reason, is dated March, then you have an exactly analagous situation. You simply:

▸ Increase (debit) **Accrued income**.

▸ Increase (credit) **Retained profit (Christmas fair sales)**.

And then in March, you enter the sales invoice and reverse the accrued income entry. Have a look at the model balance sheet chart [page 69] and note that accrued income is on the assets bar. This is because it *is* an asset. It reflects money you are owed. It is the equivalent of trade debtors when you haven't actually got an invoice.

Deferred income

So what happens if you invoice a customer in February, but you've invoiced them in advance, so the sale is actually taking place in March?

Guess what? It's exactly the same but the other way around and with different words. Look at Table 5.3 and, as before, read it a column at a time (rather than reading across rows).

Table 5.3

	0 Balance sheet before accrual	1 Enter sales invoice	2 Defer the income	3 Balance sheet at end of Feb	4 Reverse the deferred income	5 Balance sheet at end of March
Assets						
Debtors	10,000	1,200		11,200		11,200
Total	10,000	1,200	0	11,200	0	11,200
Claims						
VAT liability	1,000	200		1,200		1,200
Deferred income	0		1,000	1,000	(1,000)	0
Share capital	1,000			1,000		1,000
Retained profit	8,000	1,000	(1,000)	8,000	1,000	9,000
Total	10,000	1,200	0	11,200	0	11,200

Note the following:

- ▶ The 'deferred income' journal in column 2 cancels out the impact of the invoice on retained profit in February.
- ▶ It is the reversing of the deferred income journal that has the effect of 'recognising' the sale in retained profit during March.
- ▶ The deferred income nominal account is a claim over the assets. This is logical if you think about it. We've invoiced the customer, which is saying the customer owes us. But we haven't given the customer the goods/service yet, so we owe them either the goods/service or their money back, so they have a claim over the company's assets.

Deferred expenses ('Prepayments')

We have the exact same thing if a supplier invoices us in advance of providing the goods or services. We want to 'defer' the expense into a subsequent period. Note that this nominal account is usually called **Prepayments**. This can be confusing to beginners because it implies there was an actual payment (as we saw with SBL in Transaction 13). More often than not, though, the 'double entry' is a purchase invoice, so deferred expense is a better description.

Cash payments or receipts with no source document

If you have a bank loan or overdraft, the chances are that the bank will simply take the interest each month or quarter out of your bank account and show it on your bank statement. There's no separate document about it. This means that the entry in your bank statement is doing two things:

- ▶ Recognising the interest transaction (and acting as the source document).
- ▶ Settling (i.e. paying) the interest transaction.

You could, if you wanted, enter this as two separate transactions (using the journal functionality of your accounting system):

- ▶ Recognise the interest expense:
  - – Increase (credit) **Liability to the bank**.
  - – Decrease (debit) **Retained profit (Interest expense)**.

- ► Settle the payment of the interest:
  - – Decrease (credit) **Cash**.
  - – Decrease (debit) **Liability to the bank**.

In practice, this is usually done in one go, using a feature of your accounting system called something like 'Bank payments'. Whatever it's called, it is different from the 'supplier payment' feature that pays invoices in the Purchase ledger. The entries this function makes are direct to the nominal ledger and are just:

- ► Decrease (credit) **Cash**.
- ► Decrease (debit) **Retained profit (Interest expense)**.

The important thing, when entering each cash payment and receipt, is to make sure you are clear whether it is:

- ► merely settling an invoice in the system; or
- ► both recognising a new transaction and settling it.

Cheque payments and receipts

If I pay people by cheque, Chris, do I use the cheque stub as my 'source document' for that payment or do I wait until I see the payment going out of my bank account (i.e. making the bank statement the source document)?

You *could* use either (but whatever you do, be consistent). However, it's *much* better practice to use the cheque stubs. This is because you really want your accounting system to be able to tell you at any given time how much cash you have 'available'. Now if you write a cheque to someone and send it in the post, it might be days before they cash that cheque. If you use the bank statements as your source document, your accounting system won't know you've written that cheque, so for those few days, you will be led to believe you have more cash available than you actually do.

What about when I receive money by cheque? I could either use the stubs from the paying-in book or the bank statements. Your logic would suggest I should use the bank statements for this because I can't spend the money until it's cleared my bank account, even though I know I've got the money 'coming'.

Well, you make a good point, although remember that cheques do bounce, so you may be *fairly sure* you've got the money coming, but you're not 100 per cent certain until it's cleared. As it happens, most people run this risk and use the paying-in book stubs. This is because they are pretty sure they've 'got' that money and want the best picture of their cash position.

Bank account reconciliation

This discussion about cheques brings me onto a very important subject – **bank account reconciliation** (accountants say 'bank rec'). All this means is seeing whether, at any given point in time, your bank balance according to your accounting system is the same as your bank balance according to your actual bank statement. And if the figures are *not* the same, explaining *why* they are not the same.

This is an incredibly important part of the accounting process for a couple of reasons:

- ► Running out of cash is a disaster for a business, so you have to know exactly how much you have at all times.
- ► Many of the mistakes you might make when doing your accounting (and we all make them) will show up when you try to reconcile your bank account(s).

Some companies with big accounts departments reconcile their bank accounts *every day*. You *must* at least do it whenever you do your accounts.

Now, even if you don't ever make a mistake, you will, if you issue and/or receive cheques and are using the stubs as your source documents, often find a difference between the accounting system figure and the bank statement figure because the accounting system will reflect *all* cheques right up to the balance sheet date, whereas the bank statements will only show those that have cleared. Given the much reduced usage of cheques these days, this is less of an issue than it used to be.

Modern accounting systems all have a feature to help you do your bank reconciliations (and I use the plural because you must do them for each bank account you have). Personally, while I use this feature, I still like to make a list of the cheques or whatever that haven't cleared that make up the difference between my accounting system and my bank statements.

Fixed assets and depreciation

We saw in Transaction 3 that one of the costs incurred by SBL did not immediately affect retained profit. This is because it was an asset that was going to be 'consumed' by the company over the course of a few years. Instead of decreasing retained profit, we therefore increased fixed assets on the asset bar. Subsequently, we did reflect some of the cost of the asset in the current year's retained profit by allowing for **depreciation**. In the jargon, we **capitalised** the cost, as opposed to **expensing** it or **writing it off**. Management of companies often like to capitalise as much cost as they can get away with, because it effectively spreads that cost over a few years, which is obviously good for the current year's profits (which are what determines this year's bonus!).

The chances are that you will enter the cost of any fixed asset by way of an invoice being entered into the purchase ledger. There's no problem with telling the purchase ledger to make the entry to fixed assets. So what it does is:

- ▶ Increase (credit) **Trade creditors**.
- ▶ Increase (debit) **Fixed assets**.

Some accounting systems have a special module for fixed assets, which is another 'supporting module' like the sales and purchase ledgers. This will keep track of your assets, do the depreciation calculations and enter the depreciation into the nominal ledger each month for you. If you don't have such a module, you can easily enter depreciation using the journal functionality:

- ▶ Decrease (credit) **Fixed assets**.
- ▶ Decrease (debit) **Retained profit**.

As I mentioned earlier, companies would typically have separate nominal accounts for different types of fixed asset. The other thing you should do, which I didn't mention, is to keep the depreciation for each asset type separate from the original cost of those assets. This helps when it comes to producing statutory accounts, as we will see when we look at Wingate. So, what you get in fact is:

- ▶ When you buy a fixed asset (e.g. a vehicle):
  - – Increase (credit) **Trade creditors**.
  - – Increase (debit) **Cost of vehicles**.

- ▶ When you want to post depreciation of a vehicle:
  - – Decrease (credit) **Vehicles – Accumulated depreciation**.
  - – Decrease (debit) **Retained profit (Vehicle depreciation expense)**.

So the net value of your Vehicle fixed assets on your balance sheet is the cost box less the accumulated depreciation box. In terms of debits and credits, you can see the cost box is a debit balance, which is what we expect because it is on the assets bar. The accumulated depreciation box is a credit balance because it is effectively reducing the value of the Vehicles on the assets bar.

Stock

Another cost you might incur that you won't want to immediately 'post' (as accountants say) to retained profit is stock purchases. As we saw with SBL's transactions, we treat the stock as an asset and only recognise in retained profit the cost of the stock that has actually been sold.

The practicalities of how you do this will vary. Most accounting systems allow you to set up all your products (and raw materials for that matter) in yet another 'supporting' module. And if you create your sales invoices in the accounting system, which most allow you to do, you will specify which products are being sold and how many. Then, when the system posts the sale, it will also automatically:

- ▶ Update the product module for the products that have been sold.
- ▶ Enter the cost of the sale on the nominal ledger:
  - – Reduce (credit) **Stock**.
  - – Reduce (debit) **Retained profit (Cost of goods sold)**.
- ▶ Enter the transaction onto the audit trail.

This is all very efficient and the work involved in setting up the product module is usually worth the effort.

The important conceptual point here is that all the cost you have *ever* incurred on stock must appear in one of two places:

- ▶ in the Stock box; or
- ▶ in the Retained profit box.

If you don't use a product module, then you need some way of making sure you have the right amount of cost in each place. One way some people do this is as follows:

- ► All spending on stock is initially treated as cost of goods sold. So when you enter each purchase invoice relating to stock into the purchase ledger, you tell it to apply the cost to the cost of goods sold nominal account (which is part of retained profit, obviously):
  - – Increase (credit) **Trade creditors**.
  - – Decrease (debit) **Retained profit (Cost of goods sold)**.
- ► At the end of each month, you work out (perhaps in a spreadsheet) the cost of the stock you have left in stock. You then, in non-accounting language, take that amount of cost out of the retained profit box and put it into the stock box. In accounting language, you would make a journal entry as follows:
  - – Increase (credit) **Retained profit**.
  - – Increase (debit) **Stock**.

As long as you have the right figure in the stock box, you *must* have the right figure in retained profit. Bear in mind with this journal that you might have a value in the stock box left over from last month, in which case the journal has to be for the right amount such that the resulting figure in the stock box is the value of the stock at the current month end.

'Proving' your balance sheet

This is the second most important thing I'm going to tell you in this session. In my old life, I used to check the work of lots of different book-keepers and accountants, including properly qualified ones. You would simply not believe how often I would find mistakes in their work within, literally, minutes of starting my review. And the reason for this was always that they didn't *check* their work. They simply followed their process and assumed the answer must therefore be correct. But, as I said, everyone makes mistakes.

If you ask most people who keep their accounts for their own business how they check their accounts, they will say they look at the P&L and see if the sales, expenses and profits look about right. This is obviously a sensible thing to do. However, it's not enough. There are all sorts of possible errors that might not be immediately obvious.

What you need to do comes back, as always, to the balance sheet. If you can prove to yourself (or your boss) that every box other than retained profit on the balance sheet is correct, then, because the balance sheet balances, you *know* the retained profit box is correct. So you know you are not over- or under-stating profit.

So how do you check each box on the balance sheet? The answer is that you need 'backup' for each box that 'proves' the figure. So, for example:

- ▶ For fixed assets, you might have a spreadsheet showing all the assets you have, what they cost and each month's depreciation. Netting all this out will give you the net value of the fixed assets which should be the figure on your balance sheet.

- ▶ For trade debtors, print out what's known as an 'aged' listing. This shows how much you are owed by each customer and how old the debts are. Look for:

  - – negative figures, which suggests you've posted cash received to an invoice twice;

  - – very old debts. If these are right, you might want to get on the phone and ask for your money. If you know you're not going to get the money, you need to allow for the bad debt in your accounts.

- ▶ Ditto for trade creditors.

- ▶ For each of accruals, accrued income, deferred income and deferred payments, you should have a spreadsheet listing all the items that make up the balance in each of these nominal accounts. When you review these spreadsheets, any that should not be on the list will jump out at you. Failing to reverse entries in these nominal accounts is one of the most common errors people make and this backup will immediately highlight this fact.

- ▶ For stock, which is another area where mistakes are *frequently* made, you need to have some system for convincing yourself that the stock figure is correct. This will often be a spreadsheet with a list of your stock items, the quantities in stock at the end of the month and the cost values. Every £ your stock figure is wrong by is a £ that your retained profit is wrong by.

► Your bank reconciliation will prove the balance of the cash box is correct.

And so on.

Once you have a system in place, this checking process is really quick (and, believe it or not, quite satisfying).

That's it for practical accounting today. I hope this has helped you understand what's going on inside your accounting system and that the accounting process is just a matter of steadily working your way to a balance sheet that is correct at the relevant month end.

Summary

Here's what you need to keep in mind when finding your way around your accounting system

► Accounting systems have a lot of helpful functionality but, ultimately, it's about getting every transaction entered onto the balance sheet.

► In the accounting system, the balance sheet is actually made up of a lot of nominal accounts which reflect the cumulative effect of every transaction the company has *ever* made.

► The TB is nothing more than a list of the nominal accounts and the balance in each of them, so it is in effect a very detailed balance sheet.

► There are all sorts of things that make the real world a bit more complicated than the most simple world we could imagine. Provided we think about them individually, they are not difficult to deal with.

► Your accounting for the month is not done until you have 'proved' your balance sheet is correct. If it is correct, then retained profit must be correct and your P&L will therefore be correct.

PART 2

Interpretation and analysis of accounts

CHAPTER SIX

Wingate's annual report

- ► Different types of accounts
- ► The reports
- ► Assets
- ► Liabilities
- ► Shareholders' equity
- ► The P&L and cash flow statements

The first five sessions were devoted to the basics of accounting: the fundamental principle, the balance sheet, double entry, the derivation of the P&L and cash flow statement from the balance sheet. If you're absolutely clear on everything we've done so far, then you know about 80 per cent of everything you'll ever need to know about accounting.

From here on, it's just about understanding the rules and terminology that have developed over the years. The terminology is no problem; the rules can get very complicated, as they have to deal with all sorts of special situations. But these special situations are not important at the moment. What you and I need is a broad understanding of the rules. As you will see, there is nothing inherently difficult about any of them.

What we are going to do is work our way through Wingate's annual report and I'll explain anything we haven't already covered. Just before we do that, though, let's just talk about the difference between **management accounts** and **statutory accounts**.

Different types of accounts

Management accounts are the accounts companies prepare for the use of their directors and management. These accounts, if they are prepared properly, are based on the fundamental principle of accounting and the two basic concepts we discussed earlier (the accruals basis and the going concern assumption). There are, however, no other requirements as to how they should be laid out, how much detail there should be, etc. These things are up to the company to decide. Often, of course, they will obey many of the rules for statutory accounts. They are not available to members of the public (unless the company chooses to publish them for some reason).

Statutory accounts are the accounts which companies have to file with Companies House each year and make available to their shareholders. There are many rules for such accounts and in fact there are different *sets* of rules for different categories of company.

Statutory accounts filed with Companies House are available (at a cost) to the public. Note, though, that small and medium-sized companies (as defined by the Companies Act) are entitled to file **abbreviated accounts** (although they still have to produce full accounts for tax purposes and for their shareholders). Abbreviated accounts provide considerably less information. For example, in the case of small companies, no P&L is required – all you get is a balance sheet. What we're going to look at here are the statutory accounts of Wingate, also known as its Annual Report.

The reports

Let's start by looking at the reports, of which there are always at least three.

The strategic report

The **strategic report** is a recent introduction to company accounts. It is meant to provide shareholders with information that will enable them to assess how the directors have performed their duty to promote the success of the company. In particular, the report should explain:

- the company's business model, strategy and objectives;
- the principal risks faced by the company;
- the company's past performance.

In practice, some companies provide a lot of information in this report, while others provide as little as they can get away with.

The directors' report

All companies are required by law to provide a directors' report with their annual accounts (although they can be omitted from abbreviated accounts). Now the strategic report exists, the directors' report usually contains very little of interest.

The auditors' report

Most substantial companies have to have their annual accounts **audited**. This just means that a firm of accountants comes in and makes an independent examination of the company's books.

When the accounts are produced for the shareholders (or **members** as they are formally called), the auditors have to provide a report, expressing their opinion on the company's financial statements.

The auditors' report usually states, rather long-windedly, that:

- ► They have audited the accounts.
- ► In their opinion, the accounts give a true and fair view of the company's state of affairs and the changes over the relevant period.
- ► The accounts have been properly prepared in accordance with the appropriate accounting standards and the Companies Act.
- ► They're not responsible for anything.

Other than the last part, this is what you would hope and expect. But do always read what they say under the last three headings:

- ► Opinion on financial statements
- ► Opinion on other matters prescribed by the Companies Act 2006
- ► Matters on which we are required to report by exception.

If they say anything other than 'it's all fine' under any of these headings, you need to sit up and take notice. In the extreme, the auditors will give a 'qualified' opinion, which means they are not entirely happy with some aspects of the accounting. This is nearly always a bad sign, so watch out for it.

Assets

The real substance of the annual report is in the three main financial statements and the notes to those statements.

We will now review these in detail. As always, we will start with the balance sheet [page 272], looking first at the assets and then at the claims on those assets. As we go down the balance sheet, we will refer to the relevant notes to make sure we cover everything.

Tangible fixed assets

As you will recall, fixed assets are assets for use in the business on a long-term continuing basis. **Tangible fixed assets** are, as the name implies, fixed assets that you can touch, such as land, buildings, machinery, fixtures and fittings, vehicles, etc.

If you look at the balance sheet on page 272, you can see that there is a single tangible fixed assets figure for each of the two years (£5,326k in year five and £4,445k in year four). This tells us that the tangible assets went up by £881k during the last year.

If you look at Note 8 on page 277, you will see, as I pointed out earlier, that there is a table giving much more detail about the fixed assets.

The first thing to notice about this table is that there are three columns separating the fixed assets into different categories. The three categories are then added together in the fourth column to give the total.

If you look at the bottom right-hand corner of the table, you will see the figures £5,326k and £4,445k. These are the net book value figures that appear on the balance sheet. As I explained earlier, net book value is simply the cost of the assets less the total depreciation on the assets up to that point in time.

The rest of the table shows how the assets came to have the net book values that they do. To see how this works, we will work our way down the 'Total' column.

Look at the top of the table. The first section, headed 'Cost', shows what the company paid originally for its fixed assets:

▶ At the start of year five the company had fixed assets which had cost it a total of £6,492k to buy.

▶ During the year, the company bought fixed assets which cost it another £1,391k.

▶ Some fixed assets were sold during the year, however. These assets had originally cost £35k. Note that this is *not* what the company received for the assets when it sold them.

▶ Thus the original cost of the fixed assets still owned by the company at the end of the year totalled £7,848k (being 6,492 + 1,391 − 35).

The next section shows how the total cumulative depreciation to date was arrived at:

▶ By the start of year five, the fixed assets of the company had been depreciated by £2,047k. In other words, the company was saying that the fixed assets had been used and were worth less than when they were new.

▶ Some of that depreciation (£20k), however, related to the fixed assets that the company sold during the year. Since the company no longer owns the assets, we must remove the relevant depreciation from our calculations. Hence, we deduct it from the starting depreciation figure.

▶ We then have to add the depreciation charge for the year (£495k). This is made up of depreciation on the assets which were owned at the start of the year plus some depreciation on the assets bought during the year.

▶ We can then calculate the total depreciation figure for the assets still owned at the end of the year which is £2,522k (being 2,047 − 20 + 495).

Now all we have to do is subtract the depreciation figure from the cost figure to get the net book value figure to go on our balance sheet. Naturally, you can work your way down any one of the three individual fixed asset categories in the table, using the same principles.

Sale of fixed assets

I'm not sure if this is the time to mention it but I'm slightly confused by the sale of some of the fixed assets. I can see how selling an asset will reduce the fixed assets figure on the balance sheet, but what is the other entry?

A good question, but you should be able to work it out for yourself. The note on fixed assets tells us that Wingate sold fixed assets that had an original cost of £35k and total depreciation when sold of £20k. Thus they had a net book value of £15k upon sale.

Go back to the balance sheet chart [page 69]. When we sell a fixed asset, the fixed asset box must go down by the net book value of the asset which, in this case, is £15k.

I know from Wingate's accounts (I'll tell you how shortly) that Wingate sold those fixed assets for £23k. Assume that was paid in cash at the time of the sale. Obviously, Wingate's cash box must go up by £23k. The net effect of this and the reduction of the fixed assets box is that Wingate's assets bar goes up by £8k. Something else must change. No other assets or liabilities are affected so it must be the shareholders who benefit. Thus we raise retained profit by £8k. Wingate has made a profit on the sale of the fixed assets of £8k. This profit is declared in Note 3 to the accounts [page 276].

I can see how the accounting works, but it doesn't seem right that we are claiming to have made a profit on selling an asset for £23k when it cost us £35k in the first place.

Your question shows the importance of concentrating on what the balance sheet looks like immediately before and immediately after a transaction. Let's look at what actually happened:

- ▶ The assets were bought for £35k.
- ▶ Between the date of purchase and the date of sale, the assets were depreciated by £20k. This means that the retained profit of the company was reduced by £20k during that period.
- ▶ But, in fact, Wingate sold the assets for £23k. This implies that the total cost to the company of owning the assets for the time it did was only £12k (i.e. 35 − 23).

▶ This means that retained profit was reduced by too much in the earlier years. The cost of owning these assets was not as high as £20k – it was only £12k. Hence, when we sell them we have to cancel out the overcharged amount, which we do by showing a profit on sale.

While you've been explaining that to Tom, I've been looking at the effect of this sale on Wingate's cash flow statement. I'm afraid I don't understand it.

Again, we can work it out from first principles. We have just seen that the profit on sale is the difference between what you sell the assets for and their book value in the accounts at the time of sale. Another way of writing this would be:

$$\text{Proceeds} = \text{Book Value} + \text{Profit}$$
$$£23\text{k} = £15\text{k} + £8\text{k}$$

We know that the cash box has gone up by £23k so the cash flow statement must include exactly this amount. Now, if you remember from the cash flow statement we drew up for SBL, we start a cash flow statement with the assumption that cash flow equals operating profit and then adjust it to get to the actual cash flow.

If we start Wingate's cash flow statement with operating profit, then we will automatically have included the profit on sale of the fixed assets (i.e. the £8k) because it is included in operating profit (as Note 3 tells us). Thus, to get the total cash flow effect of selling the fixed assets, we just need to make an adjustment to add in the book value of the assets sold. Then both the book value and the profit on sale will be included and we will have accounted for all the proceeds.

In actual fact, we don't do it like this. Instead, we adjust operating profit to *remove* the £8k profit on sale of the fixed assets. You can see this under the Operating activities section in Wingate's cash flow statement on page 273.

This leaves our cash flow statement without any of the cash proceeds from the sale of the fixed assets. We then include the whole £23k proceeds under the heading 'Capital expenditure'.

The result is the same whichever way you do it. It's all just down to adding and subtracting, as always with accounting. Incidentally, the entry in the cash flow statement is what told me that Wingate had sold those assets for £23k.

Stock

Accounting for stock in SBL's books was straightforward. When Sarah bought stock, we simply increased the stock box by the cost of the stock. When Sarah sold stock, we reduced the stock box by the cost of the stock being sold.

This works fine for many companies, but not for a manufacturer such as Wingate. A manufacturer buys raw materials, makes things with those raw materials and then puts the finished goods into a warehouse, ready to sell to customers. A manufacturer will thus have three types of stock:

- ► Raw materials
- ► Work in progress (goods that are partially manufactured at the balance sheet date)
- ► Finished goods (i.e. goods ready for sale)

Accounting for raw materials is simple. We can treat them in exactly the same way as we did SBL's stock.

What value should we attribute to work in progress and finished goods, though? When we manufacture goods, we take raw materials and do things to them. This involves costs such as rent, electricity, employee wages, depreciation of fixed assets. We call these costs collectively the **production costs**. Because these costs have been incurred, we have to recognise them in the accounts. The question is: what should the accounting entries be? Let's use employee wages as an example and assume the employees have been paid during the accounting period. Obviously we must decrease (credit) the cash box. What should the other entry be?

Well, these costs have made the shareholders poorer, haven't they? So we should reduce retained profit.

If the shareholders were poorer, that would be correct. However, these production costs have been incurred in turning an asset, the raw materials, into a more valuable asset. So we take the view that the shareholders are not poorer. Instead of decreasing retained profit, therefore, we actually increase the value of the stock box (either work in progress if we're still manufacturing the goods or finished goods if the job is complete). When the finished goods are sold, of course, we have to reduce retained profit by the total value of the stock sold (i.e. the raw material cost plus the production costs we have added to it).

You remember the accruals concept we talked about earlier as one of the two fundamental concepts of accounting. Something called **matching** used to be a key part of that concept but some time ago the accounting authorities decided it should be given less emphasis. I think it's helpful to beginners and you may come across it elsewhere so let me explain it. Basically, matching simply means that you make sure you match costs to revenues in any accounting period. Taking our example above, if you had simply reduced retained profit by the production costs even though the stock had not been sold, you would have had cost in this accounting period but no associated sales. During a subsequent accounting period, you would have had sales but your only cost would have been the raw materials cost. That means that in neither of those two accounting periods do you have a fair view of how much profit the company made.

I see that Note 1(d) [page 275] is about stocks and it says that the costs of production are included in manufactured goods as you have just been saying. What is the rest of this note about, though?

There are two different points here. If some of the stocks are worth less than they cost the company, then, to be conservative, we must decrease their value in the balance sheet (as we say, **write them down**). Thus we say that stock is valued at the lower of cost (where cost would include any costs of production) and **net realisable value** (i.e. what we could sell the stock for).

The other point takes a little more thinking about. Let's go back to SBL, where stock was just bought in rather than manufactured. What would we have done if Sarah had bought two lots of identical stock at different prices, as follows?

- ► 50 bunches at £20 a bunch (i.e. a total of £1,000).
- ► 100 bunches at £23 a bunch (i.e. a total of £2,300).

Accounting for the purchase is easy; we simply increase the stock box by £3,300. If Sarah then sold 75 bunches to a customer for £40 a bunch, the sales figure would be £3,000, being 75 × £40. How much would her cost of goods sold be for this transaction, though?

The answer is that it depends. Different companies choose different ways of dealing with this question. Two of the most common ways are the **average method** and **FIFO**.

In the **average method**, we simply take the average cost of stock during the period. In our example this would be:

$$(50 \times £20 + 100 \times £23) / 150 = £22 \text{ per bunch}$$

This means that the cost of goods sold for the transaction would be £1,650, being $75 \times £22$.

FIFO stands for 'First In First Out'. This means that the oldest stock (i.e. that purchased first) is 'used' first. In our example, the oldest stock was purchased for £20. Unfortunately, we only have 50 bunches of that stock, so we then 'use' some of the next oldest stock. Our cost of goods sold is therefore:

$$50 \times £20 + 25 \times £23 = £1,575$$

You've got the same sales in each case, but different cost of goods sold. That means you're going to get different profit figures, doesn't it?

Yes, it does. This is one of many ways in which two identical companies could have different accounts. The key point to remember is that companies are obliged to use the same method every year, so their accounts are comparable from one year to the next. The method they use will be disclosed in the accounting policies in the annual report, as you can see it has been for Wingate.

Trade debtors and doubtful debts

The next heading on Wingate's balance sheet is simply 'Debtors'. This is made up of a number of items, which are listed in Note 10 [page 278]. The first is trade debtors.

Accounting for trade debtors is simple. We saw how to do it when we looked at SBL. The only thing you have to consider is the effect of bad debts or doubtful debts. If:

▶ you know that one of your customers has gone bust owing you money which they will not be able to pay, or

▶ you have reason to believe that one of your customers is likely to go bust and not be able to pay you, then you should make an allowance for those non-payments. If you know for certain that you will not get paid, then you **write off** the debt. If you only think you might not get paid, then you make a **provision** against the debt.

Whether you are writing off a debt or just making a provision, the accounting is the same:

- ► Decrease (credit) **Debtors**.
- ► Decrease (debit) **Retained profit**.

What if you make a provision against a debt that you think may not be paid, but subsequently it is?

You have to reverse the transaction. Effectively, it will show up as an additional profit in your next set of accounts:

- ► Increase (debit) **Cash**.
- ► Increase (credit) **Retained profit**.

Prepayments

Again, the accounting treatment is identical to that which we used when constructing SBL's balance sheet.

Other debtors

This is a catch-all box for any amounts owed to the company that don't fit elsewhere.

Cash

As I explained when we were putting SBL's accounts together, the term 'cash' to a company has a different meaning from that used by individuals. An individual thinks of cash as being coins and notes, as opposed to cheques, credit cards or money at the bank.

To a company, cash means money which it can get its hands on quickly in order to pay people. Thus money in a current account would qualify as cash. Money tied up in a deposit account for anything more than about 90 days does *not* count as cash, however.

Liabilities

We have now looked at all the assets on Wingate's balance sheet. I hope you agree that there is nothing very difficult about the accounting there, as long as we stick by our fundamental principle. Now we need to look at the various liabilities.

The balance sheet itself only has two lines for liabilities:

► Current liabilities (i.e. those due to be paid in the next 12 months);

► Long-term liabilities (all others).

We can see more detail of these items in Notes 11 and 12.

Trade creditors

There is no difficulty here. The accounting is just the same as for SBL.

Social security and other taxes

Companies with employees have to pay national insurance and income tax on the wages and salaries which they pay those employees. These charges are normally paid two to three weeks after the end of each month, so they usually show up as a liability on any balance sheet which is drawn up at the end of a month.

VAT payable to HMRC is also normally included under this category.

Accruals

Accruals are exactly as I described them when we were drawing up SBL's balance sheet. They are any costs that need to be included in the accounts to satisfy our matching concept, but where no invoice has been received or where the invoice is dated after the year end. Unlike the trade creditors figure, accruals will not normally include VAT.

Cash in advance (Deferred revenue/income)

Many companies can justify charging their customers in advance of delivering the goods. Often this is just a deposit; in other cases it might be full payment for something, such as a subscription to a magazine.

We talked about how to account for this when talking about accounting in practice in session 5.

Bank overdraft

Most of us are all too familiar with overdrafts. They are simply current accounts with a negative amount of cash in them. Many companies have such accounts from which they pay all their day-to-day bills and into which they put the cash they receive from customers.

As they do with individuals, banks usually grant an **overdraft facility** to companies. This means that the company can run up an overdraft to a specified limit. There is not normally any time limit on overdraft facilities, but the banks nearly always retain the right to demand immediate repayment ('repayment on demand'). This is why they are treated as current rather than long-term liabilities.

Bank loans

Bank loans are very similar to personal loans. They are made to enable specific purchases of equipment, buildings and other assets to be made. Terms for repayment of the **principal** (i.e. the amount of the loan) and payments of interest are agreed in advance. The interest payments may be fixed amounts, but usually they will be variable. So, for example, the interest payments on a loan may be described as being at '12 month LIBOR + 3%'. **LIBOR** stands for the **London Inter Bank Offered Rate**. It is the rate at which banks lend to each other. The rates at which they do that depend on the length of the loan so 12 month LIBOR refers to the rate at which the banks would lend to each other for 12 months. When the time came to make an interest payment on my example loan, the bank would calculate the amount by adding 3 per cent to the then current 12 month LIBOR rate.

A loan agreement may have other conditions and restrictions which are known as **covenants**. Provided the borrower does not breach the covenants, the bank usually does *not* have the right to demand immediate repayment.

A bank loan is nearly always accompanied by a **charge** or **lien** over the assets of the company. A charge guarantees the bank that, if the company gets into financial difficulty, the bank can have first claim over the proceeds from selling assets which are included in the charge. If the bank has a charge over a specific asset, the charge is known as a **fixed charge** or **mortgage**. This is identical to the charge that the building society has over your house. If the bank's charge is over other assets of the company, such as stock or debtors, where the actual, specific assets change from day to day as the company trades, it is known as a **floating charge**. Charges generally are known as **security** or, in the USA, **collateral** and bank debt is often referred to as **senior debt**, because it is 'senior' to all other creditors when it comes to getting their money back.

In Wingate's case, you can see:

- ► £525k of bank loans are under current liabilities, meaning this amount is due to be repaid in the next 12 months.
- ► £2,625k of bank loans are under long-term liabilities.

Leases

A lease is a contract between the owner of an asset (such as a building, a car, a photocopier) and someone who wants the use of that asset for a period of time. The owner of the asset is known as the **lessor**; the user of the asset is the **lessee**.

For accounting purposes, leases are divided into two sorts: **operating leases** and **finance leases**.

Operating leases

An operating lease is one where the lessee pays the lessor a rental for using the asset for a period of time that is normally substantially less than the useful life of the asset. The lessor retains most of the risks and rewards of owning the asset. Typical examples would include a company renting office space from a landlord for 10 years or a construction company renting a crane from a plant hire firm for six months. The payments are typically made monthly or quarterly and the notes to the accounts would show how long operating leases have to run and what the total of the next 12 months' payments is. You can see this in Note 16 of Wingate's accounts.

We account for operating leases using the 'straight line method'. What this means is that, if the rental payments are not all the same amount (which is normal), we smooth them out so the retained profit (i.e. the P&L) for each accounting period shows the expense as if the payments *were* all the same.

But presumably you have to make the payments as agreed, so how does the accounting work if you are then showing the expense differently?

Let's take an example. Assume you rent an office for four years. The landlord has said you don't need to pay any rent for the first year. This is known as a rent-free period and is a common inducement to get people to enter into property leases. Let's then assume the rent after the rent-free period is £3,000 per calendar quarter to be paid at the start of each quarter.

This means the total rent over the life of the lease is £3,000 × 4 quarters × 3 years = £36,000. Over the four-year life of the lease, that's £9,000 per annum. This is what we have to show in our P&L for each year. So in the first year, we need to reduce retained profit by £9,000, but what is the other entry? Cash has not changed because we haven't paid anything to the landlord yet, thanks to the rent-free period. The answer is that we have a liability to the landlord even though there's no actual bill yet. We therefore 'accrue' the expense as we did in Adjustment 15 when looking at SBL's balance sheet. So our double entry becomes:

	Debit	Credit
Reduce **Retained profit**	£9,000	
Increase **Accruals**		£9,000

So what happens in year two of the lease? We'll have actually paid £12,000 to the landlord during the year but, if I understand correctly, we want to show just £9,000 in the P&L.

That's right. The key to this (and all accounting when you're dealing with things that stretch across more than one accounting period) is to look at it cumulatively. So, by the end of year two, on a cumulative basis, we know the following:

▶ We have actually paid a total of £12,000 cash to the landlord.

▶ We want to show a total of £18,000 of expense in the P&L.

Because we want to show more expense in the P&L than we have actually paid, we need to have an accrued expense at the end of year two of the lease for the amount of the difference (i.e. £6,000).

The double entries to be made for year two are therefore as follows:

	Debit	Credit
Reduce **Retained profit**	£9,000	
Reduce **Cash**		£12,000
Reduce **Accruals**	£3,000	
TOTAL	**£12,000**	**£12,000**

So you've now made:

- ▶ *two entries reducing retained profit totalling £18,000;*
- ▶ *one entry reducing cash totalling £12,000;*
- ▶ *two entries in accruals which net out to £6,000 (£9,000 increase less the £3,000 decrease).*

Correct. You should be able to work out the entries for the next two years. By the end of year four of the lease, the total cash paid (£36,000) will equal the total expense shown in retained profit (£9,000 × 4 years), so there will be no 'balancing' accrual required, which is as it should be because you won't have any liability to the landlord at that point as you've paid in full.

*What happens if, say, your lease requires you to pay **more** up front than the straight line method requires you to show in your P&L (i.e. you've paid in advance)?*

Just what you would expect from the maths. Instead of you having an obligation to the landlord at the end of the first year, he's got an obligation to you, so you've actually got an asset. Thus we make the difference between the cash paid and the amount we show in retained profit show as a prepayment rather than an accrual. This is like Transaction 13 when we were creating SBL's balance sheet.

Finance leases

A finance lease is one where the lessee uses the asset for the vast majority of the asset's useful life. In such circumstances the lessee has most of the risks and rewards of ownership. A typical example would be a car lease. We account for finance leases in a different way from operating leases and the process is somewhat more complicated.

Let's assume you need a car that would cost £10,000 to buy outright. Instead of leasing it, you *could* obtain a loan from your bank and buy the car. If you did this, your balance sheet would show a fixed asset of £10,000 and a liability to the bank of £10,000. You would then treat the fixed asset and the loan exactly as you would any other fixed asset and loan. You would depreciate the asset at an appropriate rate, and you would pay interest on the loan. At some point you would repay the loan.

Acquiring the car this way recognises both the asset and the liability to the bank on your balance sheet. On the other hand, if you lease the car and treat it as an operating lease, neither the asset nor the liability would show up on the balance sheet. You would merely recognise each lease payment by reducing cash and reducing retained profit, as and when the payments were made.

Having such a lease and treating it like an operating lease is what is known as **off-balance sheet finance**, because you are effectively getting a loan to buy an asset without showing either of them on your balance sheet. As a result, companies can build up substantial liabilities without them appearing on their balance sheets. When we account for finance leases, we therefore make them look like a loan and an asset purchase in two separate transactions.

I understand the principle, but I don't see how the accounting works. Can you explain it in a bit more detail?

The best thing to do is to look at an example. Let's assume that you agree to pay the lessor £300 per month for 48 months to lease a £10,000 car. You would be agreeing to pay a total of £14,400 to the lessor during the life of the lease. Effectively, the lessor has lent you £10,000 (the price of the car), which you have to repay in instalments with interest of £4,400 over 48 months.

You therefore put the asset on the balance sheet at £10,000 and recognise a liability to the lessor of £10,000. The asset you simply depreciate just as you would any other asset. The lease payments are treated as two separate items. Some of each £300 payment is treated as repayment of the £10,000 'loan' and therefore reduces the liability; the rest of each payment is treated as interest on the loan and reduces retained profit. At the end of 48 months, you have paid the £14,400.

How do you know how much of each payment is repayment of the loan and how much is interest?

This is where it can get a touch complicated. You work it out so that the effective interest rate on what you have left to repay of the loan is always the same. You only really need to understand how to do this if you are actually going to produce your own accounts and you have some finance leases. The consequence of this method is that early in the lease term most of the payment is treated as interest and the nearer you get to the end of the lease term the more of the payment is repayment of the 'loan'.

What you do need to understand is what it means when you see:

▶ Something like 'Lease liability' on the balance sheet. This is the amount of the £10,000 'loan' left to pay. In Wingate's case, you can see from Notes 11 and 12 there was £171k of lease liabilities due for repayment within 12 months and £430k due after that.

▶ Something like 'Interest element of finance leases' in the P&L. This is the part of the year's lease payments that relate to interest on the £10,000 'loan'. In Wingate's case, you can see interest on finance leases of £82k in Note 5.

▶ Something like 'Capital element of finance leases' in the cash flow statement. This is the part of the year's lease payments that relates to repayment of the principal of the £10,000 'loan'. In Wingate's case, you can see there was a repayment of £152k in year 5.

Invoice discounting

There is another form of borrowing often used in small and medium-sized private companies, but also in some larger companies.

Instead of getting a loan or an overdraft from a bank, you go to an **invoice discounting house**. It lends you money that is a proportion of your **trade debtors**. When you receive the money from the customer, you immediately have to pay whatever amount was lent 'against' that invoice back to the invoice discounter. As soon as you issue a new sales invoice, you tell the invoice discounter and it lends you money against the invoice. So it is like an overdraft facility that is linked directly to the amount of your outstanding sales invoices at any point in time. It can be quite an expensive way of borrowing money, however, because, as well as paying interest on the money lent to you, you also have to pay fees for the service. But sometimes it works out better than getting an overdraft.

Why do you say this is an option instead of getting a loan or an overdraft from the bank? Can't you do both?

Not normally, no. Because both the bank and the invoice discounter will want a charge over the trade debtors and they can't both have one. It's possible, though, that you could have invoice discounting in place and get a bank loan that would be secured on other assets of the company (e.g. a freehold property).

Taxation

In principle, **corporation tax** is very simple. A company makes sales and incurs expenses in doing so. After paying interest on any loans, overdrafts, etc. the company makes a profit (profit before tax) which is 'due' to the shareholders. HMRC takes a share of that profit by taxing it. This is corporation tax. Large companies have to pay corporation tax in instalments during their financial year, while smaller companies pay it nine months after the end of the company's financial year. Thus a smaller company's balance sheet usually shows a corporation tax liability under current liabilities.

This straightforward situation is made complicated because corporation tax is actually calculated as a percentage of **taxable income** rather than profit before tax. Taxable income is different from profit before tax for all sorts of reasons and often requires complex calculations. For example, if a company has made losses in previous years, those losses can be carried forwards to reduce taxable income in the current year. HMRC also has its own way of allowing for depreciation (called **capital allowances**) so this will create a difference between taxable income and profit before tax in almost all companies. Accounting standards now require companies (excluding small ones) to give a summary of how taxable income differs from profit before tax.

In the UK, there have for a long time been two different tax rates – a rate of c. 20 per cent for small companies and a higher rate for all other companies that varies from year to year and from government to government. That higher rate has been reduced significantly recently and is currently not much different to the small companies rate.

Shareholders' equity

Share capital

There are various types of share capital that a company can have. Wingate only has **ordinary shares**, which are by far the most common type. This is good, because they are very easy to understand. Generally speaking, each share gets one vote, each share gets the same amount of dividend and if the company is acquired by another company or wound up, each share receives the same share of the proceeds.

Up until the 2006 Companies Act, the shareholders of a company had to agree the maximum number of shares the company should be allowed to issue. This is the **authorised** number of shares. While you will often still see references to authorised share capital in the accounts of companies that were in existence before 2006 (including Wingate), you won't see it in any new companies. When investors pay money into the company, shares are **allotted** to them (i.e. shares are 'issued'). Ordinary shares all have a **par** or **nominal** value. This is the lowest value at which the shares can be allotted. Although it is usual, it is not necessary for the full price of a share to be paid into the company when the share is allotted. If any shares are not **fully paid**, however, there is still a legal obligation on the investor to pay the rest on demand by the directors of the company, even if the investor might prefer not to by the time the directors ask for the money.

If you look at Note 15 on page 279, you can see that 1,500,000 shares of 5p par value have been authorised, but only 1,000,000 have actually been allotted. Those that have been allotted have been fully paid up.

Share premium

I mentioned just now that shares cannot be allotted for less than the par value. They can be, and frequently are, allotted for *more* than par value. The amount over and above par value that is paid for a share is called the **share premium**. This is recorded separately on the balance sheet.

We can see that Wingate has allotted shares with a total premium of £275k. The *total* capital put into the company by the shareholders is the sum of the called-up share capital and the share premium. In Wingate's case this is £50k plus £275k, making total capital invested of £325k.

Retained profit

Hopefully, by now, the meaning of retained profit is reasonably clear. To recap, it's the total profit that the company has made throughout its existence that has not been paid out to shareholders as dividends.

Let me say again that retained profit is *not* the amount of cash the company has. Retained profit is usually made up of all sorts of different assets.

The P&L and cash flow statement

As far as the P&L and cash flow statement are concerned, we covered many of the points when looking at SBL. There are a few things I should mention, however.

Trading in foreign currencies

Suppose you are based in the UK. You sell some products to a customer in the USA for $7,000 to be paid 90 days after the date of the transaction. You would translate the $7,000 into pounds sterling at the exchange rate prevailing on the day of the transaction and enter the transaction in your accounts. Assume the exchange rate was $1.75 to the pound; this would make the $7,000 worth £4,000.

When the American customer pays (90 days later), the exchange rate is likely to be different. Assume it is $1.60 per £; this would mean that the customer is effectively paying you £4,375, when your accounts say you should be getting £4,000. By waiting 90 days to be paid, you have made a profit of £375.

This profit is known as an exchange gain. Naturally, if the exchange rate had gone the other way, you would have made an exchange loss. These exchange gains or losses are included in the P&L and, if they are material, they will be disclosed in the notes.

Presumably, if a large proportion of your sales are overseas, your profits could be substantially affected by exchange gains or losses?

Yes, it's a major issue for some companies. When we talk about listed companies, I will explain how they deal with this.

Exceptional items

Occasionally, an event will occur in the course of the ordinary activities of a company that gives rise to an income or expense that has a significant impact on the accounts. Such items have to be disclosed separately. If the exceptional item is one of the following, it will be shown on the face of the P&L:

- ▶ profits/losses on the sale or termination of an operation;
- ▶ costs of a fundamental reorganisation;
- ▶ profits/losses on disposal of fixed assets.

All other exceptional items are set out in the notes to the accounts, except where it is considered necessary to show them on the face of the P&L in order to give a true and fair view of the year's profit/loss.

Wingate had no exceptional items in either of years four or five. To give you an example, however, if the profit on the sale of the fixed assets had been larger, this would have been disclosed as an exceptional item.

Extraordinary items

Occasionally, an event will occur that causes a company to earn some income or incur some expense which it would not expect in the ordinary course of its business and which it does not expect to recur, i.e. it is a 'one-off' event. The income or expense resulting from this event is called an extraordinary item. Nowadays, things can only be classified as extraordinary items if they are *extremely* rare.

Dividends

A company can pay a dividend to its shareholders as often as it likes provided it doesn't pay out more than its **distributable reserves**. These are defined as the net previously-undistributed, realised profits. **Realised** here means profits that have already turned into cash or where there is a promise of cash that is reasonably certain to be fulfilled (e.g. a trade debtor). In Wingate's case, distributable reserves are therefore equal to the retained profits on its balance sheet. In companies with more complex transactions, it's not always as simple as this.

New companies and companies that are growing very fast tend not to pay dividends as they need the cash to invest in the business. Private companies pay dividends if and when their owners see fit. The majority of listed companies, however, pay dividends twice a year. They will typically declare an **interim dividend** half-way through their financial year and a **final dividend** at the end of the year. The dividends are usually paid three to six months after being declared. Interim dividends can be decided by the board of directors of the company but final dividends have to be approved by the shareholders at the annual general meeting of the company. Some very large companies, and particularly American companies, pay dividends four times a year.

Notice one important thing about dividends though. We do not recognise them in the accounts of the company until they have either been paid (in the case of interim dividends) or approved by the shareholders (in the case of final dividends). Wingate pays a dividend just once a year. If you look at Note 7 [page 277] of Wingate's accounts, you will see that the dividend proposed for year five is £215k and that the proposed dividend for the previous year was £184k. If now you look at the P&L, you will see that the dividend recognised in the P&L in year five is £184k – i.e. the amount that was actually *paid* during year five, which was the amount *proposed* in respect of year four.

While we are talking about dividends, I ought to explain how these are normally presented in the accounts.

Reserves

Do you remember earlier I said the P&L ought to be called something like 'Explanation of the change in retained profit' because it shows both the profit made for the shareholders during the year *and* the amount of dividend taken out of the company by the shareholders, which are two very different things? What the accounting authorities have done is stop companies showing the dividends on the P&L. I put them on Wingate's P&L because

I wanted you to understand that the P&L is nothing more than a detailed description of how the retained profit on the balance sheet had changed during the year.

On any other company's accounts you are likely to see in the future, you will find that the P&L stops at 'Profit for the year'. You will, however, be able to make the connection between the P&L and retained profit on the balance sheet by looking at a note to the accounts called something like **'Capital and Reserves'**. If you look at Note 13 [page 278], you will see this note. What it does is explain how each of the items under Shareholders' equity has changed. So in Wingate's case, it shows that:

- ▶ There were no changes to the share capital or share premium accounts.

- ▶ The retained profit increased by £463k for the year due to the profit made in the year (which we can see on the P&L) and decreased by £184k due to the dividend paid during the year.

Why is this note called 'Capital and reserves' when it's about shareholders' equity?

Because, according to the Companies Act, all the boxes under shareholders' equity other than 'share capital' are known as reserves. Hence shareholders' equity becomes 'Capital and reserves'. I've avoided this phrase because reserves implies 'cash' in many people's minds and, as we know, it's not cash.

Reconciliation of movements in shareholders' equity

While we're at it, I might as well explain the next note to the accounts, Note 14 [page 279]. This is doing a very similar job to the Reserves note – i.e. showing how shareholders' equity changed during the year. The difference is that you don't see each of the capital and reserves accounts separately but you do see both the current year and the previous year.

Earnings per share

As we will see when we get around to talking about the valuation of companies, many investors and analysts use a measure called earnings per share (or eps) to make their valuations. 'Earnings' is another word for 'profit for the year'. If you are a small investor in a company, you know how much you paid for each share and it is often helpful to know how much profit the company made for each of those shares. This figure is shown as the last line on the P&L.

We would calculate earnings per share for Wingate in year five as follows:

$$\text{Earnings per share} = \text{Profit for year/Number of shares}$$
$$= £463k / 1m \text{ shares}$$
$$= 46.3 \text{ pence per share}$$

If Wingate had issued new shares *during* the year, we would use the time-weighted average number of shares in issue during the year. This means the average number of shares in issue, adjusted for how much of the year they had been in issue.

Recognised gains or losses/Continuing activities

What are these two statements right at the bottom of Wingate's P&L about?

I will come back to them later, when we talk about listed companies' accounts.

The cash flow statement

If you look at Wingate's cash flow statement [page 273], you will see that it is broadly similar to the one we drew up for SBL. On the next page, however, there is an extra box with a couple of additional tables in. These are part of a complete cash flow statement and provide a little more information about the net debt of the company. Net debt is the total debt (overdrafts, loans, finance leases, etc.) less the cash the company has. Usually, you can deduce these analyses yourself from the main statements and the notes but it's always nice to have someone do the work for you.

That completes our look at Wingate's accounts. We are now ready to start analysing them to try and gain some insight into what is going on.

CHAPTER SEVEN

Financial analysis: Introduction

▶ The ultimate goal

▶ The two components of a company

▶ The general approach to financial analysis

▶ Wingate's highlights

▶ Summary

Up to now, all our sessions have been about accounting. You should now be able to read the accounts of a small or medium-sized company and understand them. This does not mean, though, that the accounts tell you anything. That is where financial analysis comes in.

This weekend came about partly because Tom is worried about Wingate's financial position. The managing director would have you believe that things are going pretty well for Wingate – sales, profits and dividends are all rising steadily. However, Tom's perception is that the company is expansion crazy, cutting prices and giving very generous payment terms so as to win new contracts. What's more, the company has been spending a lot of money on new premises, etc.

I have had a look at Wingate in some detail. In fact, I've gone back over the last five years' accounts and discovered one or two interesting things. Before we go into that, though, I want to cover three very important aspects of financial analysis:

▶ First, I want to make sure we all understand the ultimate financial goal of a company; what is a company trying to achieve in financial terms?

▶ Then I want to be sure that you really understand the distinction between the two components of a company – the enterprise and the funding structure.

▶ Finally, I will outline the general approach we take to financial analysis.

At the end of this session, I'll show you some graphs of Wingate's sales, profits and dividends which, as Tom said, do paint a fairly rosy picture. We'll then take a break and in the next session have a look and see how rosy the picture really is.

The ultimate goal

If I gave you £100 and told you to invest it, you would have a choice of many places to put that £100. For example:

1. You could buy £100 worth of tickets in the lottery.
2. You could put it all on the outsider in the 2.30pm race at Newmarket.
3. You could buy some shares in a new company set up to engage in oil exploration.
4. You could buy shares in one of the top 100 companies in Britain.
5. You could put it in a deposit account at one of the big high street banks.

Two things should strike you as you go down this list:

▶ First, the choices become less risky. With number 1, you are extremely likely to lose all your money. With number 5 you are almost certain to get all your money back plus some interest.

▶ Second, the potential return (or profit) on your £100 investment gets lower. If you win the lottery, you will make millions of pounds in a matter of days. If you put the money in the bank you will earn less than £10 interest, even if you leave your £100 there for a year.

The point is that, generally, people will not take risks unless there is some reward (or potential reward) for doing so. The greater the risk, the greater the potential reward people require.

Although we could have a long philosophical debate about the role of companies in society, you can't escape the fact that the shareholders have invested money in the hope of a good return, relative to the risk they have taken. This has to be our guiding principle when we analyse a company's performance.

How high the return should be depends on the risk of the investment. Measuring risk is extremely difficult and well beyond what we can hope to cover today. What we can say, though, is that the return must be higher than we could obtain by putting the same amount of money on deposit in a high street bank, since we could do that with very little risk. What we can get on deposit in a bank has historically varied from next to nothing to 10 per cent or so, depending on the economic circumstances at the time. I tend to use 5 per cent per annum (before tax) as a simple benchmark.

So the directors of Wingate should be looking simply to maximise the return on the money invested in the business?

In principle, yes, but with two very important qualifications.

The long-term perspective

Some companies could easily increase the return they provide on the money invested in the business. Let's say you run a long established company which has a dominant market share in its industry. By raising your prices, you are likely, in the short term, to raise your profits and hence the return to shareholders. In the longer term, however, customers will start to buy from your competitors and, sooner or later, you will have lost so much business that your profits will be lower than they were before you raised your prices.

The point is obvious. Short-term gains can have high long-term costs. Directors have to make that trade-off on behalf of their shareholders.

Liquidity

The second qualification relates to the trade-off between cash flow and profitability, which is something that applies to individuals as well as companies. Assume you have £500 which you want to put on deposit at the bank. You can put it in an ordinary deposit account which pays you interest of, say, 2 per cent per annum. The bank manager, however, suggests that you put the money in a special account which will pay you 4 per cent per annum. The only condition of this special account is that you have to leave your money in the account for the whole year.

Obviously, the special account would provide you with a higher return than the ordinary deposit account. But if you have to pay the final balance on your summer holiday in two months' time and therefore need that £500 then, you would have to opt for the ordinary deposit account and accept a lower return.

Companies have all sorts of opportunities to make similar trade-offs between profit and cash flow. The most obvious relates to the terms on which they buy and sell goods. Many companies offer a discount for rapid payment, others charge a premium for giving extended credit.

Liquidity is the ability to pay your short-term liabilities. You can always get a higher return if you are prepared to reduce your liquidity. If you go too far, however, you will be unable to pay your debts on time and will go bust.

So what you're saying is that the financial objective of a company is to maximise the return it provides on the money invested, based on an appropriate trade-off between the short- and long-term perspectives, while ensuring that the business remains liquid?

Exactly.

The two components of a company

The simple view of a company

Let's look at what a company does, in the simplest terms:

1. It raises funds from shareholders and by borrowing from banks.
2. It then uses this cash to trade, which involves doing some or all of the following things:

    ► buying (and selling) fixed assets

    ► buying raw materials

    ► manufacturing products

    ► selling products and services

> ▶ paying employees, suppliers

> ▶ collecting cash from customers

> ▶ etc.

3. If trading is successful, then the company makes a pay-out to the people who funded the business. First, the bank has to be paid interest on its loans. Any remaining profit belongs to the shareholders, although HMRC demands a cut.

This is a pretty simplistic view of a business, but, in a nutshell, that's what goes on.

The point to notice is that the activities in the middle [point 2 above] are completely unaffected by *how* the funding was split between the different sources. A company needs a certain amount of funding in order to trade but the source of those funds is irrelevant. This bit in the middle, which is the underlying business or operation of the company, we call the **enterprise**.

The source of the funds does affect the share of the profit that goes to the bank rather than the shareholders and HMRC. The more debt (i.e. overdraft, loans, etc.) a company has, the more interest it will have to pay and the less there will be for HMRC and the shareholders. The way in which the funding is made up we call the **funding structure**.

I can see the principle, but I'm not sure how it relates to the financial statements. Presumably it does?

Yes, and it's actually very easy. Let's look at the balance sheet first. If we go back to our model balance sheet [Figure 7.1], we can assign all the items into one of the two categories. I have shaded all those that are part of the funding structure. If you study the chart, you will see that all the unshaded items are unaffected by the funding structure.

You've shaded the cash box, implying that it is part of the funding structure. Surely cash is not affected by the source of the funding?

No, but if you have got cash on your balance sheet, then effectively you've just got less of an overdraft. Hence we 'net the cash off ' the overdraft (or bank loans).

Why have you got employment taxes and VAT included as part of the enterprise? I thought you said that taxes were part of the funding structure.

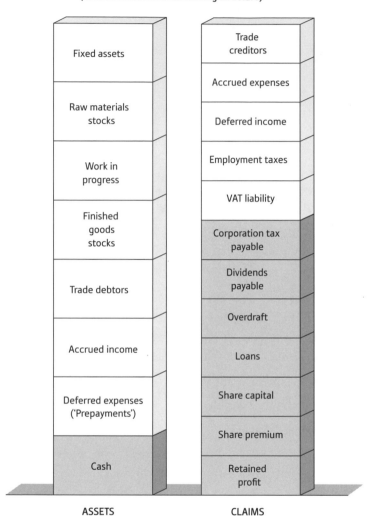

MODEL BALANCE SHEET
(Shaded items relate to funding structure)

ASSETS	CLAIMS
Fixed assets	Trade creditors
Raw materials stocks	Accrued expenses
Work in progress	Deferred income
Finished goods stocks	Employment taxes
Trade debtors	VAT liability
Accrued income	Corporation tax payable
Deferred expenses ('Prepayments')	Dividends payable
Cash	Overdraft
	Loans
	Share capital
	Share premium
	Retained profit

Figure 7.1 Model balance sheet chart distinguishing the funding structure from the enterprise

That question is a very good example of how, when applying this principle, you have to think about what things are, rather than relying on what they are called. Social security, PAYE, VAT, etc. are taxes that are determined by things to do with the underlying business, like how much you sell, how much you buy, how many employees you have and how much you pay them. These taxes are *not* affected by the source of the funds, so they must be part of the enterprise.

Corporation tax is calculated after paying interest on debt. The more interest paid, the lower the tax to pay. Hence corporation tax is affected by the amount of debt; in other words, it is affected by the source of the funding and is therefore part of the funding structure.

The balance sheet rearranged

We can actually rearrange the balance sheet to make it distinguish the enterprise from the funding structure. It's just a matter of moving certain items from one side of our balance sheet equation to the other.

As an example, look at the trade creditors box at the top of the claims bar on the balance sheet chart. We could remove this box from the claims bar and subtract the same amount from, say, the trade debtors box on the assets bar. We might then change the name of this box to 'Trade debtors minus trade creditors'. Because we have subtracted the trade creditors from both bars of our balance sheet, the balance sheet still balances.

To distinguish between the enterprise and the funding structure, we make the following adjustments to the balance sheet chart and come up with the rearranged version [Figure 7.2].

1. Leave the fixed assets box as it is, but take all the other items relating to the enterprise and combine them into one box which we will call **working capital**. What we get is:

$$
\begin{aligned}
\text{Working capital} =\ & \text{Raw materials stocks} \\
& + \text{Work in progress} \\
& + \text{Finished goods stocks} \\
& + \text{Trade debtors} \\
& + \text{Accrued income} \\
& + \text{Deferred expenses} \\
& - \text{Trade creditors} \\
& - \text{Accrued expenses} \\
& - \text{Deferred income} \\
& - \text{Employment taxes} \\
& - \text{VAT liability}
\end{aligned}
$$

*What **is** working capital though? You don't go out and buy it the way you do fixed assets, do you?*

No. Working capital is money you need to operate. Think of it as cash you *would* have in your bank account if you did not have to hold stocks, give credit to customers, make prepayments, etc. The fact that you do have to do these things means that you need to 'invest' cash in working capital.

MODEL BALANCE SHEET
Rearranged

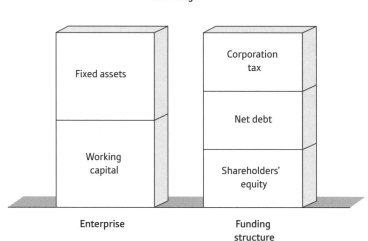

Figure 7.2 Model balance sheet chart rearranged

2. The next thing we need to sort out is the cash at the bottom of the assets bar. As we have discussed, having cash really just means you have got less of an overdraft or bank loan, since you could just pay either of them off with the spare cash. In rearranging our balance sheet, therefore, all we do is create a new box called **net debt.** This is the sum of all the debt of the company after subtracting any cash.

3. When we were looking at Wingate, we saw that shareholders' equity, which is the share of the company's assets 'due' to the shareholders, was made up of share capital, share premium and retained profit. If you think about it, dividends payable should also be included under shareholders' equity as they represent money due to the shareholders which is actually going to be paid in the near future.

*So why **aren't** dividends payable included under shareholders' equity?*

Because, once a dividend has been approved by the shareholders, it becomes a current liability like any other current liability and has to be shown as such. As it happens, most dividends get paid out quite quickly after being approved by shareholders so you're not likely to come across dividends payable on the balance sheet very often. The principle is important, though.

For the purposes of financial analysis, we do include dividends payable in shareholders' equity, which therefore represents the total funding for the company provided by the shareholders. **Shareholders' equity** thus becomes a separate box on our rearranged balance sheet.

Why are dividends payable and retained profit part of the funding provided by the shareholders? Surely the only actual money they have provided is the share capital plus the share premium.

That's true, but being owed money by a company is the same as having put that money into the company. Dividends payable and retained profit both represent money that is 'due' to the shareholders. If you like, think of the company paying out to the shareholders everything they are due and the shareholders immediately putting the money back into the company as share capital.

4. The only other thing we haven't dealt with is corporation tax. This is the same as the dividends and retained profit, in a sense. HMRC have not actually put money into the company, but by not taking what they are owed immediately, they are effectively funding the company.

We therefore leave the corporation tax in a box of its own as part of the funding structure.

If you now look at the rearranged balance sheet chart, you will see that it shows clearly:

▶ the sources of the funding for the business;

▶ the uses of that funding.

Wingate's rearranged balance sheet

We can rearrange Wingate's balance sheet at the end of year five to look like this. It will make our analysis much quicker and easier if we actually write it out now [Table 7.1]. As you can see, it has all the same numbers in it as before and it still balances.

Table 7.1 Wingate's rearranged balance sheet at end of year five

		£'000
Enterprise		
Fixed assets		5,326
Working capital		
Stocks		
Raw materials	352	
Work in progress	17	
Finished goods	862	
Total stocks		1,231
Debtors		
Trade debtors	2,125	
Prepayments	78	
Other debtors	36	
Total debtors		2,239
Creditors		
Trade creditors	(863)	
Soc sec/other taxes	(150)	
Accruals	(113)	
Cash in advance	(20)	
Total creditors	(1,146)	
Net working capital		2,324
Net operating assets (Net enterprise assets)		**7,650**
Funding structure		
Taxation		131
Net debt		
Cash	(12)	
Overdraft	933	
Loans	3,150	
Finance leases	601	
Net debt		4,672
Shareholders' equity		
Dividends payable	0	
Share capital	50	
Share premium	275	
Retained profit	2,522	
Total shareholders' equity		2,847
Net funding		**7,650**

Wingate's P&L

Distinguishing between the enterprise and the funding structure on the P&L is extremely simple. All the items down to operating profit are part of the enterprise. None of them would be affected by a change in the funding structure. Operating profit is the profit made from operating the assets, as you would expect.

All the items after operating profit such as interest, tax, dividends are related to the funding structure.

Wingate's cash flow statement

Similarly, if you look at the cash flow statement [page 273], you will see that the six different headings fall into one or other of our two categories:

- ▶ 'Operating activities' and 'Capital expenditure' relate to the enterprise;
- ▶ 'Returns on investments and servicing of finance', 'Taxation', 'Equity dividends paid' and 'Financing' relate to the funding structure.

I think I'm getting the idea, but what's the point of this distinction?

The point is simple but important. The enterprise represents the actual *business* of the company. The funding structure represents the way the directors have chosen to raise the necessary funds. By making this distinction we can:

- ▶ assess the performance of the business without the sources of the funding confusing the picture;
- ▶ analyse the implications for both shareholders and lenders of the way the company has been funded.

The general approach to financial analysis

Even when you understand how a company's accounts are put together, there is still an alarming profusion of numbers. You can't just sit down and read company accounts as you would a novel. You have to use them like a dictionary – look up the things you are interested in.

131

There are three basic steps in any financial analysis:

- ► Choose the 'performance indicator' that interests you.
- ► Look it up (and calculate it if necessary).
- ► Interpret it and, hopefully, gain some insight into the company.

By performance indicator, I mean any measure that tells you something about a company's performance. Nowadays, people use the acronym '**KPI**', which stands for **Key Performance Indicator**. Whether any given performance indicator is 'key' or not will depend on the circumstances but this acronym is widely used and understood these days and it's succinct, so I will use it from now on. There are certain useful KPIs that you can read straight from the accounts, the most obvious example being sales. In general, however, the most useful KPIs are ratios of one item in the accounts to another.

Interpretation of KPIs

There are two ways to go about interpreting KPIs:

- ► trend analysis,
- ► benchmarking.

Trend analysis is looking at how a given KPI has changed over a period of time. Trends can tell you a lot about the way a company is being managed and can help you to anticipate future performance. Usually, we look at such trends over a five-year timeframe.

Benchmarking means comparing a KPI at a point in time with the same KPIs of competitors or against universal standards (such as the interest rate on deposit accounts).

Benchmarking against competitors is particularly useful for assessing the relative strength of companies in the same industry. This is another reason we distinguish between the enterprise and the funding structure. Companies in the same industry might have very different funding structures. Some might have no debt at all, others may have a lot. If you are interested in comparing the way they run their underlying business, the funding structure is irrelevant.

Even when benchmarking against competitors, the best approach is to look at trends in KPIs rather than a point in time. It is substantially more work, but will give a more reliable picture of how the companies are performing relative to one another.

Wingate's highlights

We are now more or less ready to start our analysis of Wingate's accounts. Before we do, let's look at the KPIs that the management seem to be focusing on. These are sales, operating profit, profit before tax and proposed dividends. I have drawn graphs of each of these KPIs over the last five years [Figures 7.3 to 7.6].

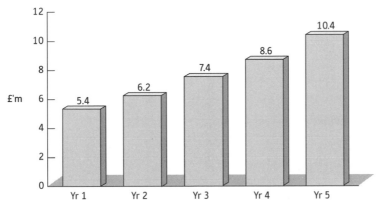

Figure 7.3 Wingate's sales

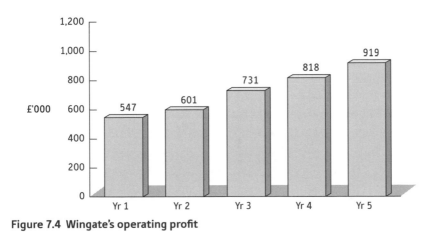

Figure 7.4 Wingate's operating profit

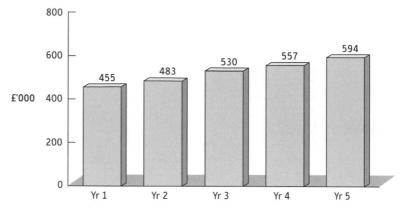

Figure 7.5 Wingate's profit before tax

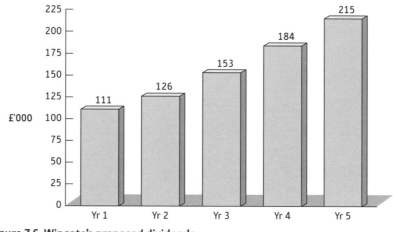

Figure 7.6 Wingate's proposed dividends

Based on these KPIs, you can see why the management can claim to be doing a reasonable job. All four KPIs are rising steadily. The question, of course, is whether these are the right KPIs to be looking at.

Summary

▶ In general, the greater the risk of an investment, the greater must be the potential reward. Otherwise, people will simply not take the risk.

▶ Companies must therefore offer a reward (or 'return') which is commensurate with the risk to the investor.

▶ The financial objective of a company is to maximise the return on the money invested in it, while making appropriate trade-offs between:
  - the short- and long-term perspectives;
  - profitability and liquidity.

▶ From a financial viewpoint, we can distinguish between the enterprise and the funding structure of a company. This distinction enables us to do three things:
  - to assess how the actual business of a company is performing without the sources of the funding confusing the picture;
  - to make more meaningful comparisons of a business with competitors;
  - to analyse the implications for both shareholders and lenders of the way the company has been funded.

▶ Financial analysis requires the selection and calculation of a number of relevant KPIs. These KPIs can then be interpreted by observing trends over a period of time or by benchmarking.

CHAPTER EIGHT

Analysis of the enterprise

- ▶ Return on capital employed (ROCE)
- ▶ The components of ROCE
- ▶ Where do we go from here?
- ▶ Expense ratios
- ▶ Capital ratios
- ▶ Summary

We are now ready to start looking in depth at Wingate's financial performance, starting with the enterprise.

What I'm going to do first is show you how we calculate the return that the enterprise is providing and see how it has changed over the last five years. We will then ask ourselves why this has happened. This will lead us on to a variety of other analyses, which will provide greater insight into Wingate's true financial performance.

Return on capital employed

When we rearranged our balance sheet to distinguish between the enterprise and the funding structure, we ended up with one side of our balance sheet showing the **net operating assets** of the business. This is the amount of money that is invested in the operation. The managers of the business are trying to make as high a return on this money as possible (or at least they should be). Net operating assets are also known as **capital employed** – the amount of capital that is employed in the operation. The measure of performance is thus usually known as **return on capital employed** ('ROCE' for short).

Calculating ROCE

Since we have already rearranged Wingate's balance sheet for the end of year five [see page 130], we know the capital employed is just the net operating assets as shown in the balance sheet, i.e. £7,650k.

We also know that the return is the profit made by operating those assets. This is the operating profit, which we can read directly off the P&L as being £919k in year five.

Thus the return on capital employed is as follows:

$$919 / 7,650 = 12.0\%$$

What I want you to do now is to work out the ROCE for the previous year. The figures are all there, alongside the figures I used to do year five. I suggest that you actually rearrange the balance sheet at the end of year four, as I did for year five. When you become more practised at doing these types of analyses, you will just read the appropriate figures from the balance sheet and the notes, but it is easy to miss something if you are not careful.

What you should have got is as follows:

$$\text{Operating profit} = £818k$$
$$\text{Capital employed} = £6,055k$$
$$\text{Return on capital employed} = 13.5\%$$

Surprisingly, we got that. I do have a question, though. Why are you using the capital employed at the end of the year? If I put £1,000 in a bank deposit account for a year and earn £40 interest, I would calculate my return based on the £1,000 at the start of the year not the £1,040 I have at the end (i.e. I would say I got a return of 4 per cent, not 3.8 per cent).

Technically, you're right, Sarah. People tend to use the year-end figure, though. They do this because capital employed at the end of the year is usually larger than at the start of the year. This means that they get a lower ROCE, which therefore presents a more conservative view of the company.

You can use the capital employed at the start of the year, if you want. You will get slightly different answers, but they are unlikely to change any decisions you will make as a result. Some people use the average of the starting and ending capital employed, on the grounds that the capital employed has been constantly changing throughout the year and the average is therefore a better measure. Whichever approach you take, the most important thing is to be *consistent*. Let's now look at what ROCE tells us.

ROCE vs a benchmark

As we've said before, the whole point of investing in businesses is to make a higher return than we could from putting our cash in a deposit account. Thus the first thing we can do is to compare the ROCE with the interest rate we could get at the bank. If you remember, I suggested using 5 per cent as a crude benchmark.

At 12.0 per cent in year five and 13.5 per cent in year four, the business is certainly outperforming a bank deposit, though not by that much given the relative risks of a bank deposit and a small company's shares. If we had the accounts of some competitors we could compare their ROCE with Wingate's, which would tell us how they are performing relative to each other.

Trend analysis of ROCE

As we have just seen, ROCE has declined by 1.5 per cent from 13.5 per cent to 12.0 per cent. This difference is not sufficient to enable us to draw any real conclusions. You might well find that a company with two such ROCE figures would achieve, say, 16 per cent next year.

What we do, therefore, is to get old copies of the annual report and look at what has happened over the last few years to see if there is an identifiable trend. I've plotted a graph for you of Wingate's ROCE over the last five years [Figure 8.1].

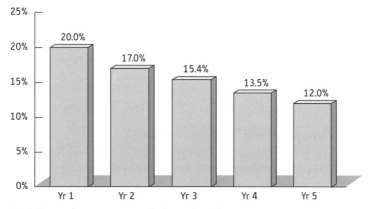

Figure 8.1 Wingate's return on capital employed

This suggests that the ROCE has gone down drastically, Chris! Are you sure it's right?

It is right and it's pretty worrying. There is a very clear, steep downward trend here. If that keeps going, you are going to end up with a business which is not even giving as high a return as you could get by putting the money in the bank.

But if Wingate's profits grew every year for the last five years, how can ROCE possibly be falling so fast?

This is the whole point of being concerned with **profitability** rather than profit. Remember that ROCE is profit divided by capital employed. Although your profit has been growing, the capital employed must have been growing faster. The result is a decline in ROCE.

The components of ROCE

We have discovered that ROCE is declining alarmingly. We now ask ourselves why.

We look at ROCE because we are interested in what profits can be generated from a certain amount of capital employed. What actually happens in a business is that we have a certain amount of capital employed in the operation. Using this capital, we generate sales to customers. These sales in turn lead to profits.

$$\text{Capital} \rightarrow \text{Sales} \rightarrow \text{Profits}$$

Two pretty obvious questions come out of this:

- ► How many sales am I getting for every pound of capital employed?
- ► How much profit am I getting for every pound of sales?

These questions can be answered with two simple ratios.

Capital productivity

The first of these ratios, which tells us how many sales we get from each pound of capital, is called **capital productivity**. To calculate it, we simply take the sales for the year and divide them by the capital employed. Sales for year five were £10,427k and capital employed was £7,650k. Thus we get:

$$\text{Capital productivity} = \text{Sales/Capital employed}$$
$$= 10,427 \,/\, 7,650$$
$$= 1.36$$

And what exactly is that supposed to tell us, Chris?

Well, not very much, as it stands. We can't really measure it against any universal benchmark, as all industries will be different. We could (and should) compare it with other companies in the industry. What we are trying to understand, though, is why ROCE is falling. Obviously, we should look at capital productivity over the last five years which, you will be glad to know, I have done for you [Figure 8.2].

As you can see, capital productivity has fallen substantially, although it appears to be levelling off now.

Presumably, we want capital productivity to be as high as possible?

Yes, in principle. The more sales we can get from a given amount of capital the better, but we have to be careful. We are only interested in profitable sales. It's nearly always possible to get more sales out of a given amount of capital just by selling goods very cheaply. The problem with that is that your profit will go down, which is likely to result in your ROCE going down rather than up.

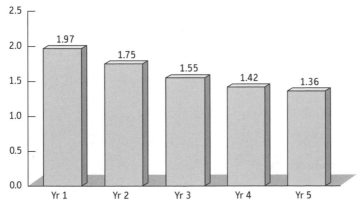

Figure 8.2 Wingate's capital productivity

What we should say, therefore, is that, all other things being equal, we want capital productivity to be as high as possible.

Return on sales ('ROS' for short)

We have just seen how we assess the amount of sales we get from a certain amount of capital. The next thing we need to know is how much profit we get from those sales. We calculate this by dividing operating profit by sales. This gives us the following:

$$Return\ on\ sales\ =\ Operating\ profit/Sales$$
$$=\ 919\ /\ 10,427$$
$$=\ 8.8\%$$

And here's a chart of Wingate's return on sales over five years [Figure 8.3].

This chart shows some evidence of a downward trend, although not as marked as that of capital productivity. Naturally, with all other things being the same, we want to make as much profit out of each pound of sales as we can, so we want return on sales to be high.

I've absolutely no idea if 9–10 per cent is an acceptable return on sales or not. Are there any universal benchmarks I can use?

The answer is no and anyway it's irrelevant. ROCE is the true measure of a company's financial performance. Some of the best retailers have relatively low returns on sales but, because they have high capital productivity, their

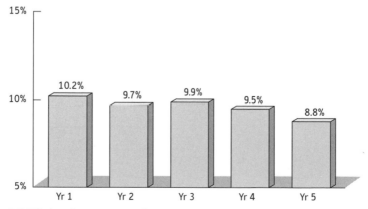

Figure 8.3 Wingate's return on sales

ROCE is high. You would be much better off owning a company like that than one that had high ROS but low ROCE.

The arithmetic relationship

Hopefully, the logic of going from ROCE to looking at capital productivity and ROS is clear. The relationship between these three ratios can be expressed arithmetically as well:

$$\text{Profit/CE} = \text{Profit/Sales} \times \text{Sales/CE}$$
$$\text{ROCE} = \text{ROS} \times \text{Capital productivity}$$
$$12.0\% = 8.8\% \times 1.36$$

Where do we go from here?

So far we have discovered that Wingate's ROCE has fallen substantially. We have also established that this is the result of getting fewer sales for every pound of capital employed and less profit for every pound of sales. Of the two causes, the fall in capital productivity is the more significant.

Naturally, we now ask ourselves why these ratios have declined as they have. We will therefore look at each of the ratios in turn and see what we can find out:

> ► Since operating profit is what we have left after paying the operating expenses, it obviously makes sense to analyse the operating expenses and see if there is anything we can learn.

> ► The capital employed in a business is made up of both fixed assets and working capital. Working capital is, in turn, made up of various different elements. We can therefore analyse each of these different elements.

In the same way that we looked at how many sales we got for each pound of assets and how much profit we got for each pound of sales, we will analyse all the expenses and the constituents of capital employed in relation to sales.

Expense ratios

The P&L lists three types of expense: cost of goods sold, distribution and administration. Let's look at these three first.

Cost of goods sold, gross margin

As you will remember, the cost of goods sold ('COGS') is exactly what it says – the cost of buying and/or making the goods to be sold. From the P&L, we know that Wingate's cost of goods sold in year five was £8,078k. We can therefore divide this by the sales of £10,427k to give us cost of goods sold as a percentage of sales ('COGS%').

$$COGS\% = COGS/Sales$$
$$= 8,078 / 10,427$$
$$= 77.5\%$$

We also saw earlier that the profit left after subtracting cost of goods sold from sales is known as gross profit. Gross profit as a percentage of sales is known as gross margin.

$$Gross\ margin = Gross\ profit/Sales$$
$$= 2,349 / 10,427$$
$$= 22.5\%$$

Gross margin and the cost of goods sold percentage effectively tell you the same thing. You will find that most people talk about gross margin.

How does this relate to 'mark-up' then, Chris?

People in business don't use mark-up much, but if you have something that cost you 77.5 pence and you sell it for £1, your cost of goods is 77.5 per cent and your gross margin is 22.5 per cent, just as we have seen for Wingate. **Mark-up** is the percentage that you add on to your cost to get your selling price, which we calculate by dividing your gross profit by your cost:

$$Mark\text{-}up = Gross\ profit/Cost$$
$$= 22.5 / 77.5$$
$$= 29.0\%$$

Let's now look at how Wingate's gross margin has changed over the last five years [Figure 8.4]. As you can see, there has been a steady decline in gross margin.

So what this says is that every year a pound's worth of sales is costing us more to produce than the previous year?

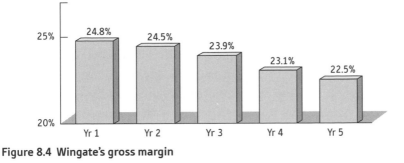

Figure 8.4 Wingate's gross margin

Yes, but the way you phrase it makes it sound as if the fault must lie with the director in charge of manufacturing. If the factory is badly run, then you may well be right, but there is an alternative explanation.

What you have to remember with all these analyses is that **sales value** (i.e. the figure for sales in the accounts) is made up of **sales volume** (i.e. the number of packets of biscuits or whatever that you sell) and **price** (the price of each packet of biscuits).

$$\text{Sales value} = \text{Sales volume} \times \text{Price}$$

Obviously, your cost of manufacturing is not affected by the price you charge your customers, but it is affected by the volume you sell. Take a very simple situation. Assume you sold one million packets of biscuits last year at a price of £1 per packet. These biscuits cost you 70p per packet to produce. What we see is:

Sales	£1m
COGS	£700k
Gross profit	£300k
Gross margin	30%

If, this year, the production director gets the cost of manufacturing down to 65p per packet, but the sales director only manages to sell the same volume of biscuits, despite a lower price of 90p per packet, then we would see:

Sales	£0.9m
COGS	£650k
Gross profit	£250k
Gross margin	28%

So, despite the production director having done a great job, the gross margin has fallen!

The decline in Wingate's gross margin coincides with Tom's tales of the price cuts that the sales department have been making to achieve the growth in sales. Clearly this is more than offsetting any gains they may have made in manufacturing costs. If Wingate is expecting to be able to raise prices once it has won these contracts and built some customer loyalty, then this trend should be reversible. If not, then Wingate had better start manufacturing even more efficiently in the very near future.

Overheads

The other two expenses itemised on Wingate's P&L are distribution and administration. We can calculate these as a percentage of sales, just as we did for cost of goods sold.

Let's look first at distribution. This will include the cost of the sales team as well as the cost of physically transporting the goods to customers. The picture over the five years looks like this [Figure 8.5].

What is interesting about this graph is that it is almost 'flat'. Given the price cutting, this suggests that distribution has become more efficient, which is good.

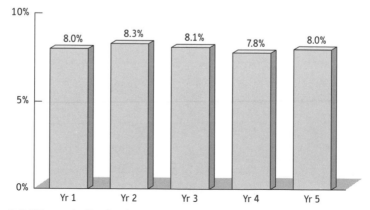

Figure 8.5 Wingate's distribution costs as a percentage of sales

Administration costs are actually showing a decline relative to sales:

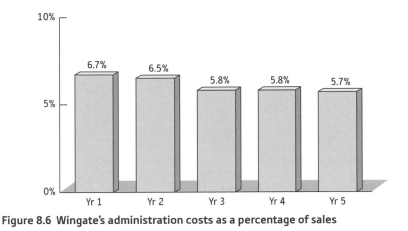

Figure 8.6 Wingate's administration costs as a percentage of sales

This reduction explains why the return on sales has not fallen as dramatically as the gross margin: savings have been made in administration. Obviously, there is a limit to the amount by which administration costs can be reduced, so the outlook for return on sales and thus return on capital could be even worse than the historic trends suggest.

One interesting thing about these administration costs is the sudden drop in year three. Do you know of anything that happened around then, Tom?

I believe that was when we moved all the office staff into the new building.

And I presume the old building was rented and the new one is owned by the company?

Yes.

So in fact all that has happened from an accounting point of view is that Wingate has reduced its operating expenses because it is no longer paying rent, but the capital employed in the business will have gone up as a result of building new offices and therefore having much larger fixed assets on the balance sheet. The effect of this is to improve ROS, but decrease capital productivity. The net impact on the key measure, ROCE, will probably be very small; for all we know, it could have got worse, not better. In other words, this reduction in administration costs is actually nothing to get excited about.

Employee productivity

As well as the expenses itemised on the P&L, the notes to the accounts also provide information which can help to explain why operating profits are behaving as they are.

Note 4 [page 276] shows the number of employees in different categories. From this we can calculate the **sales per employee**. As a general rule, we would expect that, in a well-managed company, sales per employee would be rising faster than sales due to improvements in efficiency and technological innovation. We can also calculate this ratio for each of the different types of employee itemised.

A comparison of these ratios with competitors' can be particularly revealing about efficiency and productivity gains in different companies.

Capital ratios

To understand why the capital productivity has declined, we need to look at the constituents of capital employed and understand how they have been behaving.

Fixed asset productivity

As we have seen before, total capital employed is made up of fixed assets and working capital. We can thus look at how 'productive' these two groups of capital have been. For example, to calculate **fixed asset productivity** we simply divide sales by the fixed assets (at the end of the year):

$$\text{Fixed asset productivity} = \text{Sales/Fixed assets}$$
$$= 10{,}427 \, / \, 5{,}326$$
$$= 1.96$$

This says that Wingate got £1.96 of sales out of each £1 of fixed assets. The following graph [Figure 8.7] shows how this has changed over the five years.

As with capital productivity, we would like fixed asset productivity to be as high as possible. In Wingate's case, it has declined from 2.50 to 1.96, a drop of about 22 per cent. As you can see, it does seem to have flattened out in the last year. Whether this is a reversal of the trend remains to be seen – it could be just a temporary blip.

We could, of course, now look at how the productivities of the individual fixed asset categories have changed, which may provide further insight.

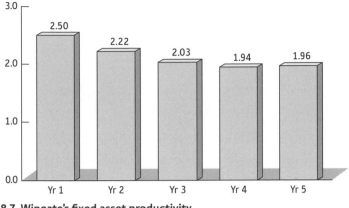

Figure 8.7 Wingate's fixed asset productivity

Working capital productivity

We calculate this exactly as we did fixed asset productivity (i.e. sales divided by working capital). The five-year picture is as follows [Figure 8.8].

Working capital productivity has declined from 9.3 to 4.5, which is a fall in productivity of about 52 per cent.

That's appalling isn't it? No wonder ROCE has fallen.

Well, let's just think about that for a second, Tom. If you owned £10,000 worth of shares in one company and £100 worth of shares in another, you would be much more concerned if the first shares fell by 10 per cent (since you would have lost £1,000) than you would if the second fell by 50 per cent (since you would have only lost £50).

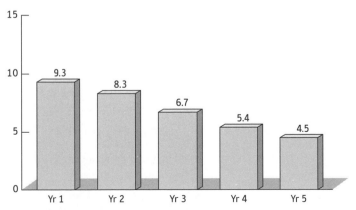

Figure 8.8 Wingate's working capital productivity

The point I'm making is that you have to look at the relative scale of things. Working capital is only a small part of Wingate's capital employed; the bulk is fixed assets. We are still getting £4.50 of sales for every pound of working capital, whereas we only get about £2 of sales for every pound of fixed assets.

Presumably, if you can avoid paying your creditors for a long time and persuade your debtors to pay you quickly, you can get an incredibly high working capital productivity?

You can, but remember what I said about profit versus cash flow. To get a high working capital productivity, you will probably have to give your customers a discount for early payment and you will have to pay your suppliers more to take deferred payment. As a result, you would be cutting your profit margins.

There is a more important point here as well. Let's assume you do get your working capital down to a very low level (and therefore its productivity is very high). If, suddenly, some of your customers decided not to pay quickly, you might find yourself without any cash coming in to pay your suppliers. If you are already taking a long time to pay them, they could get very impatient very quickly. If you have no cash in the bank and/or no overdraft facility available from a bank, this could be a real problem.

Having said all that, this level of decline in working capital productivity is pretty dreadful. Let's see what has been going on by looking at the productivity of some of the individual constituents of working capital.

Trade debtor productivity, trade debtor days

We calculate sales for every pound of trade debtors exactly as we did for the other capital ratios. What we get is shown in Figure 8.9.

Analysts tend to look at this ratio another way. We know what Wingate's sales were for the year. If we assume these sales were spread evenly throughout the year, then we can calculate what the average daily sales were. Knowing what customers owed Wingate at the year end, we can say how many days' worth of sales that represents. Hence for year five:

$$\text{Daily sales} = \text{Annual sales/Days in a year}$$
$$= 10,427 / 365$$
$$= £28.6k$$

Trade debtor days = Trade debtors/Daily sales
$$= 1{,}771 / 28.6$$
$$= 62 \text{ days}$$

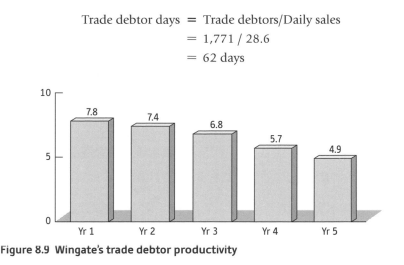

Figure 8.9 Wingate's trade debtor productivity

This suggests that Wingate is waiting on average 62 days before being paid.

Where do you get the figure 1,771 from? Wingate's trade debtors at the end of year five were £2,125k.

You have to remember that the trade debtors figure will include VAT, whereas the sales figure will not. I have assumed that the VAT rate is 20 per cent and have therefore divided the £2,125k figure by 1.20 to get the trade debtors figure excluding VAT.

Over the five-year period, we can see that Wingate has been giving its customers longer and longer to pay [Figure 8.10].

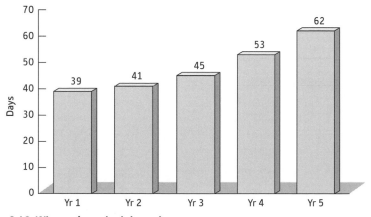

Figure 8.10 Wingate's trade debtor days

Trade creditor productivity

The trade creditor productivity (again calculated as sales divided by trade creditors) has risen over the five-year period [Figure 8.11].

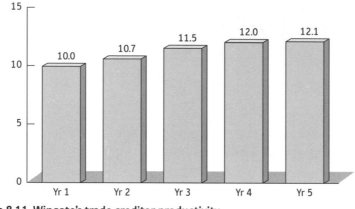

Figure 8.11 Wingate's trade creditor productivity

This is not good, however, from the point of view of getting a high return on capital. Creditors reduce working capital. Hence we want creditor productivity to be as low as possible. This chart suggests that Wingate has been paying creditors more quickly than it used to. This is probably to get better prices but it may be that the finance department just hasn't been trying hard enough!

Stock productivity, stock days

Let's see how Wingate has been managing its stock over the last five years by looking at stock productivity (sales divided by stock) [Figure 8.12].

Sales per pound of stock have been declining, contributing to the reduction in working capital productivity.

As we did with debtors, we can determine the number of days' worth of finished stock that Wingate has in its warehouse. We know that the amount of stock sold each day is simply the cost of goods sold for the year divided by the number of days in a year.

The number of days of finished goods is then easily calculated:

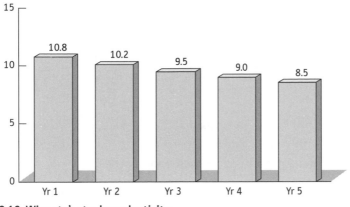

Figure 8.12 Wingate's stock productivity

Daily stock sales $=$ Annual COGS/Days in a year
$$= 8{,}078 \: / \: 365$$
$$= \text{\pounds}22.1\text{k}$$

Finished stock days $=$ Finished stock/Daily stock sales
$$= 862 \: / \: 22.1$$
$$= 39 \text{ days}$$

As you can see from my next chart, the number of days' worth of finished stock has been rising steadily over the last five years [Figure 8.13].

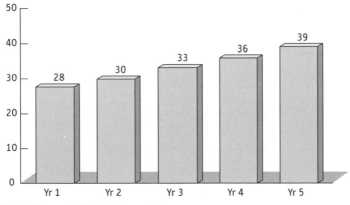

Figure 8.13 Wingate's finished stock days

Enterprise cash flow

All in all, Wingate has not been managing its working capital at all well and has been spending heavily on fixed assets. We can see the effect of this on cash by looking at the cash flow statement. The two categories relating to the enterprise are:

▶ cash flow from operating activities, which shows a cash inflow of £692k in year 5, which compares with the operating profit generated by the enterprise of £919k in the same period;

▶ capital expenditure, which was a massive £1,368k outflow.

The enterprise thus showed a net cash outflow of £676k (i.e. £692k − £1,368k).

Figure 8.14 shows the cash flow of the enterprise over the last five years. The solid bars show the cash flow before taking account of the cash spent on new fixed assets. The hatched bars show the cash flow after spending on fixed assets.

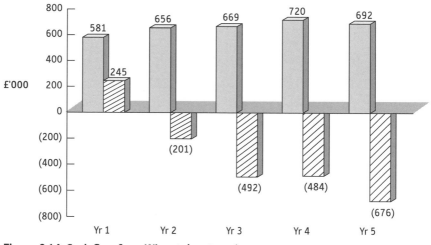

Figure 8.14 Cash flow from Wingate's enterprise

As you can see, net cash flow from the enterprise ('operating cash flow') has been pretty consistently negative and there is no sign of the cash flow reversing and the enterprise actually increasing the amount of cash in the business. Even if it could reach a situation where the cash generated from operations was equal to the capital expenditure requirement ('cash neutral' as they say), there's still more than £600k of interest, dividends and tax to pay as things stand.

Operating cash conversion

One way of looking at the enterprise cash flow is to see how it compares to operating profit. So what we do is divide the operating cash flow by the operating profit, which, in year 5 gives us:

$$\text{Operating cash conversion} = -676 / 919 = -74\%$$

Frankly, in Wingate's case, this doesn't tell us much we didn't know already – i.e. that Wingate is spending a lot more cash than it's earning in profit. That's because Wingate is investing heavily in new equipment, etc., which (presumably) isn't going to go on for ever. Ideally, we would calculate this ratio using a cash flow figure which only took account of 'maintenance' capital expenditure ('capex' for short) – i.e. the capex that is required to maintain the assets that are producing the current level of profit. We would ignore 'investment in the future' capex. This breakdown of capex is not normally available from outside the company. You will find, however, that most companies are not investing as heavily as Wingate, so calculating this ratio and looking at it over a few years may tell you something. What you are looking for is as high a cash conversion ratio as possible (and definitely not negative). And obviously you prefer to see it trending upwards rather than downwards.

EBITDA cash conversion

We can look at an alternative cash conversion ratio, which ignores capex and thus is really only measuring the impact of working capital on cash flow. To do this, we need to amend both the top and bottom of the ratio.

First, we add back depreciation to operating profit (because depreciation is the cost that arises from the capital expenditure and we are choosing to ignore it). This is known as **EBITDA**, which stands for **Earnings Before Interest**, **Tax**, **Depreciation** and **Amortisation**. You could just as easily call this 'operating profit before depreciation'. Amortisation is another word for depreciation, but is used when talking about the depreciation of intangible assets rather than tangible fixed assets. Intangible assets are things like patents, trademarks, etc. We will talk more about these later. So, in year 5, we have:

$$\text{EBITDA} = £919k + £495k = £1,414k$$

Our cash flow figure this time is just the cash flow from operating activities – i.e. ignoring the capex cash flow. So our EBITDA cash conversion in year 5 is:

$$\text{EBITDA cash conversion} = £692k / £1,414k = 48.9\%$$

Is that good or bad?

Certainly not good by pretty much any standard. But you need to bear in mind two things when thinking about cash flow relative to profit:

- ▶ **The effect of growth**. Profit is earned across the whole year. Cash flow is dependent on profit and the *change* in working capital during the year. So if trade debtors are higher at the end of the year than the beginning, that reduces the cash flow in the year. Now, in a growing company, the trade debtors at the end of the year, which are typically related to the sales in just the last two or three months of the year, will be high relative to the year as a whole. The same may well apply to stock if the company is stocking up for yet more growth next year, although this will perhaps be offset by higher trade creditors if the company hasn't yet paid the suppliers of the stock.

  So, all other things being equal, we would expect EBITDA cash conversion to be lower in a growing company than in a steady state company.

  So would I be right in thinking that EBITDA cash conversion in a steady state company would be 100%?

  Yes, very good. If debtor days, stock productivity and trade creditor productivity don't change and sales and EBITDA are 'flat', then working capital at year end will be the same as at the beginning of the year and so this measure of cash flow will equal EBITDA.

- ▶ **Industry characteristics**. The other thing you have to think about when considering EBITDA cash conversion is the nature of the industry the company is in:

  - At one extreme, you have service companies where customers pay in advance, there is no stock and suppliers are not paid until customers have received the service. In this situation, the company will have **negative working capital.** In other words, rather than having cash 'tied up' in working capital, they have cash in the bank due to working capital. And the consequence if they are growing is that the working capital will be more negative at the end of the year than the beginning of the year and so cash flow will be *higher* than operating profit, so EBITDA cash conversion will be greater than 100%. One good example of this is a travel company selling summer holidays in January.

– At the other extreme, you have companies whose customers don't pay until many weeks after receiving the goods or services, where high stocks are required and suppliers offer little or no credit. Such companies will have very high working capital and so growth will result in cash flow being substantially less than profit. And that leads to an inability to invest in growth opportunities and potentially to difficulties in paying your bank, your suppliers or even your staff.

If you ever think of starting any other business, Sarah, think hard about its working capital characteristics. It's a lot easier to grow a business with low or negative working capital than it is one with high working capital.

When analysing a company, the best thing is to look at cash conversion over time. Figure 8.15 shows Wingate's EBITDA cash conversion.

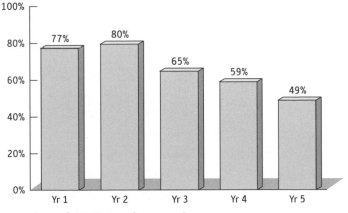

Figure 8.15 Wingate's EBITDA cash conversion

As you can see it has declined substantially. While it's true that sales are growing, a large part of this reduction in cash conversion is down to the increase in trade debtors. The company is simply not getting paid as quickly as it used to.

Let's now pull it all together and summarise what we have found out about Wingate.

Summary

► Wingate's return on capital employed, which is the key performance measure of the enterprise, has been declining dramatically since the new management took charge – although operating profit has been growing, capital employed has been growing faster.

► The decline in ROCE can be explained by a decline in both return on sales and capital productivity.

► The fall in ROS is due to a steady decline in gross margin, probably caused by the management's price-cutting policy. The gross margin decline has been offset to some extent by a reduction in administration costs (only made possible, however, by investing in new buildings).

► Capital productivity has fallen because both fixed assets and working capital are growing faster than sales.

► The disproportionate need for additional working capital is because the company is not collecting its debts from customers as quickly, is holding more stock than it used to and is paying its suppliers sooner.

CHAPTER NINE

Analysis of the funding structure

- ▶ The funding structure ratios
- ▶ Lenders' perspective
- ▶ Gearing
- ▶ Shareholders' perspective
- ▶ Liquidity
- ▶ Summary

We have looked at Wingate's underlying business and discovered that it is a much less attractive picture than the management would have you believe, Tom. Now we need to look at the funding structure and see how that affects our views of the company. What I am going to do first is show you how we summarise the funding structure in a simple ratio. We will then look at the implications of that structure from the different points of view of the lenders (i.e. the banks) and the shareholders.

The funding structure ratios

When we rearranged Wingate's balance sheet in session 8, we established that the funding for the business was a combination of tax payable, debt and equity [Table 9.1].

Table 9.1 Wingate's funding structure

WINGATE FOODS LTD		
Funding structure at the end of Year 5		
		£'000
Taxation		131
Net debt		
Cash	(12)	
Overdraft	933	
Loans	3,150	
Finance leases	601	
Net debt		4,672
Shareholders' equity		
Dividends payable	0	
Share capital	50	
Share premium	275	
Retained profit	2,522	
Total shareholders' equity		2,847
Net funding		**7,650**

The total amount of funding is, as it has to be, the same as the capital employed in the enterprise. We have seen how to calculate the return on this capital. What we are interested in now is the way the funding is made up, i.e. what proportion of the funding comes from each of the different sources.

In practice, tax payable is usually very small in comparison with debt and equity. This is certainly true of Wingate, as you can see from Table 9.1 which shows tax payable to be £131k against debt of £4,672k and equity of £2,847k. Tax only complicates the situation and, since it is so small, we just ignore it and concentrate on the debt and the equity.

The debt to total funding ratio

Ignoring tax payable, the total funding of a business is the sum of the debt and the equity. The **debt to total funding ratio** is the debt divided by the total funding, i.e. it shows what percentage of the total funding is debt:

$$\text{Debt to total funding} = \text{Debt/Total funding}$$
$$= 4{,}672 \,/\, [4{,}672 + 2{,}847]$$
$$= 62.1\%$$

I'll come on to the implications of this figure later, but to give you an idea of what is normal:

▶ Anything over 50 per cent is considered pretty high.

▶ The average for the top 100 companies in Britain is around 25 per cent.

The debt to equity ratio (or 'gearing')

The debt to total funding ratio shows you at a glance how much of a business is funded by debt and, by deduction, how much by equity. Many people prefer, however, to summarise the funding structure in a slightly different way. They divide the debt by the equity and express it as a percentage. This ratio, known as the **debt to equity ratio** or **gearing**, shows how large the debt is relative to the equity.

$$\text{Debt to equity} = \text{Debt/Equity}$$
$$= 4{,}672 \,/\, 2{,}847$$
$$= 164\%$$

This tells us that Wingate's debt is 1.64 times bigger than its equity. The two benchmark figures of 25 per cent and 50 per cent, which I just gave you for debt to total funding, are the equivalent of debt to equity ratios of 33 per cent and 100 per cent respectively.

The debt to equity ratio is probably the more common of the two ratios. Personally, I find the debt to total funding ratio much more intuitive, so I have used it in my analysis of Wingate.

Wingate's five-year debt to total funding ratio

Over the last five years, Wingate has increased the amount of debt in its funding structure markedly [Figure 9.1].

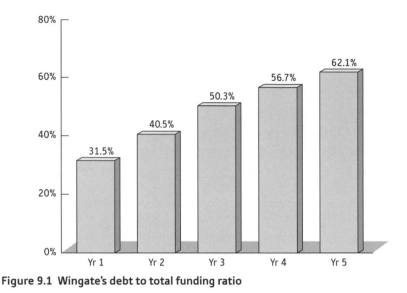

Figure 9.1 Wingate's debt to total funding ratio

Back in year one it was at a fairly conservative level; currently it is over the 50 per cent threshold at which people start to look at the company very carefully. Let's now see why people care about this ratio; we'll start by looking at it from the perspective of lenders (i.e. the banks).

Lenders' perspective

Security of debt

When a bank lends money to a company, it is making an investment. People and companies put their spare cash into current accounts, deposit accounts, etc. at their banks. The banks then lend this cash to other people and companies who need it. The banks make a profit by paying a lower interest rate to the people depositing their money than they charge to the people who borrow from them.

This sounds like money for old rope and it is, provided that everyone who borrows money from the bank repays it eventually. The banks only make a few percentage points out of each pound they lend. By the time they have paid all their costs, their profit is a fraction of a percentage point of the money they lend. If, therefore, someone doesn't repay the loan, it wipes out all the profit on hundreds of their other loans.

Because of this, banks always look for some **security** – anything that gives them confidence that they will get their money back.

As I mentioned when we were looking at Wingate's accounts in detail [session 6], most companies with overdrafts or loans will have given the bank a charge over their assets. This means that if the company goes bust, the bank has first right to sell the assets and take the cash.

The proceeds from selling assets will not always be enough to cover the bank's debt if a large percentage of the funding structure is debt. Hence the debt to total funding ratio gives an idea of the bank's risk.

Surely the assets must always be worth more than the debt?

Not necessarily, Sarah. Remember the going concern concept. A company might buy an asset which is no use to anyone else in the world and therefore has no resale value. We would still give this asset a value in the company's books, as it is of use in the company's ongoing operations.

On top of that, a bank will only want to sell a company's assets when the company is effectively bust. In that situation, even assets that are of use to other people will be hard to sell for their full value.

But presumably some of the assets, like debtors, you would get most of their book value for, and others, like specialised machinery, you would get next to nothing for?

Of course. In practice, bankers do much more detailed checks and analyses to ensure their loans are secure, but the debt to total funding ratio does give a quick idea of the position.

Wingate's bankers were probably told by the company's management that by investing in fixed assets and expanding sales rapidly, the company could reduce its unit costs and make bumper profits. If I were a banker, after watching the ROCE decline for four years and the debt to total funding ratio rise, I would be getting extremely sceptical by now. I would be looking for some convincing evidence that the company's cash flow and return on capital were going to turn round very soon.

Interest cover

Lenders are concerned at the security of their debt and rightly so. Good bankers, however, do not make loans in the expectation that they will have to sell the company's assets to get their money back. Their hope and expectation is that the company will pay the interest on the debt for as long as required, and then repay the principal.

One of the other key measures used by lenders is interest cover. This is calculated by dividing operating profit by the interest payable:

$$\text{Interest cover} = \text{Operating profit/Interest payable}$$
$$= 919 / 325$$
$$= 2.8\text{x}$$

Operating profits are applied first to paying interest on the debt. This ratio shows literally that Wingate could have paid 2.8 times as much interest as it did in year 5. What a banker would think of this depends on the economic climate at the time. In the mid-1980s, banks were lending money in situations where their interest cover was as low as 1.5 times. In the recession that followed, banks were demanding interest cover of greater than five times.

Gearing

We can now see why the funding structure is important to lenders. We have also seen that the bankers might be getting a little worried by Wingate's situation. Before looking at the shareholders' perspective, you need to understand the concept of **gearing** and its implications. A while ago, I told you that gearing was another word for the debt to equity ratio, which it is. 'Gearing' is also used more generally to describe the concept of borrowing money to add to your own money to make an investment. You will also hear the American word 'leverage' used to mean the same thing.

Let's see how this can affect your wealth by looking at a simple example. Assume you have been given an opportunity to invest in some rare stamps. The dealer has told you that they will probably go up in value by 15 per cent during the year. You know, however, that there is a risk that they will only go up by 5 per cent. You decide to take the risk.

The dealer has £500 worth of the stamps available, but you have only £100 to spare. Let's look at several different scenarios.

Scenario one – no debt

Assume for our first scenario that you decide just to invest the £100 you have. We will call this £100 your 'equity'.

If things go well, the stamps will go up in value to £115 at the end of the year. The profit on your equity will be £15, which is a return of 15 per cent on your investment.

If things go badly, your profit will only be £5, which is a 5 per cent return.

Scenario two – some debt

Let's assume instead that you decide to borrow an additional £100 from the bank to enable you to buy £200 worth of the stamps. The interest you will have to pay on the loan is 10 per cent per annum. Now the total investment is made up of your equity of £100 and debt of £100.

If things go well, the profit on the total investment is now £30. Out of this profit, however, you have to pay the bank's interest, which will be £10. You will be left with £20 profit from your £100 equity, giving you a return of 20 per cent.

If things go badly and the stamps only go up by 5 per cent to £210, the profit on the investment is only £10. You *still* have to pay the bank its £10 interest, which would leave you with nothing.

So could I end up actually losing money?

Let's see.

Scenario three – mostly debt

Assume you borrow £400 from the bank to go with your £100, thereby enabling you to buy all £500 worth of the stamps.

If things go well, the investment will make a profit of £75. Of this profit, £40 will go to the bank as interest on their £400 loan. The balance of the profit will be yours. You will make £35 profit on an investment of £100, which is a return of 35 per cent. If things go badly, though, the investment will only make £25 profit. Unfortunately, you will still owe the bank £40 interest, so you will have to find the extra £15 to pay them. You have made a loss of £15 on your £100 investment, which is a return of minus 15 per cent.

This is the situation in which many people during the recession of the early 1990s found themselves with regard to their homes. They put some of their own money towards buying their house. This is what building societies euphemistically called a 'deposit'. The rest of the money needed to buy the house came as a loan from the building society. In the good times of the early to mid-1980s, people could borrow the majority of the price of their houses, knowing that house prices would rise and they could sell the house, pay off the building society and pocket a nice profit.

In the recession, many houses fell in value so that, if the owners sold the house, they ended up owing the building society more than they got for the house, i.e. they had 'negative equity'. It's exactly the same principle.

Risk and return

Let's just summarise the return you would have made in each of the different scenarios:

	If the market went ...	
	Well	**Badly**
Increase in value of assets	15%	5%
Return on your investment		
Scenario one – No debt	15%	5%
Scenario two – Some debt	20%	0%
Scenario three – Lots of debt	35%	−15%

What this shows is that if you do not take out any debt at all, your return will match that of the underlying asset. As soon as you introduce some debt, then the returns become **geared**. The more debt you include, the higher the return you will make in the good times, but the lower the return you will make in the bad times. In other words, you have to take a greater risk to get a greater return.

How do you define the good times versus the bad times?

Simple. Provided the underlying asset gives a return greater than the interest on the debt, then gearing will lead to higher returns for the equity. In our example, provided the underlying asset provides a return of more than 10 per cent, then you would make a better return if you had some gearing.

So how does all this apply to companies?

Think of the stamps as being the enterprise. They are the operating assets, which may or may not make a good profit. The money that you put towards buying the stamps is equivalent to the equity in a company's funding structure; the money that the bank put towards buying the stamps is the debt in the company's funding structure.

Presumably, the more geared you are, the more a change in interest rates affects you?

Yes, it works in the same way as a change in the return of the enterprise. Unfortunately, a rise in interest rates is often accompanied by worse performance in the enterprise, so you get a 'double-whammy' effect. Naturally, you benefit when interest rates go down.

Shareholders' perspective

Debt to total funding ratio

As we have just seen, gearing affects the risk of and potential returns to shareholders. Shareholders ought, therefore, to control the level of debt a company takes on but, in practice, the management tends to decide. The shareholders can, of course, remove the management of a company if they don't like what they see.

Given that Wingate's debt to total funding ratio has risen from 31.5 per cent to 62.1 per cent, the shareholders' risk has risen considerably.

Return on equity

So Wingate's shareholders have a much more risky company than five years ago. What about the return they are getting?

We know from our analysis of the enterprise that the return on capital employed of the enterprise has fallen to 12 per cent. But that is the return on the total funding. Shareholders, ultimately, are interested in the return on the money they have invested, i.e. the **return on equity** (known as **ROE**). We calculated this earlier when we were looking at the investment in stamps.

We can do the same calculation for Wingate. We know what the equity is – we can read it off Table 9.1 [page 160]. The return is the profit after paying the interest on the loans, i.e. profit before tax.

$$\text{Return on equity } = \text{ Profit before tax/Equity}$$
$$= 594 \,/\, 2{,}847$$
$$= 20.9\%$$

So you're using the equity at the end of the year, as you did for the ROCE?

Yes. As with ROCE, you could use the equity at the start of the year if you wanted to – just make sure you are consistent.

Why are you using the profit before tax? Surely the actual profit to the shareholders is the profit for the year, i.e. profit after tax?

Arguably, but so far we have been calculating returns before tax. For example, we talked about getting 5 per cent per annum before tax on a deposit account and our calculation of return on capital employed for the enterprise did not take account of tax. In a minute we are going to compare the return on capital employed with the return on equity and obviously they must be calculated on the same basis.

You will, I admit, often see return on equity calculated using profit after tax or profit for the year. This does have one benefit, which is that it takes into account the company's ability to reduce the tax it pays, and some companies do manage to pay consistently less tax than others. In general, though, I think you will find that using profit before tax is more helpful.

Let's now see how Wingate's ROE has changed over the last five years [Figure 9.2].

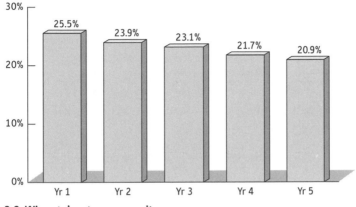

Figure 9.2 Wingate's return on equity

There are two things to notice about this chart:

- ► The ROE is consistently higher than the ROCE [page 139]. This is because the return on the enterprise is greater than the interest rate Wingate is paying. In other words, gearing has improved the returns to the shareholders.

- ► The ROE is declining, but not as fast as the ROCE. This is simply because the company is increasing the gearing of the company so quickly. The decline in the ROCE is being offset by the positive impact on ROE that the gearing is having.

Naturally, this trend cannot continue. Ultimately, the return on capital employed would fall below the bank interest rates and the company would be in serious trouble.

Average interest rate

Companies whose shares are listed on the Stock Exchange have to tell you what their average interest rates were during the year. Private companies don't have to. You can make a guess, however, just by knowing what base rates were at the time and adding a few percentage points.

You can also get a very crude estimate from the accounts by taking the interest paid during the year and dividing it by the average debt at the start and end of the year. You have to be careful about this calculation as companies' overdrafts can vary substantially during a year, depending on the seasonality of the business, and you don't usually know when loans were drawn down or repaid, so the result you will get from this calculation depends on the balance sheet date.

There is probably not much seasonality in Wingate's business as it is a food company, so let's do the calculation anyway. Wingate's net debt was £3,357k at the start of year five and £4,672k at the end. The average debt is therefore £4,015k.

$$\text{Average interest rate} = \text{Interest/Average debt}$$
$$= 325 / 4,015$$
$$= 8.1\%$$

If we look at Wingate's average interest rate over the last five years [Figure 9.3], you can see why, despite large rises in debt, Wingate has been able to report ever-increasing profit before tax: quite simply, the interest rate has gone in its favour.

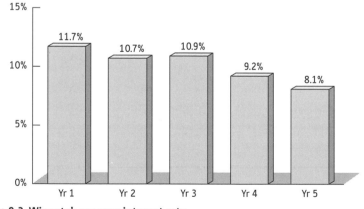

Figure 9.3 Wingate's average interest rate

Let's see what Wingate's profit before tax in year five would have been if the average interest rate were still 11.7 per cent. The extra interest Wingate would have had to pay in year five is £4,015k × (11.7 − 8.1) per cent which is £145k of extra interest. This would have reduced profit before tax in year five from £594k to £449k, less than Wingate made in any of the last five years.

Dividend cover, payout ratio

Although ROE measures the return to shareholders for having invested their money in a company over the last year, they do not actually get all this return out of the company in the form of cash. Remember that profit is not cash. The company is probably still waiting to collect cash from debtors and has manufactured more stock for next year, etc. Some of the profit, however, is paid out in the form of dividends.

Some shareholders rely upon these dividends as a key source of income and they are naturally interested to know how safe the dividends are. One measure of this is **dividend cover**, which is calculated as profit for the year divided by the dividend. When we do this calculation, remember what I said about dividends in an earlier session. Dividends recognised in the accounts are dividends that have been paid (or at least approved by the shareholders). We are really interested in comparing the dividends that relate to a given financial year with the profit for that financial year.

Sorry, I'm not sure I'm with you.

OK, look at Wingate's P&L. This shows a dividend in year five of £184k. However, that was the dividend that was proposed by the board for year four. It's shown in year five because it wasn't approved and paid until year five had started. The dividend that is proposed in respect of year five is shown in Note 7. This is £215k. This is the dividend we want to compare with the profit for year five. Thus we get:

$$\text{Dividend cover} = \text{Profit for the year/Dividend for the year}$$
$$= 463 \ / \ 215$$
$$= 2.2\text{x}$$

You will sometimes find people using a measure called the **payout ratio**. This is simply the inverse of dividend cover expressed as a percentage. It shows what percentage of the profit for the year is paid out as dividends:

$$\text{Payout ratio} = \text{Dividend/Profit for the year}$$
$$= 215 / 463$$
$$= 46\%$$

Let's now look at Wingate's dividend cover over the last five years [Figure 9.4].

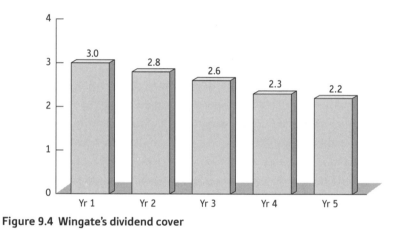

Figure 9.4 Wingate's dividend cover

As you can see, it has been falling quite markedly. This explains why the shareholders are happy. Although the profit attributable to shareholders has not been growing very fast, the dividends have been doing so as a result of paying out an ever-increasing percentage of the profits. Obviously this is not sustainable in the long run.

Liquidity

You summed up the financial objectives of a company very neatly earlier, Sarah. What you said was:

'A company's financial objective is to maximise the return it provides on the money invested, based on an appropriate trade-off between the short- and long-term perspectives, while ensuring that the business remains liquid.'

We have been analysing the returns that Wingate has been providing, both on the total capital employed in the business (ROCE) and on the shareholders' capital (ROE).

We have not paid much attention to liquidity so far. As you will remember, liquidity is the ability of a company to pay its debts as they fall due. Analysing a company's liquidity is extremely difficult. There is no single KPI that tells us very much.

There are two ratios which are commonly used as measures of liquidity which I will mention briefly but they are by no means perfect.

Current ratio

The **current ratio** is calculated by dividing the current assets by the current liabilities. The logic behind this is that the current assets should all be convertible into cash within one year, and the current liabilities are what you have to pay within one year. Provided your current assets are greater than your current liabilities, you should not have a liquidity problem.

We can calculate the current ratio for Wingate very easily:

$$\text{Current ratio} = \text{Current assets/Current liabilities}$$
$$= 3{,}482 \,/\, 2{,}906$$
$$= 1.2$$

In other words, Wingate's current assets are 1.2 times greater than its current liabilities. Typically, analysts look for this ratio to be greater than 2.0 to give a good margin of safety.

What is wrong with the current ratio as a measure of liquidity?

The major problem is that liquidity crises tend to have a much shorter time horizon than a year. If you have to pay some bills this week to continue trading, it is no comfort to know that your customers will be paying you in two months' time. The safety implied by a given current ratio figure will depend on the nature of a company's business.

You can always look at the trend in a company's current ratio, but you have to be very careful about companies which find ways to redefine short-term liabilities as long-term liabilities, thereby improving their current ratios. Switching between overdrafts and loans is one easy way to do this.

Quick ratio

The **quick ratio** is identical to the current ratio except that stock is not included in the current assets, on the basis that stock can be hard to sell. All the other assets (principally debtors and cash) are 'quick'.

The quick ratio suffers from exactly the same problems as the current ratio.

*So how **do** you assess liquidity?*

Ideally, you make week-by-week or month-by-month forecasts of exactly what bills are going to have to be paid when, and what customers are going to pay when, etc.

This, of course, is impossible from outside the company. If you only have the annual reports, I recommend looking at the cash flow statement.

The cash flow statement

We've already looked at what the cash flow statement tells us about the cash flow of the enterprise. That wasn't a particularly encouraging picture due to the high capital expenditure.

However, capital expenditure is usually a discretionary expense. You can simply stop it. What you can't stop is paying tax and servicing your debt – i.e. paying the interest and making the repayments due. So let's look at year 5, ignoring capex [see Table 9.2].

I've assumed that the finance lease debt was obtained from a separate company to the bank, which is normal. So, even if we ignore the capital

Table 9.2 Year 5 cash flow, ignoring capex

		£'000
Cash flow from operating activities	692	
Tax paid	(130)	
Finance lease repayments and interest	(234)	
Cash flow available for debt service		328
Bank interest	(243)	
Bank loan repayments	(350)	
Debt service		(593)
Excess/(deficit) in debt service		(265)

expenditure, that leaves just £328k of cash generated in year 5 to service the debt. The debt service was considerably more than this. Now we know from note 11 that the coming year's debt repayments are £525k, so the bank is probably quite worried about its loans right now.

I see you left the dividend payments off this table, Chris.

Yes, because they are entirely discretionary. The company can, if it has to, simply stop paying dividends.

My general point here is that the cash flow statement will give you some insight into a company and it is always worth studying it.

Summary

▶ Wingate's gearing (as measured by the debt to equity and debt to total funding ratios) has been rising rapidly and is now well above average levels.

▶ This means that the lenders' security has diminished and they are unlikely to lend further funds.

▶ The rise in gearing has also affected the shareholders' position:

   – Their return (as measured by ROE) has not fallen as fast as it would otherwise have done.

   – Their risk has risen substantially, however.

Summary (continued)

► Without a decline in interest rates, Wingate's profit before tax would have been lower than in any of the previous four years.

► Dividends are only growing strongly because the company is paying out an ever-increasing proportion of its profits.

CHAPTER TEN

Valuation of companies

- ▶ Book value vs market value
- ▶ Valuation techniques
- ▶ Summary

So far we have talked about how to construct, interpret and analyse company accounts. Someone like you, Tom, who is thinking of buying shares in a company is really interested in the value of those shares (which is what most people mean when they talk about the value of a 'company').

I will start by explaining why **book value** and **market value** of shares are usually different and then I will describe briefly four ratios that are used a lot when valuing companies.

Book value vs market value

Book value

Book value is simply the value that an item has on the balance sheet (i.e. 'in the books'). We know that the book value of the shares of a company is the value of the equity, which is the difference between the assets and the liabilities. At the end of year five, Wingate's equity, and therefore the book value of the shares, was £2,847k.

If you own just a few shares in the company, this figure does not tell you very much, so we can express it on a 'per share' basis. We know that Wingate has one million shares in issue, all of which have an equal right to the net assets, so the book value per share is as follows:

$$\text{BV per share} = \text{BV/Number of shares}$$
$$= \text{£2,847k / 1m}$$
$$= \text{£2.85 per share}$$

Market value

The balance sheet tells us what our shares are worth in the eyes of the accountants. The fact is, though, that we live in a market economy, where things are worth what someone will pay for them, not what anyone's 'books' say they are worth. Some companies are worth less than their book value, but most are worth more.

Why would anyone pay more than book value?

There are two possible reasons:

▶ It may simply be that the market value of one of the assets of the company is much higher than the book value. The most common example of this is land and buildings. If you knew a company had an asset that was worth much more than its value in the books, you might be prepared to pay more than book value for the company so you could sell off the assets and pocket a nice profit.

▶ In general, though, people don't invest in a company in order to wind it up. They invest in a company because they believe it will provide a good return on the investment. If they can pay more than book value for the shares and still get a good return on their money, then it makes sense to do so.

Let's take Wingate back in year one as an example. In those days, the company was making a good return on capital employed with a reasonable level of gearing, resulting in a good return to the shareholders, as measured by return on equity calculated as follows:

Profit before tax	£455k
Equity	£1,782k
Return on equity	25.5%

An investor looking at the company might have said, 'This is a well-run company in a good market position. I would accept a lower return than 25.5 per cent from such a company; I would accept 22 per cent'.

Such an investor would be saying:

$$22\% = \text{Profit before tax/Equity value}$$
$$= \pounds455k \,/\, ?$$

Hence:

$$\text{Equity value} = \pounds455k \,/\, 22\%$$
$$= \pounds2{,}068k$$
$$= 207 \text{ pence per share}$$

The investor would therefore be prepared to pay up to 207p per share, which compares with the book value per share at the time of 178p ($\pounds1{,}782k\,/\,$1m shares $= \pounds1.78 = 178p$).

Naturally, different investors and analysts will have different opinions on what return is acceptable from a company and therefore arrive at different valuations. Bear in mind as well that the returns we can calculate from the accounts are what has happened in the past. When we value a company we are, implicitly or explicitly, predicting the future, which results in even greater variation in different people's valuations.

Valuation techniques

There are many different techniques used to value companies. Unfortunately, since the value of a company depends on future events, none of these techniques is perfect. The techniques vary from simple ones, which rely on the calculation of a single KPI, to extremely complex ones, which require quantitative analysis of risk and the forecasting of a company's performance for the next ten years.

My personal experience is that the complex techniques are just as bad as the simple ones. It seems that most people have had the same experience, because the simple ones are by far the most common. It may be, of course, that we are all just lazy and have convinced ourselves that the simple way is best. Whatever the reasons, I'm only going to cover the simple ones. If you are interested, there are plenty of books on more complex techniques.

Price earnings ratio (PER or P/E)

The method our hypothetical investor used to decide to pay more than book value for Wingate shares probably seems like a fairly reasonable way to go about putting a value on a company. You assess the company's management, competition, markets, financial structure, etc. and say 'I'm prepared to accept a return of x per cent or more from this company'. The more you pay for the shares, the lower your expected return, so you buy shares up to a price at which the expected return falls to x per cent.

This method is the approach used by the vast majority of analysts and investors, except that they turn the ratio upside down. Instead of dividing the profit by the value of the shares, they divide the value of the shares by the profit. They also use a different profit figure. Instead of using profit before tax, they use profit for the year, which, as we saw earlier, is also known as earnings. This ratio thus becomes the **price earnings ratio**.

Let's suppose that the market value of each Wingate share was 500p. The price earnings ratio (based on profit for year five) would be:

$$\text{P/E ratio} = \text{Price/Earnings per share}$$
$$= 500 \, / \, 46.3$$
$$= 10.8$$

But what is this ratio measuring and how do you interpret it?

If you think about it, the ratio is literally measuring the number of years the company would have to earn those profits in order for you to get your money back. So after 10.8 years of earning 46.3p per share, Wingate would have earned 500p per share.

In practice, investors don't think of this ratio in quite these terms. Investors are typically comparing one investment opportunity with many others. They therefore compare the P/E ratios of all the companies and assess them relative to one another. Companies that have good prospects of increasing profits in the future and/or are low-risk tend to be on higher P/Es than companies whose profits are not growing and/or are perceived to be high-risk.

There are some *extremely* crude benchmarks which you may find helpful:

- ▶ A company that people believe to be in danger of going bankrupt will be on a P/E of less than 5.

▶ A company performing poorly would be on a P/E between 5 and 10.

▶ A company which is doing satisfactorily will be on a P/E of between 10 and 15.

▶ A company with extremely good prospects will be on a P/E of greater than 15.

Let me stress, though, that these figures vary hugely by industry and economic conditions, so don't rely on them for any important decisions.

It seems a little odd to use a ratio based on historic profit figures to tell you the value of the company when it obviously depends on what is going to happen in the future.

True, but what people actually do is to interpret P/Es in the light of what they know about the expected future performance of a company.

It is quite common also for people to calculate the P/E using their forecasts of the next year's earnings. This is known as a **prospective P/E** or a **forward P/E**. A P/E based on historic profits is often called the **historic P/E** to make it clear which year's earnings are being used.

PEG

Because the P/E of a company reflects, at least in part, its growth prospects, it makes sense to look at something that relates these two things to each other. This is what a PEG does. It is the P/E ratio of a company divided by the growth in its earnings per share.

$$PEG = PE/EPS \text{ growth}$$

If the PEG is low, that suggests you have found a company on a low PE relative to its growth rate. This may suggest that the company's shares are undervalued.

As with the PE itself, you can either use the prospective growth in EPS (which is of course, uncertain) or you can use the historic growth from the most recent annual report.

So what is a low PEG?

Well, there's no hard and fast rule, but most of the people who use PEG's extensively for investment decisions are looking for PEG's that are definitely below 1.0 and preferably below 0.7–0.8.

Dividend yield

When you invest your money in a deposit account, the bank pays you all your interest. You might decide to leave it in the account and earn interest on the interest the next year, but you can choose to take it out if you want.

Companies tend not to pay out all of the year's profits to their shareholders. Companies that are expanding rapidly need cash to enable them to expand and tend not to pay out much. They have low payout ratios. Other companies, such as utility companies like telephone, water, gas and electricity, tend not to grow all that fast and thus are able to pay out a higher percentage of their year's profits.

Such companies are often valued using **dividend yield**. This is calculated as the dividends for the year divided by the market value of the shares. The average dividend yield of the large companies in Britain is around 3 per cent. Low-growth companies such as utility companies typically pay yields of 5–6 per cent.

Market to book ratio

There is one further simple measure you can use to compare the valuations of companies.

I started this session by explaining why the market value of shares is usually higher than the book value. This leads us to a simple valuation technique, which is to compare the market value with the book value.

What we do is divide the market value of the shares by the book value, which gives us the **market to book ratio**.

Let's assume that someone is prepared to pay 500p per Wingate share. We know that the book value is 285p. Hence we get:

$$\text{Market to book ratio} = \text{Market value/Book value}$$
$$= 500 / 285$$
$$= 1.75$$

We could then compare this with the market to book ratios of other companies and decide whether it seemed reasonable or not. If it seemed low, then we would say the market value should be higher. We might therefore decide to buy some shares. If the ratio seemed too high, we would take that as an indication to sell the shares.

The problem with this method is that there is very large variation in these ratios in different industries and even within the same industry. Investors therefore have difficulty in comparing them. This ratio is useful, however, when valuing companies whose business is just investing in assets (as opposed to operating them). Such businesses include property investment companies and **investment trusts**. Investment trusts are companies that invest in other companies' shares.

Summary

- Accounts tell us the book value of a company's shares.
- The market value of shares is usually different from the book value.
- There are many different methods for valuing companies, from the very simple to the extremely complex.
- The most common methods are the price earnings ratio and dividend yield.
- The price earnings ratio can be based on either historic or expected future earnings.
- The PEG relates the price earnings ratio to the growth in earnings of the company.
- Dividend yield is an important valuation metric, particularly in more mature companies.
- The market to book ratio can be useful, particularly for valuing companies like investment trusts.

PART 3

Listed company accounts

CHAPTER ELEVEN

Listed company accounts: Introduction

- ► Introduction
- ► The primary statements
- ► Terminology and jargon
- ► Accounting standards
- ► Fair value vs historical cost
- ► Summary

Introduction

In our review of Wingate's accounts, we covered most of the items you will see in the accounts of a small private company. When you look at the annual reports of larger companies, and in particular **listed** companies (i.e. where their shares are **listed** or **quoted** on a stock exchange so anyone can buy or sell them), you will notice four things:

1. They become very long. While Wingate had just three reports plus the accounts and the notes to those accounts, a **listed company** might have as many as 20 different reports, plus of course the accounts themselves and the related notes. Having said that, the broad approach is the same as for Wingate – the reports all fall into one of three categories:

   ► **Strategy,** which for Wingate was a single report, but for a listed company will be several reports on the business, its markets, strategy, employees, risks, finance, corporate responsibility, etc.

   ► **Governance,** which includes the directors' report and the auditors' report plus reports on things like directors' remuneration and corporate governance.

> ► **Financials,** which is the accounts and the related notes (which themselves can be over 100 pages long).

2. The accounts are usually described as 'consolidated'. This tells you the company whose accounts you are looking at owns one or more companies (each of which might own other companies, etc.). This may be because they have bought the companies or because they have started new businesses through separate companies. It's too much to expect investors to look at the accounts of each individual company in this 'family tree' of companies, so the top company in the tree (known as the **parent**) is obliged to produce **group accounts** or **consolidated accounts.** Essentially it's one set of accounts that presents the financial picture of the entire group of companies *as if* it were just one company.

3. The companies enter into all sorts of transactions that we didn't encounter with Wingate.

4. The accounting for some of these transactions can appear, and sometimes be, quite complex.

All this can make such companies' annual reports more than a little daunting. However, you should not be put off. All the strategy and governance stuff is generally written in reasonably plain English. Some jargon does appear, but hopefully I will have covered most of it by the end of this session. Where you're going to need a little help is when you get to the financials (i.e. the accounts themselves). My goal over the next two sessions is to get you to the point where you can look at a typical listed company's accounts and think 'I know what's going on here' instead of 'Which ancient language is this stuff written in?'

And there is some good news. There is a lot more explanation of the accounting than there used to be. Provided you understand some of the language they use, you will be able to follow how things are being accounted for.

In the first of these two sessions on listed company accounts, I'm going to give you a general introduction to listed companies' accounts and expand on one of the crucial concepts we've been working with. In the second session, I will run through a longish list of new things you are likely to encounter if you start looking at listed companies.

The primary statements

As you will recall, I described the balance sheet as the 'definitive statement' of a company's financial position and the P&L and cash flow statement as important, but nonetheless merely 'descriptive statements'. These three statements are called **primary statements.** This means they have to be separate from the notes and given equal prominence in the accounts. There are also two other primary statements that didn't appear in Wingate's accounts.

I've created the five primary statements for an imaginary company called Listco so I can refer to them as I explain the various items in the next session. Let's start by having a quick look at these five primary statements [see pages 280 to 286 and/or print out larger copies from the author's website **www.accountsdemystified.com**].

Profit and loss (Income statement)

[See page 280] This should look familiar, but there are a few points to note:

- ▶ It might be called the income statement, the profit and loss or the statement of comprehensive income (which I will explain shortly).

- ▶ It is described as 'Consolidated'. As we just discussed, this means it is the P&L of a group of at least two companies.

- ▶ I've added line numbers down the side to help direct you more easily to the line I'm talking about. You won't see these when looking at some real accounts. You will also find that real accounts have a much fancier layout (usually dreamt up by the company's investor relations adviser). Far more often than not, in my experience, this just makes them harder to follow.

- ▶ The profit from '**Continuing operations**' is shown separately from the profit from '**Discontinued operations**'. This arises where a company has sold or is in the process of selling a meaningful bit of its business. The idea is to enable the reader to see the performance of the continuing businesses. Sometimes, the P&L will have three columns of figures for each year, where column 1 is Continuing operations, column 2 is Discontinued operations and column 3 is the total group. In Listco's case, the discontinued operations profit is shown as a single line (line 15). The notes would give more details about the discontinued operations' P&L.

▶ You might also see P&Ls which have lines showing 'adjusted profit', 'headline profit', 'underlying profit' or something similar. This is where a company believes that presenting its P&L in accordance with the accounting rules does not give a useful picture of the underlying performance of the company. It therefore adjusts the figures as it sees fit to show 'adjusted profit'. The adjustments made will be explained in the notes. Again, you sometimes see a three-column layout, showing the adjusted P&L, the adjustments and then the total. In Listco's case, they have not shown adjusted profit on the P&L at all, but *have* made some adjustments and thus have come up with adjusted earnings per share, which you can see on line 33.

▶ I will explain in the next session all the following new things:

    – share of profit of associated undertakings on line 11;

    – the split of profit between the parent's shareholders and non-controlling interests on lines 19 and 20;

    – the various earnings per share figures.

▶ Finally, note that, as mentioned when discussing Wingate, dividends are not shown on the P&L.

Balance sheet (Statement of financial position)

[See page 282] Apart from the fact that this is called the **Statement of financial position** rather than the balance sheet and fixed assets are called **non-current assets**, the top section of the balance sheet will look familiar. There are, of course, some line items you don't understand yet, but we'll come to those.

The bit that is really different is the shareholders' equity section. With Wingate we had three boxes:

▶ share capital and share premium, which represented the money put into the company by the shareholders to get it going;

▶ retained profit which was all the profit the company had made since it started trading that it had not (as yet) paid out to shareholders as dividends.

In Listco, we have a heading called Equity, which has two sub-headings:

▸ Shareholders' equity,

▸ Non-controlling interests.

Ignore the Non-controlling interests for the moment. I will come back to this.

Under shareholders' equity, we have nine boxes (compared with Wingate's three). As you can see, I have divided them into two categories:

▸ 'Share related': boxes in this category relate in some way to the money shareholders have put into the company.

▸ 'Profit related': boxes in this category relate to profit made by the company.

Note that you won't see these two category headings on a real company's accounts. I have added them to help explain things later.

Cash flow

[See page 284] The cash flow statement is similar to Wingate's in that it starts with profit and then explains why the cash increase/decrease was different from profit.

You will notice, however, that there are only three category headings, whereas Wingate had five. The logic of having just three categories is based on a very simple view of a company's activities:

▸ finance the company;

▸ invest the funds raised in various assets;

▸ operate those assets.

The categories don't matter, as there are generally enough individual lines that you can re-arrange the cash flow statement how you want. Sometimes, you will find the detail of the operating activities category is in the notes rather than in the actual cash flow statement.

Shareholders' equity, retained profit and the P&L

So those are the three main statements we've come across before. Before we look at the two new statements, we need to revisit a basic concept we've been taking as read since our very first session.

Let me just recap that basic concept:

▶ The balance sheet lists all the assets of the company and all the claims over those assets.

▶ The claims are made up of the claims of creditors (these are therefore the liabilities of the company) and the claims of the shareholders (which is whatever is left after the liabilities have been paid). So we say

$$\text{Assets} = \text{Liabilities} + \text{Shareholders' equity}$$

or

$$\text{Assets} - \text{Liabilities} = \text{Shareholders' equity}$$

▶ Shareholders' equity is made up of what the shareholders put into the company (i.e. share capital + share premium) plus the cumulative profits the company has made that have not been paid out to shareholders as dividends (i.e. retained profit).

▶ The change in retained profit from one year end to the next year end is shown by the P&L.

With a listed company's accounts, there are two crucial differences from this nice and simple situation.

▶ First, as we saw when we glanced at Listco's balance sheet, there may be additional boxes making up shareholders' equity.

– The first five, including the share capital and share premium boxes we already know about, all relate to the company's shares. Some transactions a company makes *effectively* increase or decrease the value and/or number of shares in issue and these adjustments are put in separate boxes in order to help the reader understand what has gone on.

– The bottom four boxes, including the retained profit box we know about, all relate to transactions where the shareholders have actually become richer or poorer through the company making a gain or a loss of some sort. While such transactions *can* (usually) be recorded in the retained profit box, some companies prefer, again for the sake of clarity, to have separate boxes for particular types of transactions.

► The second crucial difference is that any transaction that affects one of the boxes under shareholders' equity is categorised as one of the following:

1. A transaction that affects 'real' profits or losses of the company in the relevant year.

2. A transaction that represents some other gain or loss the company has made in the relevant year, but which is not considered (yet, at least) to represent 'real' profit or loss of the company. It's more of a 'paper' profit or loss, which may even reverse at some point.

3. A transaction that is actually a 'transaction with owners', i.e. with some or all of the existing shareholders or with new shareholders. So these kinds of transactions are not about profit or loss but about shareholders' actual investment in the company and/or how the value attributable to the shareholders is divided among the shareholders.

Having categorised transactions as above, we treat them as follows:

– Any transaction in category 1 will increase or reduce the retained profit box and will be included in the P&L.

– Any transaction in category 2 will either affect the retained profit box or one of the other 'profit' boxes (such as revaluation reserve or translation reserve). Regardless of which box on the balance sheet it goes into, however, the transaction is *not* included in the P&L. Instead, it is classified as being **other comprehensive income** (a slightly odd choice of words, if you ask me – think of it as including any gains and losses the shareholders have made that *don't* go into the P&L).

– A transaction in category 3 doesn't relate to gains or losses the company has made that affect the shareholders' wealth and so will go in a box under shareholders' equity but will not be included in the P&L and nor will it be classified as Other comprehensive income.

I understand your category 1, but what kinds of transactions are you talking about in the other two categories?

Well, for example, when you buy a building, you include it on your balance sheet at what you paid for it, as we saw with Wingate. After a few years, however, it may well be worth considerably more than you paid for it, because land and buildings do tend to appreciate rather than depreciate. So companies are allowed to revalue buildings to their 'fair' value. While that's good for shareholders, because that increase in value has definitely made them wealthier, at least on paper, it's not *really* related to the underlying profitability of the actual business and neither is it a 'realised' gain – it's just a paper gain until the building is sold. So it goes in my second category as a gain that's not a 'real' profit in the year.

As for category 3, we have already seen examples of such transactions:

- the issue of shares to investors in return for cash;
- the payment of dividends to shareholders.

Another category 3 example is where the company buys back its own shares from shareholders. This isn't about the company making a gain or loss – it's actually more like a dividend because the shareholders are taking money out of the company, but at the same time their claim over the assets of the company is reduced.

OK, I sort of understand each point as you've made it but I'm not sure I can put it all together without getting completely confused.

Don't worry. I think it will become clear as we work through some examples. First, we need to get to grips with the two new primary statements.

Statement of changes in equity

Look at this one first [page 286]. There are lots of numbers, but don't worry about most of them for the moment. Just observe the following:

- The headings across the top are identical to the headings under Equity on the balance sheet. That is because each column of this statement is explaining the changes in each of the boxes under Equity from one year end to the next. Which has to be useful.
- If you look at the row headings down the left-hand side, you will see that we have:
  - on line 1, the balance of each of the Equity boxes at the end of Year 4 (which is of course the beginning of Year 5);

- from lines 3 to 25, the descriptions of the transactions that have resulted in the changes to each Equity box during the year: you can see that these are separated into the three categories I mentioned:

    A. Profit for the period (i.e. as shown on the P&L) (line 5);

    B. Other comprehensive income (lines 6–12);

    C. Transactions with owners (lines 14–23);

- on line 27, the balance of each of the Equity boxes at the end of Year 5.

▸ Now look at the fourth column from the right. This is labelled 'Retained profits'. Up to a few minutes ago, you would have expected the change in this box during the year to be just the retained profit shown in the P&L, wouldn't you? In fact, though, if we look down this column, we can see that:

- The profit for the year on the P&L *is* included in this column (line 5).

- There are, however, other entries in this column relating to trans-actions falling into category 2 (Other comprehensive income) and category 3 (Transactions with owners).

▸ Now look at the column headed 'Revaluation reserve' (just to the left of Retained profits). You can see that this has increased by £8.0m from £3.4m to £11.4m. This is an accounting entry that:

- does notionally increase shareholders' wealth, so must show as an increase in shareholders' equity on the balance sheet;

- doesn't warrant inclusion in the P&L, because it's not reflective of the real underlying business of the company, so is categorised as Other comprehensive income.

We don't need to go through every column now. At this point, I just want you to remember the following:

▸ In terms of understanding what's going on, we need to focus on the balance sheet. This is *always* true. Don't let anyone ever tell you otherwise.

▸ While it was nice and easy to think that the P&L explained all the change in retained profit in a given year, it doesn't matter that it doesn't, because we have the statement of changes in equity to reconcile it all for us.

- ▶ And while it was nice and simple just having three boxes under shareholders' equity, it doesn't matter if there are more, because we get an explanation of how and why each has changed.

- ▶ And, of course, there are pages and pages of notes with all the detail.

Statement of comprehensive income

Now look at this statement [page 281]. This is very straightforward (ignoring the details of the particular transactions for the moment). We have:

- ▶ On line 1, the profit for the year, as per the P&L (line 16).

- ▶ Various other items of gains and losses under the heading 'Other comprehensive income'.

- ▶ On line 19, the **Total comprehensive income for the year** (being, obviously, the sum of the profit for the year and the other comprehensive income).

Ignore, for the moment, the bit at the bottom where it says 'Attributable to . . . .' I will explain this when we talk about group accounts shortly.

OK, but what about these sub-headings 'Items that will not be reclassified blah, blah, blah'?

Again, I will explain these when we come to talk about the specific items. One final thing I should mention is that the P&L and the statement of comprehensive income are sometimes combined into one statement, either because:

- ▶ the company chooses to do it that way; or

- ▶ there is no 'other comprehensive income' to report.

Terminology and jargon

As you may have discovered already, there are a lot of different terms for the same thing in the accounting world. Even more confusingly, some terms mean different things to different people. I started out in our first couple of sessions using terminology that I felt best described what we were talking about. In discussing Wingate, I have tried to stick with the same terminology as far as possible.

Here are a few examples of alternative terminology you will come across when looking at listed companies' accounts. As you can see, they are mostly intuitive, so you aren't generally going to be confused.

Term I've used	Alternatives
Balance sheet	Statement of financial position
Profit and loss account	Income statement
Turnover	Revenue
Fixed assets	Non-current assets
Tangible fixed assets	Property, plant and equipment
Stocks	Inventories
Trade debtors	Trade receivables
Trade creditors	Trade payables
Shareholders' equity	Capital and reserves, Equity, Shareholders' funds

I actually prefer, from a beginner's point of view, some of the alternative terms because they describe the thing more accurately. 'Statement of financial position' is definitely better than balance sheet, but it's a bit of a mouthful, so I will mostly stick with balance sheet.

Jargon

As I said, modern listed company accounts do include a *lot* of explanation of the various items in their accounts and how they have been accounted for. The problem for beginners is that these explanations often involve the use of jargon, which is great when you're used to it but hopeless when you're not. There's one bit of this jargon I want to talk about as it turns up a lot and it's important to understand it.

We discussed how transactions that affect one or more of the boxes under shareholders' equity are either:

▸ included in the P&L; or

▸ are included in Other Comprehensive Income; or

▸ are not included in either of those statements.

You will come across lots of jargon describing which of those categories a transaction fits into. So:

- ▶ 'goes through the P&L' or 'is recognised in the P&L' or 'is charged to the P&L' refer to a transaction that affects retained profit on the balance sheet and is included in the P&L;

- ▶ 'goes to/through other comprehensive income' or 'is taken to other comprehensive income' refer to a transaction that affects retained profit (or one of the other 'profit' boxes on the balance sheet) but which, rather than being included in the P&L, is included in other comprehensive income (which I may call 'OCI' for short from now on);

- ▶ 'goes directly to reserves' or 'goes directly to equity' means a transaction that affects shareholders' equity in some way, but does *not* affect either the P&L or OCI.

Apologies if this seems obvious to you at this point, but I don't want you to start thinking of the P&L and OCI as somehow separate from the balance sheet. They are still descriptive statements and you should concentrate first on how transactions affect the balance sheet and only then on which descriptive statement they will appear in. To keep emphasising this point, when I describe the accounting for the transactions we're going to come onto, I will continue to refer to the two balance sheet boxes that change, but I will show in brackets if the transaction appears in the P&L or in OCI or goes direct to equity. For example, the revaluation of a property would be described as follows:

- ▶ Increase (debit) **Fixed assets.**
- ▶ Increase (credit) **Revaluation reserve (through OCI).**

There are a couple of other bits of jargon you will come across regularly and I might even use later:

- ▶ **'Carrying value'** simply means the value at which an asset or liability is included in the balance sheet. Historically, we would say 'book value', but that suggests cost values and, as we are going to see, lots of items are not 'carried' in the balance sheet at their cost value.

- ▶ An **'instrument'** is essentially a piece of paper conferring rights and obligations on parties. So shares, loans, trade receivables are all instruments.

- ▶ **Component of equity/Reserves.** As we have seen, there can be a lot of lines making up 'Shareholders' equity'. I've been calling these 'boxes', really just to keep the balance sheet chart in your minds. As I mentioned when looking at Wingate's accounts, these boxes (other than 'share capital') are known as **'reserves'** by many people. Accounting standards, which we should talk about briefly, simply refer to them as **'components of equity'**.

Accounting standards

What appears in a company's accounts is determined by 'accounting standards'. These standards cover:

- ▶ What transactions we have to account for.
- ▶ How we account for them.
- ▶ How much additional information we have to disclose (i.e. in the notes to the accounts).
- ▶ How we present the information.
- ▶ The terminology we use.

In the UK, the accounting standards regime starts with the Companies Act 2006. This says a company must prepare its accounts either:

- ▶ in accordance with international accounting standards; or
- ▶ in accordance with the rules set out in the Companies Act itself and also with additional standards issued by the body or bodies designated for the purpose by the relevant Secretary of State. This combination of rules and standards is known as 'UK GAAP' (pronounced 'gap' and standing for 'Generally Accepted Accounting Practice').

Because most of the large company accounts you are likely to look at are listed companies, which *have* to use international standards, I'm going to focus on these standards. You just need to be aware if you look at a private company's accounts that the standards they are using might well be a bit different.

International accounting standards are produced by a body called the **International Accounting Standards Board ('IASB').** A set of their standards has been adopted by the EU, so all EU companies that are required to use international standards are using this one set of standards. Ultimately, it is hoped that all listed companies in all countries will use the same standards, but, as things stand, we are some way off this, particularly since the USA currently uses its own standards.

The standards issued by the IASB are identified either as:

- ► IAS xx (e.g. IAS 22, meaning International Accounting Standard 22); or as
- ► IFRS xx (e.g. IFRS 5, meaning International Financial Reporting Standard 5).

What's with having two sets of references?

Because the first lot (the IASs) were issued by the body that preceded the IASB. When the IASB took over, they kept many of the IASs but all new standards were given the IFRS designation. To add to the confusion, despite being made up of these two different sets of documents, international standards as a whole are usually just referred to as 'IFRS'. You will also come across references to **IFRICs** and **SICs,** which are interpretations of the respective standards, issued to clarify particular aspects of the standards.

As well as the additional primary statements we've already had a look at, the international standards have one other major difference from what we saw in Wingate's accounts. This is that lots of items on the balance sheet are included at **fair value.**

Fair value vs historical cost

Have a look at Note 1(a) of Wingate's accounts [page 275]. You can see that it says that the accounts were prepared under the **historical cost convention.**

What this means is that all the assets on our balance sheets to date have been based on the actual cost of the asset at the time it was bought, i.e. the 'historical' cost. However, the international standards have moved to reporting many assets and liabilities at fair value rather than at cost. Fair value is defined, more or less, as the price at which you could buy the asset or 'sell' the liability in an 'orderly' market at the market conditions on the balance sheet date.

Doesn't that just complicate things?

Yes, it does somewhat, but:

- ► companies today enter into a lot of transactions where the resulting assets and liabilities change value significantly (and sometimes very rapidly) depending on what's happening in the world economy;

▶ there is a big difference in the value 'today' between an amount of money you are due to pay in the next few days or weeks and the same amount of money that you don't have to pay for three years or whatever. This is known as the **time value of money.** If you can delay paying someone for several years, that is valuable because you can invest the money in the meantime.

We adjust for the time value of money by **discounting** future cash flows to give us their value 'today', which is known as the **present value.** The discounting is done by applying an annual percentage discount rate to the future cash flow. Because money in the future is less valuable than money today, this always gets you to a lower figure than the undiscounted figure. Discount rates used by companies in their accounts vary, depending on what's being valued, from as low as 1 per cent up to as much as 15–20 per cent. The discount rate makes a big difference to the present value, so the notes to the accounts often show the impact on fair value of changing the discount rate by, say, 1 per cent.

If, say, a company has included in its balance sheet at discounted fair value a cash outflow that is two years away, then, in its balance sheet a year later, the actual cash outflow will be one year nearer. This therefore affects the time value of money calculation. The present value of the outflow will now be higher and this has to be reflected in the balance sheet. What you get is:

▶ Increase (credit) **Future obligation.**

▶ Decrease (debit) **Retained profit (through P&L – Finance expenses).**

This is referred to as the **unwinding** of the discount and you will come across it a lot.

Impairment

As well as fair value appearing all over a listed company's accounts, you will also see frequent references to '**impairment**'.

Where there are assets that are *not* restated to fair value at each balance sheet date, there is an over-riding requirement to consider **impairment.** This means that if the **recoverable amount** or fair value of such an asset is actually lower at the balance sheet date than the standard accounting treatment shows (i.e. the asset is 'impaired'), the company is obliged to write down the value of the asset to the fair value.

But you don't ever increase such an asset's value?

No. Although, if you reduce the carrying value of an asset for impairment at one balance sheet date, and then, at a subsequent balance sheet date, you believe the asset has recovered some value, you can write the value back up. But you can never write the value back up above the original value at which it was included on the balance sheet. Otherwise, you would effectively be accounting for that asset at fair value, of course.

So presumably impairment affects the shareholders' wealth, so shareholders' equity must reduce. Does that mean the loss due to impairment is included in the P&L?

That depends on the item in question, as we will see.

Summary

I think that's enough of an introduction for us to get going. Here's what I think you need to take away from this session:

- ▶ Wingate's accounts reflected a nice simple situation where the balance sheet gave us the definitive position of the company at a point in time and the P&L explained how the shareholders got richer or poorer during the year and the cash flow explained why cash had gone up or down during the year.
- ▶ Listed company accounts are not quite as simple as Wingate's, but:
  - – The balance sheet is still the definitive statement of the company's financial position.
  - – The cash flow still explains the change in the cash balance.
  - – While the P&L doesn't fully explain the change in retained profit, we have the two additional primary statements that enable us to understand exactly what's going on.
- ▶ International accounting standards lead to some slightly more sophisticated accounting, but provided we focus on the balance sheet and read the notes, we should be able to follow it.

CHAPTER TWELVE

Interpretation of Listco's accounts

- ▶ Intangible assets
- ▶ Groups of companies
- ▶ Accounting for subsidiaries
- ▶ Accounting for associates and joint ventures
- ▶ Accounting for investments
- ▶ Property, plant and equipment
- ▶ Capital/Funding
- ▶ Equity
- ▶ Debt
- ▶ Financial instruments
- ▶ Foreign currencies
- ▶ Hedging
- ▶ Pensions
- ▶ Corporation tax
- ▶ Share buy backs/Treasury shares
- ▶ Share-based payments
- ▶ Earnings per share
- ▶ Conclusion

OK, it's time to start looking at Listco's accounts in a bit more detail. I'm going to keep it brief on most subjects, but I've written more detailed explanations of a lot of this, which you can find on my website. I should probably start by explaining about the 'consolidated' aspect of accounts, but to do that, I really need to discuss intangible assets first.

Intangible assets

In plain language, intangible assets are things you can't touch like computer software, patents, copyrights, brand names, trademarks, customer relationships and customer lists.

If you buy an intangible asset from a third party, you capitalise it (which, to remind you, means treat it as a fixed asset) and then depreciate it over a number of years. As it happens, we use the word **amortise** to mean 'depreciate' when talking about intangible assets.

If you generate intangible assets internally (i.e. as opposed to buying them), you capitalise them when certain pretty strict conditions are met (and then amortise them over their useful life). Otherwise you have to expense the cost as incurred.

So should I capitalise my expenditure on my website or do I write it off like an ordinary expense?

Good question. The answer is that it depends. Broadly speaking, if your website is just providing information about your company, it's no different from any other marketing materials, so you would just recognise the costs in the year in which they are incurred (i.e. you would 'expense' them). If, however, it's a transactional website, meaning that customers can buy (or sell) online via the website, and provided you can reasonably expect enough trading through it to more than cover the costs of building the website, then you capitalise it (and, of course, amortise the asset over the next few years).

Groups of companies

OK, now we've dealt with intangible assets, we can talk about consolidated accounts.

A company can, just like an individual, buy just a few of the shares in another company or it can buy *all* the shares in another company. There's obviously quite a big difference between these two extremes. If you own just a small percentage of the shares in a company, you don't have any control over it and its business can't really be considered to be part of your business.

On the other hand, if you own 100 per cent of a business, then it clearly is your business and the performance of that business should be reported in detail in your accounts.

So most investments in other companies are put into one of three categories:

▶ **Subsidiaries** (technically '**subsidiary undertakings**'). A company is a subsidiary of yours if you control it. This includes control by way of owning more than 50 per cent of the voting rights of the subsidiary, but also by way of powers arising from contractual rights.

▶ **Associates** (technically '**associated undertakings**') and **joint ventures.** A company is usually an associate of yours if it is not a subsidiary, but you exert a significant influence over the company. If you own 20 per cent or more of the voting rights of a company, you would normally be considered to exert significant influence over it but this threshold is determined on a case-by-case basis.

▶ **Investments.** This includes any investment in another company's shares that is not in one of the categories above.

Let's now look at how we account for each of these in turn.

Accounting for subsidiaries

The objective is simply to present the accounts as if the investor company (known as the **parent**) and its subsidiaries were all actually just one company. This gives you the **consolidated accounts** (often known as the **group accounts**), which make it much easier for someone interested in the group as a whole to get the full picture.

Goodwill

As we discussed when talking about the valuation of companies, people often pay more than net asset value when buying shares in companies. I gave a couple of reasons why people might do that. A slightly different way to think about why they might do this is that the company has lots of valuable things that aren't in the balance sheet at all. Obviously, if those valuable things were included as assets on the balance sheet, the net assets would be higher. Such assets might include:

- ► an organisation of skilled employees with procedures, culture, know-how, experience, etc.;
- ► relationships with customers and suppliers;
- ► brand names.

When a company buys another company, the difference between what it pays and the net asset value of the company it's buying is known as **goodwill**. When we create consolidated accounts, we have to include this goodwill figure on the consolidated balance sheet in order to make the balance sheet balance (because of the gap between what the parent paid and the net assets of the subsidiary).

*I'm not **quite** sure I get that, Chris.*

OK, let's look at a very simple example. Assume a company (the 'parent') buys, for £800k, a company (the 'subsidiary') which has no liabilities and whose only asset on its balance sheet is a building. The building is in the books at £300k, which means the net assets of the subsidiary are £300k. If we look at the overall effect of this transaction on the accounts of the parent in combination with its new subsidiary, we would conclude the accounting must be:

	Debit	Credit
Decrease **Cash**		£800k
Increase **Fixed assets**	£300k	

But that leaves us with a balance sheet that doesn't balance. We can't change the cash figure, because that's a fact. That money is gone. We are left with two options. Either we have to change the value of the building to £800k or we have to do something else. The something else is that we create an asset called **goodwill** to the value of £500k. So what you get is:

	Debit	Credit
Decrease **Cash**		£800k
Increase **Fixed assets**	£300k	
Increase **Goodwill**	£500k	
TOTAL	**£800k**	**£800k**

So when you see goodwill on a company's consolidated balance sheet, you now know what it is – it's a 'plug'.

When, as they often do, companies buy subsidiaries that have lots of different businesses, they have to split the goodwill up and apportion it among what are actually called '**cash generating units**' or **CGUs**.

What happens to the goodwill in the years after you make an acquisition is one of the areas where IFRS differs markedly from UK GAAP. Under the latter, the goodwill is '**amortised**' like other intangible assets. So under UK GAAP, you would pick an estimated life for the goodwill and decrease the value of goodwill pro rata in each year over that period.

Under IFRS, the goodwill on the balance is *not* amortised. It simply sits there on the consolidated balance sheet. Each year, the directors of the parent have to review the goodwill figure. If they have reason to believe it is not worth as much as it was at the start of the year, it has to be written down (i.e. an impairment charge is made). This lowers goodwill and lowers retained profit (and the charge is included in the P&L). The impairment assessment is done on a CGU by CGU basis, which means that if one CGU should have its value written down, you can't say 'yes, but some other parts of the subsidiary have much more value than we allocated to them so it all balances out and we can leave it as it is'.

Revaluation of assets on acquisition

When I said that goodwill is the difference between the price the parent paid and the net assets of the subsidiary, that wasn't quite the full picture.

Not for the first time where you're concerned, Chris.

Fair comment, but I'm hoping it's easier, if a bit slower, to deal with one thing at a time. What in fact happens is that the parent has to revalue to fair value all of the assets and liabilities of the subsidiary. It then uses *those* figures in its consolidated balance sheet.

As part of this process, the parent also gives a value to various intangible assets of the subsidiary, even though those intangible assets may not appear on the subsidiary's own balance sheet. So, for example, the subsidiary may have, over the years, created a strong brand name. Because that was generated internally (rather than being bought), the subsidiary does not treat it as an asset on its balance sheet. For the purposes of the group consolidated balance sheet, though, that brand *is* treated as an asset and is included on the balance sheet.

The goodwill figure then becomes the difference between what the parent paid and the net asset figure after the revaluations. Because this revaluation process will *generally* increase the net asset figure, the goodwill figure after this process is generally smaller than it would otherwise have been.

So how would this work with your building example?

Well, let's see. Assume that:

- ▶ The fair value of the building at the time it was bought was actually £600k.

- ▶ The subsidiary owned a brand name that wasn't included in its balance sheet but was established to be worth £50k.

Then what you get is the following:

	Debit	Credit
Decrease **Cash**		£800k
Increase **Property assets**	£600k	
Increase **Intangible assets**	£50k	
Increase **Goodwill**	£150k	
TOTAL	**£800k**	**£800k**

As you can see, we've still got some goodwill, but it's less than it was before.

*This business with the intangible assets. Does this not create a bit of an anomaly? If the parent has been trading for some years and has created its own brand name or names, those are **not** going to appear on the consolidated balance sheet, but the brand names of any subsidiaries it has bought will do, surely? So you've got apples and pears, haven't you?*

Correct. And, what's more, I don't believe it's possible to make accurate valuations of some of these intangible assets. So, personally, I think it's all nonsense and the only thing it achieves is to generate yet more fees for the accountants who come up with the valuations.

Of course, you can get an apples and pears situation anyway with intangible assets, because if you buy an intangible asset, you capitalise it, whereas if you generate it internally, you often don't. This is an area you should think about when studying a company's accounts.

Non-controlling interests (Minority interests)

You will recall that I said you only had to own more than 50 per cent of a company's shares for it to be described as a subsidiary. Regardless of how much of a subsidiary the parent owns, the consolidated accounts will always be prepared *as if* the parent company owned 100 per cent of the subsidiary. Obviously, though, where the parent owns less than 100 per cent, that would lead to overstating the parent's shareholders' claims over the assets, so an extra line is added to the balance sheet to show the portion of the assets that is 'claimed' by whoever owns the rest of the subsidiary. These are called the **non-controlling interests** (or what used to be called **minority interests).** You can see this on line 51 of Listco's balance sheet.

Similarly, the consolidated P&L and the statement of comprehensive income have a line showing the portion of the consolidated profits that is attributable to the non-controlling interests and thus, of course, the profit that is attributable to the parent's shareholders.

Accounting for associates and joint ventures

Associates are not, by definition, controlled by the parent company and so we don't include all the individual assets and liabilities of the associate on the group's balance sheet. Instead, we just put the net figure in one line.

So if a company invests, say, £12m to buy 25 per cent of a company which has total net assets at the time of £20m, then the investor company has paid £12m for £5m worth of net assets. We would account for this initially as follows:

	Debit	Credit
Decrease **Cash**		£12m
Increase **Investment in associates**	£12m	

So if the investor company has paid more than net asset value for the shares it has bought, it is effectively paying for some previously unrecognised intangible assets and/or 'goodwill' but these are all just included in the one line 'Investment in associates'?

Correct. Subsequently, at each period end, the parent adds its share of any increase or decrease in the net assets of the associate during the period to the 'Investment in associates' line. So you get, assuming the associate made a profit:

- ▶ Increase (debit) **Investment in associates.**
- ▶ Increase (credit) **Retained profit (through P&L – Share of profits of associated companies).**

The group P&L and, if any of the increase/decrease is unrealised, the statement of comprehensive income show the share of the associate's profit. You can see this in line 11 of Listco's P&L. If at any time, the directors of the parent believe the value of their investment has declined, then they would have to recognise an impairment charge.

What happens if the associate pays a dividend?

In that case the group accounts would reflect the cash from the dividend and the reduction in the investment in the associate:

- ▶ Increase (debit) **Cash.**
- ▶ Decrease (credit) **Investment in associates.**

If the associates/joint ventures are significant to the group, the notes will contain additional information. This information is not going to be sufficient to enable you to analyse the associate properly, however; for that you need a copy of the associate's own annual report.

This way of accounting for associates is known as the **equity method.**

Accounting for investments

Where a company invests in the shares of another company but not such that it is a subsidiary or an associate/joint venture, we account for it as follows:

- ▶ If the shares are listed on an exchange such that you can determine the fair value of the shares easily, the investment should be recognised on each balance sheet at its fair value on that date. Any increase or decrease since the last balance sheet is included in the P&L.
- ▶ If the fair value of the shares is not easily determined, then the shares are carried on the balance sheet at cost (subject to impairment testing).

Company vs consolidated accounts

The last thing I want to mention for now about consolidated accounts is that you will also find some information about the parent company's individual (i.e. unconsolidated) accounts. This is often only a balance sheet with some limited notes. In other cases, you may have full accounts and notes, often presented alongside the consolidated accounts. Generally, the parent's accounts will not be of much interest to you. The consolidated statements are where you should focus your attention.

Property, plant and equipment

I explained when we were looking at SBL and Wingate how we account for property, plant and equipment (what we called tangible fixed assets). In summary, we record the asset at cost and then depreciate it over its expected life. The depreciation is included in the P&L. When an asset is sold, we recognise the difference between its carrying value and what we sell it for in the P&L (which may be a profit or a loss, of course).

There are a couple of other things to know.

First, if the company believes an asset is included in its balance sheet at more than its **recoverable amount,** then you have to recognise an **impairment loss.** If you have to do this, then the accounting entries are simply:

- ▶ Reduce (credit) **Property, plant and equipment.**
- ▶ Reduce (debit) **Retained profit (through P&L).**

Second, as I touched on when talking about fair value, you are allowed, if you want, to account for property, plant and equipment at fair value (rather than at cost less cumulative depreciation), subject to a few conditions, including the following:

- ▶ You must treat all assets of the same type in the same way (e.g. if you want to account for one building at fair value, you have to do the same for all buildings).
- ▶ You have to revalue the assets on a regular basis.
- ▶ Any gain or loss since the last revaluation is shown in OCI, not in the P&L, unless it is a loss that takes the carrying value of the asset

down below what its depreciated cost would have been by now if it had never been revalued *and* that reduction in value is expected to be permanent, in which case that element of the loss has to be shown in the P&L, as it is considered a 'real' loss for the shareholders.

So the accounting in a simple revaluation upwards is:

- ► Increase (debit) **Property, plant and equipment.**
- ► Increase (credit) **Retained profit (through OCI).**

Alternatively, you might want or, in the UK, be required to show this revaluation not in the retained profit box, but in a special box called a **revaluation reserve.** Then the accounting is:

- ► Increase (debit) **Property, plant and equipment.**
- ► Increase (credit) **Revaluation reserve (through OCI).**

This latter approach is how Listco treated the revaluation of some of its assets.

The choice to use fair value is mostly applied in respect of land and buildings, which companies often own for many years and which tend to increase in value over time, unlike most plant and equipment.

Investment properties

If a company owns properties that it holds purely for investment purposes rather than for use in its business, then the accounting is, or at least may be, different to the above.

You can choose to include your investment properties at either fair value or at cost less depreciation (i.e. as per the above). If you choose the fair value approach, then:

- ► Any increase or decrease in value from the previous year *is* shown in the P&L. This is because, if you're holding a property as an investment, then you've chosen that asset with a view to it going up in value as a part of your business plan, so any gain or loss is a 'real' gain or loss for the shareholders.
- ► You must apply the same approach to *all* your investment properties, except where, in exceptional circumstances, you can't measure fair value easily.

Capital/Funding

If we think back to Wingate for a second, we saw that it obtained its funding (or **capital**, as it is often known) from two sources – the shareholders and the bank. The cash the shareholders put in was ordinary share capital. It was a long-term investment that could only pay a dividend if the company did well. The better the company did, the better would be the shareholders' **return** (i.e. the profit on their investment). This form of funding we call **equity** or **share capital.**

Hold on. I thought 'equity' was all the claims of the shareholders over the assets of the company. Now you're using the same word to mean just the part of shareholders' equity that is actually invested by the shareholders (i.e. you're excluding all the retained profits).

Exactly right. It's not a confusion I can do anything about, so we will have to live with it. *Generally,* it is clear what someone is talking about from the context.

Now, the rest of the funding came from the bank. This was different from the shareholders' investment in that the length of the loan (the **term**) was known and the return (the interest) on the loan was not only known but *had* to be paid by the company, unlike dividends on share capital. This kind of capital is known generally as **debt.**

There are many different forms of both equity and debt and quite often you get things that look like a combination of the two. Together, **equity instruments** and **debt instruments** are known as **capital instruments.**

Ranking of capital instruments

One subject that will inevitably come up when talking about companies' capital instruments is **ranking.** We touched on this when talking about Wingate's bank loans. If a company ceases trading for whatever reason (but usually because it is bust), an official is appointed to sort out the company's affairs. The official could be an **administrator,** a **receiver** or a **liquidator,** depending on the company's circumstances, but they are all essentially doing the same thing. Their job is to **realise** (i.e. turn into cash) the assets of the company and then distribute the proceeds to the creditors of the company and, if there is any money left over, to the shareholders.

This is where ranking comes in. When we talked about Wingate's bank loans, I mentioned that the bank would have charges over the assets of the company, to ensure that it got its money back before any other creditor. Only once all the creditors have been paid do any holders of shares get any money. And, as we will see, the holders of some types of shares get their money back before holders of other types. Not many public companies actually go bust, but it does happen and plenty of private ones do. Ranking is therefore very important to the banks and other lenders of money and investors in shares.

Let's now look at some of the most common capital instruments.

Equity

Ordinary shares

Like Wingate, Listco has only one type (or **class** as it is known) of share capital – ordinary shares. We talked about these earlier.

Sometimes you will see companies that have, for example, A ordinary shares and B ordinary shares. These two classes of shares might have identical rights except that, say, the B shares might have no right to vote. The notes to the accounts have to summarise the rights of the different classes of shares.

Preference shares

The shares you are likely to encounter most often after ordinary shares are **preference shares.** They are different from ordinary shares in that:

- ► They usually have a fixed annual dividend, which must be paid before any dividend is paid on the ordinary shares. Unlike interest, though, these dividends cannot be paid unless the company has positive distributable reserves.

- ► If the company is wound up, the preference shareholders usually get their money back before any money is returned to the ordinary shareholders – i.e. they rank ahead of, or are 'senior to', the ordinary shares. The amount they get back will, however, be the amount they put in or some other predetermined amount. The ordinary shareholders get what is left over, which may be a lot more than they put in or a lot less.

The result of this is that preference shares are less risky than ordinary shares because they come before the ordinary shares in everything (hence the name preference), but there is less opportunity for the preference shares to become worth a huge amount.

There are many variations on simple preference shares. For example:

- ► Sometimes a company may not be performing very well and may not be able to pay a dividend in a particular year. **Cumulative preference shares** entitle the holders to get all their dividends due from past years, as well as the current year's, before any dividends can be paid to ordinary shareholders.

- ► Sometimes preference shares include conditions whereby the dividend on the shares will be increased (e.g. when the company does particularly well). These are known as **participating preference shares**.

- ► Some preference shares have a fixed date on which the company must return the capital invested by the preference shareholders. These are known as **redeemable preference shares**.

- ► Some preference shares can be converted into ordinary shares at a certain time and certain price per ordinary share. These are known as **convertible preference shares**.

- ► Indeed, you could have a preference share that has all of these features.

Other types of shares

A company can issue shares with more or less any terms and conditions it chooses (provided the shareholders agree) and these shares can be called whatever the company chooses.

You will now also come across shares that, although *legally* shares, have to be treated as debt in a company's accounts. This is because they behave more like debt than equity.

How do you tell the difference?

Well, if you are reading a set of accounts, the company will have classified the instruments appropriately and the notes will explain. Broadly speaking, however, they are classified according to the following rule of thumb:

- ► If the holder of the instrument has the right to *demand* cash (or another instrument) either as a sort of interest payment or to wholly or partly 'redeem' the instrument, then the instrument is more like debt and is thus treated as such.

▶ If the *company* can decide if and when any such payments are to be made, then the instrument is more like equity and should be treated as such.

This can, however, become very complicated and some instruments are treated in the accounts as partly equity and partly debt.

So, going back to the preference shares, would any that are redeemable on a specific date be treated as debt, because the company has no choice but to return the money?

Yes, well spotted. And if the company is *obliged* to pay an agreed dividend on a preference share, then those shares would also look more like a loan and be treated as such.

Why does it matter whether a preference share is treated as debt or equity? It represents a claim over the assets of the company either way, doesn't it?

Yes, it does. It really only makes a difference in two ways:

▶ If it's treated as debt, then any dividend on the preference shares will actually be treated as interest and will be included in the P&L in the finance costs line.

▶ The various funding structure ratios, such as the debt to equity ratio, will be different.

Debt

Bank debt

Wingate had two types of bank debt – an overdraft and a loan. You may also come across a **revolving credit facility (RCF)**. This is very similar to an overdraft, in that the company can draw down funds from the bank up to the limit and then repay them and then draw them down again and so on as often as it likes. But whereas an overdraft is almost always 'repayable on demand' (i.e. immediately the bank asks for its money back), an RCF is typically a 'committed' facility. This means the bank can't demand its money back until the end of the agreed term unless the company breaks one or more covenants relating to the RCF.

Corporate bonds

Larger companies, as well as borrowing money from banks, often 'issue debt' to investors (typically to big institutions such as pension funds or insurance companies but also to individuals). This means that the company borrows money from investors in return for paying interest at regular intervals at an agreed rate. On an agreed date, the principal is returned to the investors. These kinds of borrowings are known collectively as '**corporate bonds**', but you will also see other terms such as:

- ► **notes,** which tend to be of shorter 'term' than bonds;
- ► **commercial paper,** which tends to be of even shorter term than notes (usually less than one year).

Companies, helped by their bankers, issue their debt to investors via the **bond markets.** These are electronic market places, where investors can:

- ► buy 'new' bonds from companies that need to raise funding;
- ► buy and sell previously-issued bonds among themselves: this is the 'secondary' market.

The vast majority of corporate bonds are issued in US$ or euros. They are typically issued in tranches of $1,000 or €1,000 'face value'. The face value is the amount of principal used to calculate how much interest is paid. So if the interest rate on a bond is 3.250 per cent and I have bought bonds with a face value of $10,000, I will receive $325 of interest each year.

This may seem blindingly obvious, but there is a point I am getting to. As an investor, you would not necessarily have paid $10,000 for those bonds. Depending on the market conditions at the time, those bonds might be selling for, say, $11,000. So, as the investor, you would still be getting the $325 of interest and you will still only get $10,000 back at the end of the bond's term, but you would have handed over $11,000 for those rights. You would, *in effect*, be accepting a lower interest rate.

Presumably, if you buy 'new' bonds from the company issuing the bonds, you pay face value for them?

No, usually you don't. The prices of bonds change by the second and companies can't change the interest rate on their new bonds' paperwork to exactly match the price investors would be prepared to pay at the moment they are going to be issued. So a company will pick an interest rate that is *roughly* right and then issue the bonds for as high a price as they can get at the time. This might be slightly more or slightly less than the face value.

Bond prices are quoted by reference to a '**par value**' of 100. So if a bond is quoted at 100, that means you will pay $1,000 for every $1,000 of face value. If the bond is quoted at, say, 102.4, that means you will pay $1,024 for every $1,000 of face value.

So let's say a company issues bonds with $1m worth of face value, repayable in 2022, at an interest rate of 3.250 per cent and the issue price is 102.4. Am I right in saying that that means the company will actually receive $1,024,000 of funding 'today', but will only have to pay annual interest of £32,500 (i.e. 3.25 per cent × the $1m) and will only have to repay $1,000,000 in 2022 rather than the $1,024,000? And if so, how does the company enter that transaction on its balance sheet?

You are 100 per cent right about how it works. And it's not immediately obvious how one therefore enters this on the company's balance sheet. It is in fact done using something called the '**effective interest rate method**', a term you will see regularly in listed companies' accounts. We have actually come across this before – when we looked at finance leases.

On issue of the bonds, you would account for them as follows:

	Debit	Credit
Increase **Cash**	$1,024,000	
Increase **Liabilities to bond-holders**		$1,024,000

At the end of the first year, you would make three entries:

	Debit	Credit
Decrease **Cash**		32,500
Decrease **Retained profit (Interest expense)**	24,700	
Decrease **Liabilities to bond-holders**	7,800	
TOTAL	**32,500**	**32,500**

Don't worry about the exact numbers. The point to notice is that, while you are paying $32,500 of 'interest' out in cash, some of that is attributed to reducing the principal amount you owe and some of it is making the shareholders poorer and thus lowering retained profit. This continues each year, until, by the end of the bond's term, the liability to bond-holders has reduced to the $1,000,000 you are actually going to repay them.

The $7,800 that goes to decreasing the liabilities to bond-holders is known as the **amortisation of the premium** on the bond (i.e. by getting a price of 102.4, rather than 100).

On Listco's balance sheet, the bank debt and corporate bond liabilities are all included in line 21 or line 27. The notes provide lots of detail about all the different borrowings.

Convertible bonds

Companies also issue bonds that are the same as we've just been discussing with the additional feature that the holder of the bond can convert the bond, at a prescribed price, into ordinary shares in the company.

Companies benefit from making a bond convertible because buyers of the bonds will accept a lower interest rate during the time before the bond is converted into shares. Buyers, obviously, have to believe that the bond will be worth converting into shares, otherwise they would simply buy a non-convertible bond that would give them a higher interest rate.

Other corporate debt

Companies also 'issue' debt to investors in less standardised form than cor-porate bonds. Usually, such debt will not be traded and may have many much more complicated terms than 'vanilla' corporate bonds. This kind of debt may well be called bonds, notes or commercial paper, but you will also come across other terms such as:

- ► **loanstock;**
- ► **debentures,** which in the UK means a long-term loan secured on some of the assets of the company, but in the USA and elsewhere means a short-term loan that has no security.

Financial instruments

Financial instruments is a broad category made up of **financial assets** and **financial liabilities.** We have already talked about investments made in other companies' shares and about bank and corporate debt. These would be financial assets and financial liabilities respectively. But we should talk about financial instruments more generally now.

A financial asset is any contract between you and a third party that is an asset in your books and is either a financial liability or an equity instrument (e.g. shares) in the other party's books. So financial assets include:

- ► trade receivables;
- ► investments in another company's shares;
- ► loans receivable;
- ► derivative contracts that, at the relevant balance sheet date, are favourable to you.

A financial liability is any contract between you and another party that is a liability in your books and an asset in their books. Financial liabilities include:

- ► trade payables;
- ► loans payable;
- ► derivative contracts that, at the relevant balance sheet date, are unfavourable to you.

Derivatives

What is a derivative contract? Aren't they the things that caused all the trouble in the banks?

Derivative contracts (or 'derivatives' for short) are contracts between two parties whereby one party gains and the other loses depending on what happens to some underlying 'variable'. The variable could, for example, be a particular interest rate, a commodity price, a share price, a bond price or the value of an index like the FTSE All-Share Index (an index of the combined share prices of all the companies listed on the London Stock Exchange).

Table 12.1 describes some of the most common derivatives and some examples.

Table 12.1 Common derivatives and examples

Name	Description	Examples
Forward	Agreement to buy or sell a specified quantity of something on a specified date at a specified price. When the settlement date arrives, the 'something' is actually delivered or the two parties agree a cash amount to settle the contract.	▶ Agreement to sell 200 tonnes of wheat on a particular date at a price of £150 per tonne. ▶ Agreement to sell €500k on a particular date in exchange for GBP at a rate of €1.30 per GBP (i.e. for £384,615).
Future	The same as a forward, except that futures: ▶ are standardised contracts; ▶ are traded in huge volumes on exchanges around the world; ▶ are consequently always settled by cash rather than delivery of the underlying item.	▶ As for forwards.
Option	▶ One party pays the other party an amount of money now (the 'premium') for the right (but not the obligation) to buy a quantity of something during a specified time period at a specified price. ▶ Or, as above except the party paying the premium has the right to *sell* a quantity of something. ▶ Might be settled by delivery or by a cash payment. ▶ Many are standardised and traded on exchanges; many others are custom-written between the two parties.	▶ The right to buy 1,000 shares in a listed company at a price of 150 pence at any time in the next three months. ▶ The right to sell €500k to the other party at a price of €1.30 per GBP at any time in the next six months.

▶

Table 12.1 (*Continued*)

Name	Description	Examples
Interest rate swap	▶ Agreement to exchange one set of interest payments on a loan for another set of interest payments.	▶ The bank agrees to give me the six-monthly interest payments on a notional loan of £1m at an interest rate of LIBOR + 2% in return for me giving them the six-monthly interest payments on a notional £1m based on a fixed interest rate of 3.0 per cent.

When used properly, these derivatives are extremely valuable to businesses, because they can give the business certainty about the future. So:

- ▶ If I know that in the course of the next financial year, I am going to make sales in euros to the tune of, say, €10m, I might well be worried about the exchange rate moving against me and hurting my profits. So I can enter into a forward contract today that fixes the price in £ that I will get in three, six, nine, 12 months' time. Of course, come the time, I may win or I may lose, but I don't care. I have obtained certainty.

- ▶ Similarly, farmers might want to fix now the price they get for at least some of the wheat they will have ready to sell in the autumn, so they enter into a forward contract with the grain wholesaler. Alternatively, they might just enter into some futures contracts through their stockbroker, which will benefit them if the price of wheat falls from today's price (thus offsetting the lower price they get for their actual wheat sales) and vice versa.

- ▶ If I have borrowed £1m from a bank for the next five years at a variable interest rate of, say, 2.0 per cent above LIBOR, then I am at risk of interest rates rising and making my interest payments unmanageable. I therefore enter into an interest rate swap agreement with the bank (or even an entirely different bank) to pay me the difference on a notional £1m. This effectively cancels out any change in the interest rate on my actual loan, so I've now effectively got a fixed interest rate.

These kinds of arrangements are known as **hedges**.

Accounting for financial instruments

A company has to classify all its financial instruments into various categories and then account for them in accordance with the rules for that category. The notes will explain the categorisation of a company's instruments. All you really need to understand is that there are three ways they can be treated:

▶ The instrument is carried at fair value on the balance sheet and any change since the last balance sheet affects retained profit (through P&L).

▶ The instrument is carried at fair value on the balance sheet and any change since the last balance sheet affects retained profit (through OCI).

▶ The instrument is carried at amortised cost, where amortised cost in this context means:

   – the initial investment;

   – less any repayments of principal;

   – less any impairment losses;

   – plus or minus the amortisation of any discount or premium received/paid (using the effective rate of interest method, as we discussed when talking about corporate bonds).

Here's how some of the most common financial instruments are treated:

▶ investments bought with the intention of trading them: at fair value (through P&L);

▶ trade receivables and payables: at amortised cost;

▶ loans made: at amortised cost;

▶ all derivatives: at fair value (through P&L).

Foreign currencies

Many major companies have dealings abroad which involve them in foreign currencies. There are two principal ways in which a company can be affected by foreign currencies:

- The company trades with third parties, making transactions that are denominated in foreign currencies. We discussed this when talking about Wingate.

- The company owns all or part of a business that is based abroad and which keeps its accounts in a foreign currency.

Functional currency

Functional currency is a phrase you will see a lot, so I'd better explain it briefly. Assume:

- You have a company based in France and which therefore uses the euro as its main currency.

- The French company carries out some transactions (e.g. buying and selling goods) that are denominated in US$.

- The company is owned by a UK company, which reports to its shareholders in Sterling.

We would describe the different currencies as follows:

- The French company's **functional currency** would be the euro.

- The US$ would be a **foreign currency** to the French company.

- Sterling would be the **presentation currency** of the UK parent.

Consolidating foreign subsidiaries

In order to consolidate the French company's accounts into the accounts of its UK parent, you:

- first, convert all foreign currency transactions into the functional currency;

- then convert the P&L, balance sheet and cash flows of the French company from the functional currency into the parent's presentation currency.

The conversion into the presentation currency is done as follows:

▶ The balance sheets at the period start and period end are translated at the exchange rates prevailing on those relevant balance sheet dates. This is so you have an accurate statement of the financial position of the company on the relevant dates.

▶ The transactions making up the P&L are translated at the exchange rate prevailing at the time each transaction occurred. This is so you have a fair view of how much money the company made or lost during the period.

▶ The cash inflows and outflows are translated at the exchange rate prevailing at the time the cash flows occurred.

Now think about this in the simple Wingate world where the P&L shows the change in the retained profit box on the balance sheet. You will be translating the retained profit box on the starting and ending balance sheets at rates that are different from each other and from the rate at which you translate the P&L. So, once translated, it's *highly* unlikely that the P&L is going to be equal to the change in the retained profit box. The 'hole' is known as a **translation gain or loss**.

If you look at line 46 of Listco's balance sheet, you can see a special box for this gain or loss called **translation reserve.** But the change in the translation reserve from one year to the next is not included in the P&L. Instead, it appears in OCI. You can see this in line 9 of Listco's statement of comprehensive income. You will see that it's under the heading **'Items that may be reclassified to the P&L in subsequent periods'.** This is because, if you were to sell the subsidiary in the future, any profit or loss, which would of course be affected by the exchange rate, *would* be shown in the P&L at that time. The statement of changes in equity obviously shows the change in the translation reserve during the year – see column 6.

The last thing to say is that companies are not obliged to have a separate translation reserve. Instead it can be included in retained profit. If so, you will still see the movement for the year in the statement of changes in equity.

Hedging

When we talked about derivatives earlier in this session, I explained how they are used to hedge against (i.e. offset) movements in some variable that might adversely affect the company. Separately, I explained that derivative instruments are included on the balance sheet at their fair value and any gain or loss in the period goes through the P&L. Where the underlying hedged item is also included on the balance sheet at fair value with any gains or losses going through the P&L, then any gain/loss in the underlying hedged item will be offset by the corresponding loss/gain in the derivative. Which is exactly what you want from your hedge, so that's good.

We run into a problem, however, in situations where the underlying item is *not* being included in the balance sheet at fair value or is not being included in the balance sheet at all. Then your balance sheet and P&L will reflect the change in the value of the derivative but not in the underlying item.

As an example, let's say you are going to buy 500 tonnes of aluminium next year and are worried about the price going up. You enter into a forward contract to buy 500 tonnes of aluminium at a fixed price on the date you need it. The price is a bit above the price you would have to pay today, but you don't mind that, because at least you have certainty. Although you've solved your 'real world' problem, you now have an accounting problem, because the forward contract will have to be valued on your balance sheet at the end of this year but the aluminium won't be, because you haven't actually bought it yet. If the price of aluminium has declined since you entered into the forward contract, the market value of the contract is going to have declined, so you are going to have to show a loss in your P&L. Not good for directors' bonuses!

OK, so when the underlying transaction is eventually completed and the derivative contract finished ('settled', I think you called it), presumably at more or less the same time as each other, there isn't a problem. Any gains or losses on one will offset the other. It's just at any balance sheet date between entering the hedge and the transactions being completed, that you have this 'matching' problem.

Exactly. The problem is dealt with by rules that allow companies to 'pair up' an underlying transaction (the 'hedged item') with the derivative intended as a hedge for that underlying item (the 'hedging instrument') and apply special accounting treatment. The rules about how this is done and when you can pair these transactions are complicated and we don't really need to go into them to understand the principles. The three different types of recognised hedge treatment you will come across and the way they match the gains or losses are as follows:

Hedge designated as...	Accounting
Cash flow hedge	Any gain or loss on the hedging instrument is taken to other comprehensive income (rather than the P&L) until the hedged item crystallises, at which point the gain or loss on the hedging instrument is 'recycled' into the P&L to match the hedged item.
Fair value hedge	Any gain or loss on the hedged item, which would not under the normal rules be recognised on the balance sheet, *is* recognised on the balance sheet and any gain or loss taken through the P&L, thereby 'matching' the gain or loss on the hedging instrument (which will also be included in the P&L under the normal rules).
Net investment hedge	Applies to instruments such as loans that are related to investments in foreign subsidiaries. Any gain or loss on the instrument due to foreign exchange is included in other comprehensive income rather than the P&L, thereby matching the gain or loss on translation of the foreign subsidiary's accounts as we discussed a few minutes ago.

If you look at Listco's statement of comprehensive income, lines 10–11, you can see:

- a £0.3m loss on cash flow hedges in year 5;
- the reversing of £2.4m of cash flow hedge profits from previous years because those cash flow hedges have now crystallised and are included in the P&L along with the related hedged item(s).

Pensions

There are essentially two types of pension scheme:

- **defined contribution pension schemes** (also known as **money purchase pension schemes**);
- **defined benefits pension schemes** (also known as **final salary pension schemes**).

A **defined contribution scheme** is one where the company pays an agreed amount of money each month or year into a pension scheme for each employee in the scheme. That money hopefully grows over the years and when the employee retires, their pension is based on whatever is in their personal 'pot'.

The accounting for such a pension is very easy, as the company has no liability to the employee above the payments made to the scheme (hence the phrase 'defined contribution'), so the company's accounting is simply to reduce cash by the amount of the payments and reduce retained profit (through P&L).

Defined benefits pension schemes are those where the company promises to procure or pay the employee an annual pension of £x, where x depends, among other things, on how long the employee worked for the company and what their salary was when they retired.

This leads to much more risk and accounting difficulty for the company as it has to make sure it has paid enough into the relevant pension scheme 'pot' to make sure there will be enough money to pay out the agreed amount of pension to employees during their retirement. If you are old enough, you may remember a number of companies going bust early in the new millennium with pension schemes that did not have enough money in them and lots of employees lost their entire pensions.

There are now very tight, complicated rules for working out whether a company's pension scheme has a shortfall or surplus of assets. The company's accounts then have to reflect this shortfall or surplus (at today's fair value) as at each balance sheet date. For a large company, you will often find pages and pages of notes on their pension schemes. Frankly, most of us will gain nothing from even reading them, let alone trying to understand them. The important thing to focus on is the total pension liability on the balance sheet. It *can* be a huge number that the company will be paying off for years to come.

Accounting for changes in the fair value of the pension liability (or asset, as it is occasionally) occurs in three general ways:

> ▶ If the change is due to what are called 'actuarial gains or losses', then the change goes through OCI:
>
> – Increase/Decrease **Pension liability.**
>
> – Decrease/Increase **Retained profit (through OCI).**

► If the change is simply due to the company paying some money into the scheme to reduce the liability, then we simply have:

– Decrease **Pension liability.**

– Decrease **Cash.**

► Any other changes (which include additional cost due to the service of the employees in the current year, changes to benefits of employees in respect of past years' service, paying an employee to give up their pension rights) all go through the P&L:

– Increase **Pension liability.**

– Decrease **Retained profit (through P&L).**

Actuaries are people who specialise in forecasting pension assets and liabilities decades into the future and actuarial gains/losses broadly occur where the actuaries turn out to be wrong and/or they change their assumptions.

In Listco's accounts, you can see:

► the pension liability at the period end in line 30 of the balance sheet;

► the change in that liability since the last balance sheet date due to actuarial gains or losses in:

– line 5 of the statement of comprehensive income;

– line 11 of the statement of changes in equity.

Corporation tax

Like pensions, corporation tax is, or at least can be, phenomenally complicated and like pensions, most of us aren't going to gain a huge amount by studying pages of notes about it.

All I can really do today is explain the difference between **current tax** and **deferred tax.**

Current tax is the actual tax payable on the period's profits, as we discussed when looking at Wingate [page 113]. So you see the expense for the period in the P&L and the outstanding liability on the balance sheet.

Deferred tax is tax that is not actually yet payable but may become so in the future as a result of transactions that have been recognised in the accounts. It can arise in two ways:

> ► As I said when we talked about Wingate, taxable income is usually different from profit before tax. Frequently, this is because HMRC makes adjustments which, while they reduce the taxable income in the current year, will increase it in future years. In other words, the ultimate amount of tax to pay does not change but the timing of the payments does.
>
> In such cases, companies allow for the fact that they may have to pay this extra tax some time (which can be several years) in the future by recognising an additional liability to the taxman.

> ► When assets and liabilities are revalued to fair value, a gain or loss results. Now if the asset or liability had been realised (i.e. turned into cash), the gain or loss made would increase or decrease respectively the amount of tax the company had to pay. However, most gains or losses due to restating assets and liabilities to fair value are not considered to affect current tax by HMRC. The company thus calculates what the tax impact would be and includes that in its deferred tax liability.

You will see deferred tax on balance sheets under long-term liabilities. It is really no different from corporation tax, otherwise. You can, of course, end up with deferred tax where HMRC owes *you*, in which case, your balance sheet will show a deferred tax asset. Listco has both a deferred tax asset and a liability.

Share buy backs/Treasury shares

Subject to all sorts of rules, companies are allowed to buy their own shares back from shareholders. This is known as a **share buy back.** Their reasons for doing this include the following:

> ► The company thinks its shares are undervalued in the market place. If it is right, then it is buying something cheaply today that will be worth more in the future and is therefore creating value for the shareholders who remain.

▶ It is an alternative to paying a dividend. When a company pays a dividend in respect of a particular share class, it has to pay the same dividend to each share in that class. With a share buy back, different shareholders can sell different percentages of their shareholdings back and thus some shareholders might sell no shares and others might sell all their shares.

▶ The company has promised shares to its employees as part of an incentive scheme and chooses to buy the shares now.

How do you think we would account for shares bought back in this way?

Well, it's an investment in listed shares like any other the company might buy, so:

▶ *Decrease* **Cash.**

▶ *Increase* **Investments.**

There's nothing really wrong with that, in theory. But that's not how we do it. Instead we treat it as if the company was doing the opposite of issuing shares. So we reduce shareholders' equity. This is logical if you think about it. By handing out cash to shareholders (even if only to some of them), it is like reversing the share issue transaction.

So the entries are:

▶ Decrease (credit) **Cash.**

▶ Decrease (debit) **Treasury share reserve.**

Treasury share reserve (also often referred to as **Own share reserve**) is a special box under shareholders' equity on the Claims bar that decreases shareholders' equity when shares are bought back. So it will always have a negative figure in it. You can see this box on Listco's balance sheet (line 43) and the change in it during the year is also shown on the statement of changes in equity (fourth column). The effect of purchasing additional treasury shares appears in line 17.

So what does a company do with shares it's bought back?

It may hang on to them until a reason to re-issue them arises. The most common application is for re-issuing them to employees who have earned the right to shares under an incentive programme (more about which shortly). Alternatively, the company may cancel the shares entirely. Companies generally prefer to keep shares they've bought back as there is less cost and paperwork associated with reissuing them than there is with issuing new shares.

If you look at line 18 of the statement of changes in equity, you can see that Listco did cancel some shares during Year 5. Notice a couple of things

> ▶ The cancellation of shares already 'in treasury' makes precisely no difference to the total shareholders' equity figure (see the zero in the end column). It just changes some of the numbers in various of the equity boxes.

> ▶ An entry is made in a box called '**Capital redemption reserve**'. This box is not a requirement of IFRS but of some individual countries' legislation (including the UK). If, when you cancel shares, you reduce share capital by X, then you have to also make the following entries:

>> – Increase (credit) **Capital redemption reserve** by X.

>> – Decrease (debit) **Retained profit** by X.

The logic behind this dates back a hundred years or more. Today, it's pretty much pointless and merely confuses the likes of you and me. Don't worry about it too much.

One last thing to note is that companies often set up trusts, known as **Employee Benefit Trusts** ('**EBTs'**) to hold shares for subsequent issue to employees. For the purposes of the consolidated accounts, shares in such trusts are treated as being treasury shares, which makes things much simpler for you and me.

Share-based payments

Equity-settled share-based payments

Employees of companies, as part of their remuneration package, are often promised free shares in their company if they are still with the company on a stated date. This date is known as the '**vesting date**' and the date between the date on which the shares are promised and the vesting date is the **vesting period.** The free share gift may also be dependent on various performance conditions. If the performance conditions have been met and the vesting date has passed, the shares are described as **vested** – i.e. the employee is unconditionally entitled to the shares.

Similarly, employees are often given **options** over shares. These options give the employee the right, after an agreed vesting date has passed and sometimes subject to performance targets being met, to make the company sell them shares at a price agreed at the time the options are issued to the employee (this is known as the **exercise price**). If the market price of the shares goes above the exercise price, then, if the options have vested, the option-holder can 'exercise' the option, pay the exercise price to the company, get the shares and then sell them at the market price for an instant profit.

These schemes are intended to act as an incentive to the employee to work hard to raise the share price of the company, which is what the shareholders want. Because employees usually lose their options or shares if they leave a company, these schemes also tend to encourage employees to stay with the company ('golden handcuffs', as they are sometimes known).

Accounting for a share-based payment works as follows:

- ▶ First you work out the fair value of the 'promise' to the employee without taking account of any performance conditions (except those that relate to the company's future share price). This is done using very complicated models. That is the cost to the company.

- ▶ Then you estimate, given any performance conditions that exist but which aren't related to the company's share price, how many of the 'promised' shares or options are actually likely to vest.

- ▶ This gives you an estimated cost to the company of the share-based payment. You allocate that cost across the whole vesting period, which may be a few years, and thus determine how much belongs in the period you are accounting for now.

- ▶ Then your double entry becomes

  – Decrease (debit) **Retained profit (through P&L).**
  – Increase (credit) **Share-based payments reserve.**

So you are acknowledging an expense due to the share scheme, even though you're never going to pay it out in cash, are you?

Correct. Some people think you shouldn't bother doing this accounting and just issue the shares if and when the employee becomes entitled to them.

So what happens when the options are exercised by the employee?

That depends. The company is required to give the right number of shares to the employee. It can do this in two ways:

- ▶ by issuing brand new shares to the employee;
- ▶ by transferring existing shares from the treasury share reserve to the employee.

The accounting for the first of these is quite simple – it's just the same as any share issue:

- ▶ Increase (debit) **Cash** (by the amount of the exercise price of the options).
- ▶ Increase (credit) **Share capital** (by the par value of the shares being issued).
- ▶ Increase (credit) **Share premium** (by the difference).

You can see this in line 16 of Listco's statement of changes in equity.

When existing shares are issued 'from treasury', it's a bit more complicated. You:

- ▶ Increase (debit) **Cash** (by the amount of the exercise price of the options).
- ▶ Increase (credit) **Treasury share reserve** (by whatever it cost the company to buy back those particular shares into Treasury).
- ▶ Decrease (debit) **Share-based payments reserve** (by the cost that was recognised in relation to these options).
- ▶ Increase or decrease **Retained profit** (by the balance – direct to equity).

You can see the effect on reserves on line 19 of Listco's statement of changes in equity.

Up to now, I've been talking about share-based payments where the employee gets shares. These are known as **equity-settled share-based payments.** There are also **cash-settled share-based payments.**

Cash-settled share-based payments

These are bonuses paid in cash where the cash amount to be paid is determined by reference to the company's share price. An example would be an employee bonus that is determined by the rise in the company's share price between two dates.

As before, you have to estimate the fair value of the potential bonus. This again involves complicated option-pricing models and an assessment of the likelihood of all the conditions being met.

When you have determined fair value, you can do the accounting, which, because the obligation is going to be paid in cash, is different:

- ► Reduce (debit) **Retained profit (through P&L).**
- ► Increase (credit) **Liabilities to employees** (because this is an actual liability to pay out cash, even though it's determined by reference to the share price).

The other difference from equity-settled schemes is that you have to do the fair value estimate at every balance sheet date (whereas with equity-settled schemes, you might revise the number of shares/options you expect to vest, but you would not change the initial fair value figure).

Earnings per share

Basic and diluted earnings per share

When we were looking at Wingate, we saw that earnings per share was simply the profit for the year divided by the time-weighted average number of ordinary shares in issue during the year. This is what is known as **Basic earnings per share (Basic EPS).**

Basic EPS can be slightly more complicated to calculate than it was with Wingate, because there may be adjustments to be made to both the earnings figure and to the number of shares figure. For example, if an employee is unconditionally entitled to some free shares but has not been given them yet, those shares would be taken into account.

Basic EPS is all very well for a very simple company, but most listed companies have one or more arrangements that *might* require them to issue shares, which will thus mean the profits of the company have to be shared out among more shares. So the actual issued shares will be 'diluted'. Listed companies are therefore required to calculate and present **Diluted earnings per share (Diluted EPS).**

We have already discussed four arrangements that could lead to shares being issued:

- ► convertible bonds – where loans from investors are converted into ordinary shares;
- ► convertible preference shares – where preference shares are converted into ordinary shares;
- ► contingently issuable shares – such as under an employee incentive scheme;
- ► options to acquires shares – ditto.

As with basic EPS, these arrangements can affect both the profit for the year and/or the number of shares used in the calculation of diluted EPS. And the calculations can get quite complicated. It is entirely possible that an adjustment for a particular arrangement will *increase* earnings per share. In that event, that adjustment is ignored. So only **dilutive** adjustments are made and thus diluted EPS is always *lower* than basic EPS.

Earnings per share from continuing operations

We discussed earlier the fact that, where companies cease a material operation during a year, they separate out the continuing and discontinued operations in their P&Ls. Where this applies, companies are required to present both basic and diluted EPS for the total company and for just the continuing operations. You thus see four different numbers for EPS for each year.

Adjusted earnings per share

I mentioned at the start of this session that companies often present an adjusted profit figure and adjusted earnings per share. Unsurprisingly, this is usually higher than the unadjusted figures and/or shows better growth from the previous year.

Just don't assume that the company's idea of a fair underlying picture of their performance is the right one! You can see that Listco's adjusted EPS figures are considerably higher than the unadjusted figures, so you'd want to look at the reasons pretty carefully.

Conclusion

Chris, a lot of things you've talked about in this session don't seem to have much to do with the enterprise – i.e. the actual business. They seem to be focused on the funding structure and 'financial engineering'.

It's true and what we've talked about is a pretty fair reflection of the weight of paper in the notes of the average company. It could reasonably make you wonder if companies aren't trying to compensate for poor management of the enterprise by messing about with the funding structure. While that's surely true of some companies, I don't think it's true of most. Bear in mind the following:

▶ Accounting for 'enterprise' transactions is largely straightforward, so there's less to say about them. That doesn't make them less important. The only way to give more emphasis to the enterprise would be to *de-emphasise* the funding structure information, but that wouldn't actually help you.

▶ We have only been talking about the accounts themselves here. The strategic report section of the annual report will spend much more time talking about the enterprise.

OK, I accept that, but do I therefore need to know all this stuff in this session?

Well, remember a few things:

▶ As we discussed earlier, earnings per share is the widely-used measure for valuing listed companies and all these things affect it.

▶ A number of the things we've discussed do affect the enterprise's profits (i.e. operating profit), so you need to know about them.

▶ Finally, I hope and think you will find listed company accounts less daunting if you know what they are talking about, even if you don't actually *use* the information.

What did you think of this book?

We're really keen to hear from you about this book, so that we can make our publishing even better.

Please log on to the following website and leave us your feedback.

It will only take a few minutes and your thoughts are invaluable to us.

www.pearsoned.co.uk/bookfeedback

Glossary

Synonyms are shown in brackets. Terms appearing elsewhere in the glossary are shown in *italics*.

Abbreviated accounts Abbreviated version of the *annual report and accounts* for filing at *Companies House.*

Accounting period The time between two consecutive *balance sheet dates* (and therefore the period to which the *profit & loss account* and *cash flow statement* relate).

Accounting policies The specific methods chosen by companies to account for certain items (e.g. *stock, depreciation*) subject to the guidelines of the *accounting standards.*

Accounting standards The accounting rules and guidelines issued by the recognised authority.

Accounts payable (*Trade payables, Trade creditors*) The amount a company owes to its suppliers at any given moment.

Accounts receivable (*Trade receivables, Trade debtors*) The amount a company is owed by its customers at any given moment.

Accrual (Accrued expenses) Adjustment made at the end of an *accounting period* to *recognise expenses* that have been incurred during the period but for which no *invoice* has yet been received or an invoice has been received but is dated after the relevant period.

Accruals concept Under the accruals concept, *revenues* are *recognised* when goods or services are delivered, not when payment for those goods or services is received. Similarly, all *expenses* incurred to generate the revenues of a given *accounting period* are recognised, irrespective of whether payment has been made or not.

Accumulated depreciation/amortisation The total *depreciation* or *amortisation* of an *asset* since the asset was purchased.

Allotted share capital (*Issued share capital*) The number and/or value of the *shares* that haves been allotted (issued) to *shareholders*.

Amortisation (1) The amount by which the *book value* of an *intangible asset* is deemed to have fallen during a particular *accounting period*. Amortisation therefore appears as an *expense* of that period.

(2) Reduction in the balance of a loan through a schedule of repayments.

Annual report and accounts (Annual report) The report issued annually to *shareholders* containing the *strategic report*, the *directors' report*, the *auditors' report* and the financial statements for the year.

Asset Anything of value which a company owns or is owed.

Associated undertaking (Associate) Broadly speaking, a company is an associate of an investor company if it is not a *subsidiary* but the investor company exerts a significant influence over the company. 'Significant influence' is normally assumed to occur when the investor holds in excess of 20 per cent of the company.

Audit Annual inspection of a company's *books* and financial statements carried out by *auditors*.

Audit trail Module of most accounting systems which records in chronological order the details of every *transaction posted* to the system.

Auditors Accountants appointed to carry out a company's *audit*.

Auditors' report Report on a company's financial statements prepared for the *shareholders* by the *auditors*.

Authorised share capital The total number of *shares* the directors of a company have been authorised by the *shareholders* to issue. As of the 2006 *Companies Act*, companies are not required to get this authorisation, although where it existed prior to the Act (and has not been removed by the shareholders), it still applies.

Average method Method of accounting for *stock* whereby, if a company has identical items of stock which cost different amounts to buy or produce, the average value is used.

Bad debt Money owed by a customer which will never be paid.

Balance sheet (*Statement of financial position*) Statement of a company's *assets* and the *claims* over those assets at any given moment (i.e. at the *balance sheet date*).

Balance sheet date Date at which a *balance sheet* is drawn up.

Balance sheet equation Statement of the *fundamental principle of accounting*, whereby the *assets* of a company must equal the *claims* over those assets (i.e. the *liabilities* and *shareholders' equity*).

Basic earnings per share *Earnings per share* before allowing for any additional *shares* that may potentially be issued.

Benchmarking Method of assessing a company's performance by comparing it against competitors or other benchmarks.

Bond (*Long-term loan, Loanstock*) A *loan* which is typically not due to be repaid for at least 12 months. More specifically, the bond is the certificate showing the amount and terms of the loan.

Book value (*Carrying value*) The amount at which an asset or liability is included in a company's balance sheet.

Books The records of all the *transactions* of a company and the effect of those transactions on the company's financial position.

Capital allowance When calculating *taxable income*, HMRC takes no account of *depreciation* on *tangible fixed assets*. Instead, capital allowances are made which reduce taxable income (effectively, capital allowances are HMRC's method of depreciation).

Capital and reserves (*Equity, Shareholders' equity/funds*) The shareholders' *claims* over the *assets* of the company. Consists of *share capital, share premium, retained profit,* and any other *reserves*.

Capital employed (*Net operating assets*) The total amount of money tied up in the *enterprise* in the form of *fixed assets* and *working capital*. It is also equal to the sum of the *equity*, the *debt* and any *corporation tax* payable.

Capital expenditure Money spent on *fixed assets* as opposed to day-to-day running *expenses*.

Capital productivity *Sales* divided by *capital employed*.

Capital redemption reserve A component of *shareholder's equity* used when a company cancels shares it has bought back.

Capital structure (*Financial structure, Funding structure*) The relative proportions of the funding for a company that are provided by *debt* and *equity.*

Capitalise Treat an expenditure as an *asset* (and *depreciate* it over its life) instead of *expensing* it *(writing it off)* in the *P&L* in the period in which it was incurred.

Carrying amount/value (*Book value*) The amount at which an *asset* or *liability* is included in a company's *balance sheet.*

Cash conversion ratio The *cash flow* in a period divided by the profit in that period. Shows what percentage of profit is being turned into cash.

Cash equivalents Short-term, highly liquid investments that are readily convertible to cash at known amounts and subject to insignificant risk of value changes. In practice, is usually just cash in bank accounts requiring less than 90 days' notice.

Cash flow The change in a company's cash balance over a particular period. Cash under new accounting standards includes *cash equivalents.*

Cash flow hedge A *designated hedging arrangement* in which any change in value in the underlying hedged item will not be reflected in the balance sheet and the change in value in the hedging item (usually a *derivative*) will be and the change in value in the hedging item is therefore shown in *Other Comprehensive Income* rather than in the *P&L.*

Cash flow statement A statement showing the reasons behind a company's *cash flow* during a particular *accounting period.*

Cash in advance (*Deferred revenue/income*) A *liability* a company has as a result of having received cash in payment for goods or services from a customer before those goods or services have been provided to the customer.

Charge (*Lien*) First claim over an *asset* (normally taken as *security* for a *loan*).

Claim A *balance sheet* is a list of a company's *assets* and all the claims over those *assets.* Claims are made up of *liabilities* (which are claims by *creditors* of the company) and the claims of *shareholders* (whose claims are whatever is left over once the liabilities have been paid).

Class of share Different types of *shares* are described as being different classes.

Collateral (*Security*) Assets pledged to a lender, usually by way of a *charge*, to protect the lender against losses on their loan(s).

Commercial paper A form *of short-term loan* issued by companies requiring funds.

Companies Act Act of Parliament of 2006 setting out the requirements for the creation and running of a company. Replaced the Companies Acts of 1985 and 1989.

Companies House Organisation which keeps and makes available to the public the documents that companies are required by law to file.

Component of equity Any balance sheet item that makes up part of the *equity* (i.e. the *claims* of the *shareholders* over the company's *assets*).

Consideration The amount 'paid' for entering into any contract (which might be to acquire an *asset* or to terminate a *liability*). Consideration may consist of cash, *loans, shares,* other *assets.*

Consolidated accounts Accounts prepared for a *parent company* and its *subsidiaries* as if the parent company and the subsidiaries were all just one company.

Contingent consideration *Consideration* that may be paid in future, depending on whether certain agreed conditions are met.

Contingent liability A potential *liability* that arises from past events but which may or may not crystallise into an actual liability, depending on the outcome of some future event that is not under the company's control. A contingent liability is not recognised in the *balance sheet.*

Continuing operations The operations of a company that, at period end, are still owned by the company and are not being held for sale.

Convertible loanstock/bond A *loan* that can be converted into *shares* in the company (at the option of either the company and/or the holder of the loan) instead of being repaid.

Convertible preference share A *preference share* that can be converted (at the option of either the company and/or the holder of the preference share) into *ordinary shares* in the company.

Corporation tax The tax paid by a company on its profits.

Cost of goods sold (Cost of sales) All materials costs and *expenses* which can be directly ascribed to the production of the goods sold.

Coupon (1) The *interest* payable on a *bond*.
       (2) The *dividend* payable on a *preference share*.

Covenant Condition imposed by a lender, breach of which normally enables the lender to demand immediate repayment of the *debt*.

Credit (1) Time given to a customer to pay for goods or services supplied.
       (2) In *double-entry book-keeping,* there are always at least two entries; one of these is always a credit, the other is always a *debit*.

Creditor Someone who is owed money, goods or services.

Cumulative preference shares *Preference shares* with the additional condition that, if any *preference dividends* for past years have not been paid, these must be paid in full before a *dividend* can be paid to the *ordinary shareholders*.

Current asset An *asset* that is expected to be turned into cash within one year of the *balance sheet date*.

Current cost convention Accounting convention whereby *assets* are recorded in a company's *books* based on their *market value* or replacement cost at the *balance sheet date*.

Current liability A *liability* that is expected to be paid within one year of the *balance sheet date*.

Current ratio *Current assets* divided by *current liabilities*.

Debenture A *long-term loan* issued by a company, usually with *security* over some or all of the company's *assets*.

Debit In *double-entry book-keeping,* there are always at least two entries; one of these is always a *credit*, the other is always a debit.

Debt (1) Money, goods or services owed.
       (2) Any funding which has a known rate of *interest* and *term*. Typically, a form of *loan* or *overdraft*. Some *equity instruments* are also treated, for accounting purposes, as debt.

Debt to equity ratio (*Gearing*) *Debt* divided by *equity*.

Debt to total funding ratio *Debt* divided by the sum of debt and *equity*.

Debtor Someone who owes money, goods or services.

Deferred expense (*Prepayment*) A payment made in advance of the receipt of goods or services (e.g. a deposit).

Deferred revenue/income (*Cash in advance*) A *liability* a company has as a result of having received cash in payment for goods or services from a customer before those goods or services have been provided to the customer.

Deferred shares Typically, *shares* that have voting rights but no rights to a *dividend* until certain conditions are met (e.g. profits reach a specified level).

Deferred taxation *Corporation tax* relating to profits and gains made and which the company expects to be payable in future but which is not yet recognised as payable by HMRC.

Defined benefits pension scheme (Final salary pension scheme) A pension scheme for employees whereby the company promises to procure or pay the employee an annual pension of £x, where x depends, among other things, on how long the employee worked for the company and what their salary was when they retired.

Defined contribution pension scheme (Money purchase pension scheme) A pension scheme for employees where the company pays an agreed amount of money each month or year into a pension scheme for each employee in the scheme. That money hopefully grows over the years and when the employee retires, their pension is based on whatever is in their personal 'pot'.

Depreciation The amount by which the *book value* of a *tangible fixed asset* is deemed to have fallen during a particular *accounting period*. Depreciation therefore appears as an *expense* of that period.

Derivative contract ('Derivative') A contract between two parties whereby one party gains and the other loses depending on what happens to some underlying 'variable'. The variable could, for example, be a particular interest rate, a commodity price or the value of an index like the FTSE All share index.

Designated hedging arrangement The pairing up of an underlying transaction (the hedged item) with, typically, a *derivative* (the hedging item) such that special hedge accounting rules can be applied. A designated hedging arrangement can be a *cash flow hedge,* a *fair value hedge* or a *net investment hedge.*

Diluted earnings per share *Earnings per share* adjusted to allow for any *shares* that may potentially be issued in future (thereby diluting the existing *shareholders'* share of the *assets* of the company).

Directors' report Report on a company's affairs by the directors (included as part of the *annual report*).

Discontinued operations Operations of the company that have either been sold or are being held for sale and whose financial performance is therefore reported separately from the *continuing operations.*

Discounting The mathematical process by which amounts to be paid or received in the future are ascribed a value 'today'.

Distributable reserves The amount which a company is legally entitled to *distribute* to its *shareholders,* typically as *dividends.*

Distribution Payment of a *dividend* to *shareholders* (thereby 'distributing' some of the profits of the company). Also includes a *stock* dividend.

Dividend Payment made to *shareholders* out of the *distributable reserves* of the company.

Dividend cover *Profit for the year* divided by the *dividend* for that year.

Dividend yield A company's *dividend* per *share* for a year divided by the *share price.* Alternatively, the total dividends for the year divided by the *market capitalisation* of the company.

Double-entry book-keeping Procedure for recording *transactions* whereby at least two entries are made on the *balance sheet,* thereby enabling the balance sheet to remain 'in balance'.

Doubtful debt Money due to a company that the company is not reasonably confident of receiving.

Earnings (*Profit for the year*) Profit attributable to *ordinary shareholders* (after taking account of *corporation tax, minority interests, extraordinary items, preference dividends* but before taking account of any *ordinary dividends* payable).

Earnings before interest and tax (EBIT) (*Profit before interest and tax, Trading profit, Operating profit*) The profit generated by the *enterprise* of a company, i.e. profit before taking account of *interest* (either payable or receivable) and *corporation tax.*

Earnings dilution Reduction in *earnings per share* as a result of the company issuing new *shares.*

Earnings per share *Earnings* divided by the average number of *ordinary shares* in issue during the *accounting period.*

EBITDA An abbreviation of *Earnings* before *Interest, Tax, Depreciation* and *Amortisation.* The profit before taking account of the items listed.

Effective interest rate method A way of adjusting for the fact that, when a financial instrument is bought or sold at a premium or discount, the amount to be received or repaid at the end of the term is different from the amount paid or received today. In essence the adjustment amends the actual interest rate on the instrument to the 'effective' interest rate.

Equity (*Capital and reserves, Shareholders' equity/funds*) The *shareholders' claims* over the *assets* of the company. Consists of *share capital, share premium, retained profit,* and any other *reserves.* 'Equity' is also used more loosely to mean any funding raised by a company in return for *shares.*

Equity instrument Actually the document that evidences ownership of shares in a company. Commonly used to refer to the *shares* rather than the document relating to the shares.

Equity method Method of accounting for *associates* whereby the *investment* is shown on the investor's *balance sheet* as the investor's share of the *net assets* of the associate.

Employee benefit trust A trust typically set up by a company to acquire shares in the company that are then used for the company's *share-based incentive* schemes.

Enterprise The actual business of a company, i.e. the components of the company which are unaffected by the *funding structure* (the way in which the funding for the company was raised).

Exceptional item Any item that is part of the ordinary activities of a company but which, because of its size or nature, needs to be disclosed if the financial statements are to give a true and fair view.

Exchange gain/loss Gain or loss made as a result solely of the movement in the exchange rate between two currencies.

Exercise price The price paid or received when buying or selling, for example, a *share* as a result of *exercising an option*.

Exercising an option The activation of an *option* to buy or sell, for example, the *shares* to which the option relates.

Expense Any cost incurred which reduces the profits of a particular *accounting period* (as opposed to *capital expenditure* or *prepayments*, for example). Also used as a verb to describe the accounting for a cost incurred when the cost reduces retained profit (rather than, say, increasing fixed assets). 'I'm going to expense the cost of your new laptop'.

Extraordinary item Any expense or income which falls outside the ordinary activities of a company and is not expected to recur.

Fair value Broadly, the price at which you could buy the *asset* or 'sell' the *liability* in an 'orderly' market at the market conditions on the *balance sheet date*.

Fair value hedge A *designated hedging arrangement* under which any change in value in the underlying hedged item would not otherwise be reflected in the *balance sheet* and the change in value in the hedging item (usually a *derivative*) would be, so the change in value in the hedged item *is* therefore reflected in the *P&L*.

Final dividend *Dividend* declared at the end of a company's *fiscal year*. Has to be approved by the *shareholders* and hence is not *recognised* in the *accounts* for that year.

Finance lease A *lease* where the *lessee* (i.e. the user of the *asset*) has the vast majority of the risks and rewards of ownership of the asset, i.e. the lessee effectively owns the asset. For accounting purposes, finance leases are treated as if the lessee had actually bought the asset with a *loan* from the *lessor*.

Financial structure (*Capital structure, Funding structure*) The relative proportions of the funding for a company that are provided by *debt* and *equity*.

First in first out (FIFO) Method of accounting for *stock* whereby, if a company has identical items of stock which cost different amounts to buy or produce, the oldest stock is assumed to be used first.

Fiscal year The year preceding the *balance sheet date* (used for reporting a company's results to its *shareholders*).

Fixed asset (*Non-current asset*) An *asset* used by a company on a long-term continuing basis (as opposed to assets which are used up in a short period of time or are bought to be sold on to customers).

Fixed asset productivity *Sales* divided by the *net book value* of *fixed assets*.

Fixed charge A *charge* over a specific *asset* of a company.

Fixed cost An *expense* which does not change with small changes in the volume of goods produced (examples might include rent, rates, insurance, etc.).

Floating charge A *charge* over all the *assets* of a company rather than any specific asset.

Foreign currency Any currency in which some of a company's transactions are denominated other than its *functional currency*.

Forward An agreement to buy or sell a specified quantity of something on a specified date at a specified price.

Forward P/E (*Prospective P/E*) The *price earnings ratio* calculated using a forecast of the coming year's *earnings*.

Fully diluted earnings per share *Earnings per share* calculated after taking into account unissued *shares* which the company may be forced to issue at some time in the future (as a result of outstanding *options, convertible loanstock*, etc.).

Functional currency The principal currency in which a company operates, as distinct from its *foreign currencies* and its *presentation currency.*

Fundamental principle of accounting The *assets* of a company must always exactly equal the *claims* over those assets.

Funding structure (*Capital structure, Financial structure*) The relative proportions of the funding for a company that are provided by *debt* and *equity.*

Future An agreement to buy or sell a specified quantity of something on a specified date at a specified price. Different from a *forward* inasmuch as futures are typically highly standardised and traded on exchanges around the world.

Gearing (*Debt to equity ratio*) General term used to describe the use of *debt* as well as *equity* to fund a company. The term is used more specifically to describe the ratio of debt to equity.

Going concern concept One of the basic accounting concepts: when preparing a *balance sheet*, it is assumed that the company will continue in business for the foreseeable future.

Goodwill The difference between what an investor company paid for *shares* in a *subsidiary* or an *associate/joint venture* and the net *fair value* of the *assets and liabilities* of the subsidiary/associate/joint venture.

Gross assets The total *assets* of a company before deducting any *liabilities*.

Gross margin *Gross profit* as a percentage of *turnover*.

Gross profit *Turnover* less *cost of goods sold*.

Hedging A transaction undertaken to 'cancel out' the effect of any future change in a variable that may affect a company's profits, such as interest rates, exchange rates, commodity costs.

Historic P/E The *price earnings ratio* calculated using the most recently reported *earnings* figure.

Historical cost convention Accounting convention whereby *assets* are recorded in a company's *books* based on the price paid for them (as opposed to the *market value* or replacement cost of those assets at the *balance sheet date*).

HMRC Abbreviation of Her Majesty's Revenue and Customs, a department of the UK Government responsible for the assessment and collection of taxes.

IAS Abbreviation of *International Accounting Standards*. Refers to individual accounting standards issued with a reference IAS xx, where xx is a number. These standards, together with those issued under an '*IFRS*' reference, make up international accounting standards.

IASB (International Accounting Standards Board) Organisation responsible for issuing the international accounting standards.

IFRS Abbreviation of *International Financial Reporting Standards*. Refers to individual accounting standards issued with a reference IFRS xx, where xx is a number. IFRS is also often used to mean international accounting standards generally.

Impairment The *writing down* of the value of an *asset* when the *recoverable amount* of that asset is below its *carrying value.*

Income statement (Profit & loss account) *A* statement showing how the profit attributable to *shareholders* in a given *fiscal year* was achieved.

Ineffectiveness In relation to a *designated hedging arrangement,* the amount by which the hedging item does not move exactly in step with the movement in the hedged item.

Input Raw material, equipment, service, etc. bought in by a company to enable it to produce its *outputs.*

Insolvent A company is insolvent when it is unable to meet its *liabilities.*

Instrument Essentially a piece of paper conferring rights and obligations on parties. So *shares, loans, trade receivables* are all instruments.

Intangible assets Identifiable, non-monetary *assets* without physical substance, such as computer software, patents, copyrights, brand names, trademarks, customer relationships and customer lists.

Interest The amount paid to lenders in return for the use of their money for a period of time.

Interest cover *Operating profit* divided by *interest* payable.

Interest rate cap A *derivative contract* whereby the buyer is compensated pound for pound to the extent by which interest rates exceed the agreed level, thereby 'capping' the buyer's interest payments.

Interest rate collar (Interest rate floor) A *derivative contract* whereby the buyer is compensated pound for pound to the extent by which interest rates are below the agreed level, thereby putting a 'floor' under the buyer's interest income.

Interest rate swap A *derivative contract* whereby variable interest payments are turned into agreed fixed payments or vice versa.

Interim dividend *Dividend* declared in the course of a company's *fiscal year.*

International Accounting Standards (IAS) Refers to individual accounting standards issued with a reference IAS xx, where xx is a number. These standards, together with those issued under an *'IFRS'* reference, make up international accounting standards.

International Financial Reporting Standards (IFRS) Refers to individual accounting standards issued with a reference IFRS xx, where xx is a number. IFRS is also often used to mean international accounting standards generally.

Inventory (*Stock*) Raw materials, *work in progress* and goods ready for sale ('finished goods').

Inventory turn (*Stock turn*) A measure of how much inventory a company has relative to its sales. Calculated as annual cost of sales divided by year-end inventories.

Investment An *asset* that is not used directly in a company's operations.

Invoice Formal document issued by a supplier company to its customer recording the details of the *transaction*.

Invoice discounting An arrangement whereby a financial institution lends money to a company up to a percentage of the value of the company's *trade receivables*.

Issued share capital (*Allotted share capital*) The number and/or value of the *shares* that have been issued (allotted) to *shareholders*.

Joint venture A joint arrangement whereby the parties that have joint control of the arrangement have rights to the net assets of the arrangement.

Journal entry End-of-period adjustment to a company's accounts (e.g. to *post accruals* or *depreciation*).

Last in first out Method of accounting for *stock* whereby, if a company has identical items of stock which cost different amounts to buy or produce, the newest stock is assumed to be used first.

Lease An agreement whereby the owner of an *asset* (the *lessor*) allows someone else (the *lessee*) to use that asset.

Lessee The user of an *asset* which is owned by someone else but is being used by the lessee under the terms of a *lease*.

Lessor The owner of an *asset* which is being used by someone else under the terms of a *lease*.

Liability Money, goods or services owed by a company.

LIBOR (London Inter Bank Offered Rate) The rate at which banks lend to one another. Used as a reference point for many loans that have variable interest rates. There are different LIBOR figures for different periods such as 3 months, 6 months, 12 months.

Lien (*Charge*) First claim over an *asset* (normally taken as *security* for a *loan*).

Limited company A company whose *shareholders* do not have any *liability* to the company's *creditors* above the amount they have paid into the company as *share capital*. Hence the shareholders have 'limited liability'.

Liquid assets *Assets* which are either cash or can be turned into cash quickly and easily.

Liquidate To sell all of a company's *assets*, pay off the *liabilities* and pay any remaining cash to the shareholders.

Liquidity The ability of a company to pay its short-term *liabilities.*

Listed company (*Quoted company*) A company whose *shares* can be bought or sold readily through a recognised *stock exchange.*

Loan Funding of a fixed amount (unlike an *overdraft,* which varies on a day-to-day basis), with a known rate of *interest,* an agreed repayment schedule and, usually, a *charge* over some or all of the company's *assets.*

Loanstock (*Bond, Long-term loan*) A non-bank *loan* that is typically not due to be repaid for at least 12 months.

Long-term liability (*Non-current liability*) Any *liability* which does not have to be settled within the next twelve months.

Long-term loan (*Bond, Loanstock*) A *loan* which is not due to be repaid for at least twelve months.

Market capitalisation The total *market value* of all the *ordinary shares* of a *listed company.*

Market to book ratio *Market value* of *shares* divided by *book value* of those shares.

Market value The value of an *asset* to an unconnected third party.

Marketable An *asset* is marketable if it can be sold quickly and without affecting the market price of similar assets.

Matching The principle whereby all *expenses* incurred to generate the *sales* of an *accounting period* are *recognised* in the accounts of that period.

Member (*Shareholder*) Holder of *shares* in a company.

Merger accounting A method of accounting for business combinations that is not permitted under *IFRS* and therefore rarely seen.

Merger reserve A component of *shareholders' equity* that arises when a company issues its own *shares* to the owners of an acquired business as part of the *consideration* for the acquisition.

Minority interests (*Non-controlling interests*) When a *parent company* owns less than 100 per cent of a *subsidiary,* the *consolidated accounts* will identify separately 'minority interests' to show the portion of the *net assets* and the year's profits which are attributable to the owners of the minority shareholding rather than to the *shareholders* of the parent company.

Mortgage A *charge* over a specific *asset*.

Net assets (*Net worth*) The total *assets* of a company less its *liabilities*.

Net book value The value of an *asset* as recorded in the company's *books* after allowing for *accumulated depreciation* or *accumulated amortisation*.

Net investment hedge A *designated hedging arrangement* whereby any financing (such as a loan) used to make an investment in a foreign *subsidiary* is paired with the investment, such that any changes in the value of the financing due to exchange rate movement is reflected in *Other comprehensive income* and therefore offsets the movement on translation of the investment.

Net operating assets (*Capital employed*) The total amount of money tied up in a business in the form of *fixed assets* and *working capital*. It is also equal to the sum of the *equity,* the *debt* and any *corporation tax* payable.

Net realisable value The price which could be obtained if an *asset* were sold (after allowing for all costs associated with the sale). The term is usually applied to valuation of *stock*.

Net worth (*Net assets*) The total *assets* of a company less its *liabilities*.

Nominal account Each of the different items that make up a *balance sheet* is a nominal account. In practice, companies often have many hundreds of nominal accounts which are then summarised to produce the balance sheet you see in a company's *annual report.*

Nominal ledger A book or computer program which maintains the details of each of the *nominal accounts.*

Nominal value (*Par value*) The face value of a company's *shares.* The company cannot issue shares for less than this value.

Non-controlling interests (*Minority interests*) When a *parent company* owns less than 100 per cent of a *subsidiary,* the *consolidated accounts* will identify separately 'non-controlling interests' to show the portion of the *net assets* and the year's profits which are attributable to the owners of the minority shareholding rather than to the *shareholders* of the parent company.

Non-current asset (*Fixed asset*) An *asset* used by a company on a long- term continuing basis (as opposed to assets which are used up in a short period of time or are bought to be sold on to customers).

Non-current liability (*Long-term liability*) Any *liability* which does not have to be settled within the next twelve months.

Note of historical cost profits and losses A summary statement showing the additional profit or loss that would have been recorded in the *P&L* if an unrealised gain or loss had not, in a previous year, been *recognised* and shown in the *statement of recognised gains and losses.*

Off-balance sheet finance Funding raised by a company which does not have to be *recognised* on its *balance sheet.*

Operating cash flow The change in a company's cash during an *accounting period* due solely to its *enterprise* (i.e. disregarding *interest/tax/dividend* payments, *equity/debt* issues, etc.).

Operating expense *Expense* incurred by the *enterprise* (i.e. excludes all *funding structure* items such as *interest,* tax, etc.).

Operating lease A *lease* where the *lessee* does not take on substantially all the risks and rewards of ownership of the *asset.*

255

Operating profit (*Earnings before interest and tax, Profit before interest and tax, Trading profit***)** The profit generated by the *enterprise* of a company; i.e. profit before taking account of *interest* (either payable or receivable) and *corporation tax.*

Option The right (but not the obligation) to buy or sell *shares,* commodities, etc. at a specified price (the *exercise price*) during a specified period.

Ordinary dividend *Dividend* paid to holders of *ordinary shares.*

Ordinary share (Common stock, in the USA) The most common *class of share.* Entitles the holder to a proportionate share of *dividends* and *net assets,* and to vote at meetings of the *shareholders.*

Other comprehensive income Any gains or losses made by a company during the year that are not included in the *P&L,* due, for example, to the fact that the gains or losses are not yet *realised.*

Output The product or service produced by a company.

Overdraft Funding provided by a bank. Unlike a *loan,* the amount varies on a day-to-day basis, and is usually repayable on demand. An overdraft carries a known rate of *interest,* and usually the company will have to give the bank a *charge* over some or all of its *assets.*

Overdraft facility Agreed limit of an *overdraft.*

Overheads *Operating expenses* which cannot be directly ascribed to the production of goods or services.

Own share reserve (*Treasury share reserve***)** A component of *shareholders' equity* that arises when a company buys back its own *shares* and holds them for future re-issue (or prior to cancellation of the shares).

Par value (*Nominal value***)** The face value of a company's *shares.* The company cannot issue shares for less than this value.

Parent company A company which has one or more *subsidiaries.*

Participating preference share A *preference share* whose *dividend* is increased if the company meets certain performance criteria.

Payout ratio *Dividends* divided by *profit for the year.*

PEG *Price earnings ratio* divided by growth in *earnings per share.* May be based on prospective earnings or historic earnings.

Petty cash Small amounts of cash held on a company's premises to cover incidental expenses.

Post balance sheet event An event which takes place after the *balance sheet date* but which needs to be disclosed in order that the *annual report* should give a true and fair view of the company's financial position.

Posting Entering a transaction/adjustment onto a company's *balance sheet*.

Preference dividend *Dividend* payable on a *preference share*.

Preference share *Share* which typically has a right to a *dividend* which must be paid in full before the *ordinary shareholders* can be paid a dividend. In a *liquidation* of a company, holders of preference shares typically receive their money back before holders of *ordinary shares* receive anything.

Premium (1) The amount paid in consideration for a *derivative* such as an *option*.

(2) The amount paid in excess of face value for a *bond*.

Prepayment (Deferred expense) A payment made in advance of the receipt of goods or services (e.g. a deposit).

Present value The value 'today' of one or more future cash flows after *discounting* them.

Presentation currency The currency in which a company presents its *accounts* to its *shareholders*. Not necessarily the same as its *functional currency*.

Price earnings ratio (PER, P/E) The price of a company's *ordinary shares* divided by its *earnings per share*. *Prospective PE* is the PE ratio based on today's share price and the forecast earnings per share. *Historic PE* uses the most recently reported historic earnings.

Primary statements The main statements making up a company's accounts all of which have to be given the same level of prominence in the accounts. Under *IFRS*, includes the *P&L, statement of comprehensive income, balance sheet, cash flow statement, statement of changes in equity*.

Prior year adjustment An adjustment to a prior year's *balance sheet*.

Productivity A measure of output divided by a measure of input (e.g. sales per employee, sales per pound of capital employed).

Profit & loss account (P&L) (*Income statement*) A statement showing how the profit attributable to *shareholders* in a given *fiscal year* was achieved.

Profit after tax Profit after taking account of all *expenses* including *interest* and *corporation tax* (but before taking account of any *extraordinary items* and before adjusting for *minority interests*).

Profit before interest and tax (PBIT) (*Earnings before interest and tax, Operating profit, Trading profit*) The profit generated by the *enterprise* of a company, i.e. profit before taking account of *interest* (either payable or receivable) and *corporation tax*.

Profit before tax (PBT) Profit after all *expenses* including *interest* (but before taking account of *corporation tax* and *extraordinary items* and before adjusting for *minority interests*).

Profit for the year (*Earnings*) Profit attributable to *ordinary shareholders* (after taking account of *corporation tax, minority interests, extraordinary items, dividends* on *preference shares* but before taking account of any *dividends* on *ordinary shares*).

Profitability The amount of profit made by a company for each pound of capital invested. Usually measured as *return on capital employed* and/or *return on equity*.

Prospective P/E (*Forward P/E*) The *price earnings ratio* calculated using a forecast of the coming year's *earnings*.

Provision An *expense recognised* in the accounts for a particular *accounting period* to allow for expected losses (e.g. a *doubtful debt*).

Public limited company (plc) A *limited company* which is subject to more stringent legal requirements than a private limited company. All *listed companies* are plcs but a plc need not be listed.

Purchase ledger A book or computer program in which details of suppliers and amounts owed to them are recorded.

Qualified auditors' report An *auditors' report* which has a qualification to the usual 'true and fair view' statement.

Quick ratio *Current assets* less *stock* divided by *current liabilities*.

Quoted company (*Listed company*) A company whose *shares* can be bought or sold readily through a recognised *stock exchange*.

Ranking The order in which different *creditors'* and *shareholders' claims* over the *assets* of a company are met when the company is *wound up* and the assets *distributed*.

Realisation Conversion of an *asset* into cash, or a promise of cash which is reasonably certain to be fulfilled.

Recognition The inclusion of the impact of a *transaction* on a company's *balance sheet*.

Recoverable amount In relation to an asset, the higher of (a) fair value less costs of disposal and (b) value in use.

Redeemable preference share *Preference share* which can (at the option of the company or the preference *shareholder*, depending on what is agreed) be cancelled and the capital invested by the shareholder returned to him or her.

Reserve A *nominal account*, other than *share capital*, which represents a *claim* of the *shareholders* of a company over some of the *assets* of the company. Examples include *retained profit* and *revaluation reserve*.

Retained profit/earnings The total cumulative profits of a company that have been retained (i.e. not distributed to *shareholders* as *dividends*).

Return on capital employed (ROCE) *Operating profit* divided by *capital employed*. The key measure of the financial performance of the *enterprise*.

Return on equity (ROE) *Profit before tax* divided by *shareholders' equity*. Often calculated using *profit after tax* or *profit for the year*.

Return on sales (ROS) *Operating profit* divided by *sales*.

Revaluation reserve A *reserve* created when the *net assets* of a company are increased due to the revaluation of certain of the company's *assets*.

Revenue The amount due to (or paid to) a company in return for the goods or services supplied by that company. Note that revenue is recorded in a company's accounts net of VAT (i.e. after subtracting any VAT added to the invoices).

Revolving credit facility A *loan* from a bank that behaves like an *overdraft* inasmuch as the company can draw down and repay funds as often as it chooses up to the limit of the facility, but which behaves like a *term* loan inasmuch as the bank cannot demand repayment before the end of the term unless the company is in breach of its *covenants*.

Rights issue An issue of new *shares* whereby the *shareholders* have the right to acquire the new shares in proportion to their existing holdings before the shares can be offered to anyone else.

Sales (*Turnover*) The total *revenues* of a company in an *accounting period*.

Sales ledger A book or computer program in which details of customers and amounts owed by them are recorded.

Scrip issue A free issue of additional *shares* to *shareholders* in proportion to their existing holdings. It has no effect on the *market capitalisation* of a company but reduces the price of each share.

Security (1) Rights over certain *assets* of a company given when a *loan* or *overdraft* are made available to the company. If the terms of the loan or overdraft are breached then the rights can normally be exercised to enable the lenders to get their money back.
(2) A general term for any type of *equity* or *debt*.

Senior debt Borrowings a company has made that are at the top of the *ranking* of the company's *creditors* – i.e. the holders of senior debt will get their money back first if the company gets into trouble.

Share One of the equal parts into which any particular *class* of a company's *share capital* is divided. Each *share* entitles its owner to a proportion of the *assets* due to that class of share capital.

Share-based payment Payments made, typically to employees but also to others, either in the company's *shares* or in cash where the amount is determined by reference to the value of the company's shares.

Share-based payment reserve A *component of equity* in which the future potential issue of *shares* under a *share-based payment* scheme is *recognised*.

Share capital The *nominal value* of the *shares* issued by a company. The term is also used more generally to describe any funding raised by a company in return for shares.

Share premium The amount paid for a company's *shares* over and above the *nominal value* of those shares.

Share price The *market value* of each *share* in a company.

Shareholder (*Member*) Holder of *shares* in a company.

Shareholders' equity/funds (*Equity, Capital and reserves*) The shareholders' *claims* over the *assets* of the company. Consists of *share capital, share premium, retained profit,* and any other *reserves.*

Short-term loan A *loan* which is due to be repaid within 12 months of the *balance sheet date.*

Statement of changes in equity A *primary statement* explaining the movements during the *accounting period* of each *component of shareholders' equity.*

Statement of comprehensive income A *primary statement* setting out all the gains and losses of the company during the *accounting period,* including those that are reflected in the *P&L.*

Statement of financial position (*Balance sheet*) Statement of a company's *assets* and the *claims* over those assets at any given moment (i.e. at the *balance sheet date*).

Statement of recognised gains and losses A statement that records any gains or losses *recognised* during the financial year but which do not appear in the *P&L.*

Stock (*Inventory*) Raw materials, *work in progress* and goods ready for sale ('finished goods').

Stock In the USA, the equivalent of *shares.*

Stock days The number of days' worth of *stock* a company has at the *balance sheet date.* Calculated as year-end stock divided by daily cost of sales (*cost of sales* for the year divided by 365).

Stock exchange A market on which a company's *shares* can be *listed* (and therefore be readily bought and sold).

Stock turn (*Inventory turn*) A measure of how much *stock* a company has relative to its *sales.* Calculated as annual *cost of sales* divided by year-end stock.

Strategic report Report in the *annual report* containing an overview of the company, its business and performance.

Subordinated debt *Long-term debt* that ranks behind other *creditors.* Thus, if a company is *wound up,* all other creditors are paid in full before the subordinated debt holders receive anything.

Subsidiary undertaking (Subsidiary) Broadly speaking, a company is a subsidiary of another company (the *parent company*) if the parent company owns more than 50 per cent of the voting rights and/or exerts a dominant influence over the subsidiary.

Tangible fixed asset A *fixed asset* that can be touched, such as property, plant, equipment.

Taxable income The income on which *HMRC* calculates the *corporation tax* payable by a company.

Term Duration of a *loan, redeemable preference share* or other *instrument.*

Trade creditor days The number of days' worth of purchases that have not been paid for by the company at the year end. Calculated as year-end trade creditors divided by daily purchases (excluding VAT in both cases).

Trade creditors (*Accounts payable, Trade payables*) The amount a company owes its suppliers at any given moment.

Trade debtor days The number of days' worth of sales that have not been paid for by customers at the year end. Calculated as year-end trade debtors divided by daily sales (excluding VAT in both cases).

Trade debtors (*Accounts receivable, Trade receivables*) The amount a company is owed by its customers at any given moment.

Trade investment A long-term *investment* made by one company in another for strategic, trading reasons.

Trade payables (*Accounts payable, Trade creditors*) The amount a company owes to its suppliers at any given moment.

Trade receivables (*Accounts receivable, Trade debtors*) The amount a company is owed by its customers at any given moment.

Trading profit (*Operating profit, Profit before interest and tax, Earnings before interest and tax*) The profit generated by the *enterprise* of a company; i.e. profit before taking account of *interest* (either payable or receivable) and *corporation tax.*

Transaction Anything a company does which affects its financial position (and therefore its *balance sheet*).

Translation reserve A *component of equity* that arises when a company recognises a currency gain or loss on the translation of a foreign *subsidiary's* accounts into the *presentation currency* of the *parent.*

Treasury share reserve (*Own share reserve*) A *component of shareholders' equity* that arises when a company buys back its own *shares* and holds them for future re-issue (or prior to cancellation of the shares).

Treasury shares A company's own *shares* that it has bought back from *shareholders* and not yet cancelled or re-issued.

Trend analysis Method of assessing a company by analysing the trends in its performance measures over a period of time.

Trial balance (TB) A list of all the *nominal accounts,* showing the balance in each. It is, in effect, a very detailed *balance sheet.*

Turnover (*Sales*) The total *revenues* of a company in an *accounting period.*

Value added The difference between a company's *outputs* and *inputs.*

Variable cost An *expense* which changes even with small changes in volume (e.g. raw materials costs).

Vesting The process by which an employee acquires unconditional rights under *share-based payment* schemes or pension schemes.

Wind up Cease trading and *liquidate* a company.

Working capital The amount of additional funding required by a company to operate its *fixed assets,* e.g. money to pay staff and bills while waiting for customers to pay. Working capital is equal to *capital employed* less fixed assets.

Working capital productivity *Sales* divided by *working capital.*

Work in progress Goods due for sale but still in the course of production at the *balance sheet date.*

Write up/down/off Revalue an *asset* (upwards, downwards or down to zero) or, in the case of 'write off', to put any cost into the *P&L* (i.e. reduce *retained profit*) in the current year rather than *capitalise* it (also known as *expensing*).

Appendix 1: **Wingate Foods' accounts**

Strategic report

The directors present their strategic report for the year ended 31 December, Year 5.

Review of the business

The principal activity of the company is the production and sale of confectionery and biscuits.

Although the UK market for the company's products is not showing significant growth, the company intends to continue its growth by:

- ► gaining market share in the UK through the introduction of new products to its existing UK customers; and
- ► commencing exports to new customers in France, Germany and Scandinavia.

Over the last few years, the company has invested in its production facilities in order to improve efficiency to help the company compete in a very competitive market place.

The directors use a number of key performance indicators to manage the business, the principal ones being turnover, operating profit and profit before tax.

The directors' objectives are to continue to grow turnover, operating profit and profit before tax such that the company can steadily increase its dividends to shareholders each year.

Principal risks and uncertainties

The principal risks faced by the company include:

▶ The price pressure resulting from the power of the company's major customers. This is expected to continue and the company will continue to improve production efficiency to maintain margins.

▶ The risk that the international expansion strategy will not be successful.

▶ Government changes in excise duty rates and regulation.

Performance

The directors believe the company to be in a healthy financial position. The highlights are set out below.

£'000	Year 5	Year 4
Turnover	10,427	8,619
Operating profit	919	818
Profit before tax	594	557
Dividends proposed	215	184
Net assets	2,847	2,568

This strategic report was approved by the board on 31 March, Year 6.

Directors' report

The directors submit their report and the audited financial statements for year five.

Results for the year

Sales increased by 21.0 per cent from £8.6m in year four to £10.4m in year five. Profit before tax increased by 6.6 per cent from £557k in year four to £594k in year five.

The directors propose the payment of a final dividend of 21.5p per share for year five (year four: 18.4p).

Statement of directors' responsibilities

The directors are responsible for preparing the Strategic Report, the Directors' Report and the financial statements of the company in accordance with applicable law and regulations.

Company law requires the directors to prepare accounts of the company for each financial year. Under that law the directors have elected to prepare the accounts of the company in accordance with United Kingdom Generally Accepted Accounting Practice (United Kingdom Accounting Standards and applicable law). Under company law the directors must not approve the accounts of the company unless they are satisfied that they give a true and fair view of the state of affairs of the company and of the profit or loss of the company for that period. In preparing these accounts of the company, the directors are required to:

- select suitable accounting policies and then apply them consistently;
- make judgments and estimates that are reasonable and prudent;
- state whether applicable UK Accounting Standards have been followed, subject to any material departures disclosed and explained in the financial statements;
- prepare the financial statements on the going concern basis unless it is inappropriate to presume that the company will continue in business.

The directors are responsible for keeping adequate accounting records that are sufficient to show and explain the company's transactions and disclose with reasonable accuracy at any time the financial position of the company and enable them to ensure that the accounts of the company comply with the Companies Act 2006. They are also responsible for safeguarding the assets of the company and hence for taking reasonable steps for the prevention and detection of fraud and other irregularities.

Provision of information to auditors

Each of the persons who are directors at the time when this Directors' Report is approved has confirmed that:

- ▶ so far as that director is aware, there is no relevant audit information of which the company's auditors are unaware; and
- ▶ that director has taken all the steps that ought to have been taken as a director in order to be aware of any information needed by the company's auditors in connection with preparing their report and to establish that the company's auditors are aware of that information.

Auditors

The auditors of the company are ABC Accountants. A resolution to reappoint them will be proposed at the annual general meeting in accordance with section 485 of the Companies Act 2006.

By order of the Board

ANO Secretary

Secretary

31 March, year six

Independent auditors' report to the members of Wingate Foods Ltd

We have audited the financial statements of Wingate Foods Limited for the year ended 31 December, year five, set out on pages 271 to 279. The financial reporting framework that has been applied in their preparation is applicable law and United Kingdom Accounting Standards (United Kingdom Generally Accepted Accounting Practice).

This report is made solely to the company's members, as a body, in accordance with Chapter 3 of Part 16 of the Companies Act 2006. Our audit work has been undertaken so that we might state to the company's members those matters we are required to state to them in an Auditors' Report and for no other purpose. To the fullest extent permitted by law, we do not accept or assume responsibility to anyone other than the company and the company's members as a body, for our audit work, for this report, or for the opinions we have formed.

Respective responsibilities of directors and auditors

As explained more fully in the Statement of Directors' Responsibilities, the directors are responsible for the preparation of the financial statements and for being satisfied that they give a true and fair view. Our responsibility is to audit the financial statements in accordance with applicable law and International Standards on Auditing (UK and Ireland). Those standards require us to comply with the Auditing Practices Board's Ethical Standards for Auditors.

Scope of the audit of the financial statements

An audit involves obtaining evidence about the amounts and disclosures in the financial statements sufficient to give reasonable assurance that the financial statements are free from material misstatement, whether caused by fraud or error. This includes an assessment of: whether the accounting policies are appropriate to the company's circumstances and have been consistently applied and adequately disclosed; the reasonableness of significant accounting estimates made by the directors; and the overall presentation of the financial statements.

Opinion on financial statements

In our opinion the financial statements:

- ► give a true and fair view of the state of the company's affairs as at 31 December, year five and of its profit for the year then ended;

- ► have been properly prepared in accordance with United Kingdom Generally Accepted Accounting Practice; and

- ► have been prepared in accordance with the requirements of the Companies Act 2006.

Opinion on other matters prescribed by the Companies Act 2006

In our opinion the information given in the Directors' Report for the financial year for which the financial statements are prepared is consistent with the financial statements.

Matters on which we are required to report by exception

We have nothing to report in respect of the following matters where the Companies Act 2006 requires us to report to you if, in our opinion:

- ► adequate accounting records have not been kept, or returns adequate for our audit have not been received from branches not visited by us; or

- ► the financial statements are not in agreement with the accounting records and returns; or

- ► certain disclosures of directors' remuneration specified by law are not made; or

- ► we have not received all the information and explanations we require for our audit.

ANO Auditor (Senior statutory auditor)

for and on behalf of

ABC Accountants, Statutory Auditor

31 March, year six

WINGATE FOODS LTD
Profit and loss account for year five

	Notes	£'000 Year 5	£'000 Year 4
Turnover	2	10,427	8,619
Cost of sales		(8,078)	(6,628)
Gross profit		2,349	1,991
Distribution expenses		(832)	(673)
Administration expenses		(598)	(500)
Operating profit	3	919	818
Interest payable	5	(325)	(261)
Profit before tax		594	557
Taxation	6	(131)	(130)
Profit for the year		463	427
Dividends	7	(184)	(153)
Retained profit for the year		279	274
Earnings per share (pence)		46.3	42.7

There were no recognised gains or losses other than the profit for the year.

All the activities of the group are classed as continuing.

WINGATE FOODS LTD

Balance sheet at 31 December, year five

	Notes	£'000 Year 5	£'000 Year 4
Fixed assets			
Tangible assets	8	5,326	4,445
Current assets			
Stock	9	1,231	953
Debtors	10	2,239	1,596
Cash		12	17
Total current assets		3,482	2,566
Current liabilities	11	2,906	2,192
Long-term liabilities	12	3,055	2,251
Net assets		**2,847**	**2,568**
Shareholders' equity			
Share capital	15	50	50
Share premium		275	275
Retained profit		2,522	2,243
Total shareholders' equity		2,847	2,568

The financial statements were approved and authorised for issue by the board and were signed on its behalf on 31 March, year six

....

Director A

WINGATE FOODS LTD

Cash flow statement for year five

	Notes	£'000 Year 5	£'000 Year 4
Operating activities			
Operating profit		919	818
Depreciation		495	402
Profit on sale of fixed assets		(8)	0
Increase in stock		(278)	(172)
Increase in debtors		(643)	(423)
Increase in creditors		207	95
Cash flow from operating activities		692	720
Capital expenditure			
Purchase of fixed assets		(1,391)	(642)
Proceeds on sale of fixed assets		23	0
Total capital expenditure		(1,368)	(642)
Returns on investments and servicing of finance			
Interest paid		(325)	(261)
Total interest		(325)	(261)
Taxation			
Corporation tax paid		(130)	(134)
Total taxation		(130)	(134)
Equity dividends paid			
Dividends on ordinary shares		(184)	(153)
Total equity dividends paid		(184)	(153)
Financing			
Loans drawn down		1,500	800
Loan repayments		(350)	(250)
Capital element of finance leases		(152)	(109)
Total financing		998	441
Increase/(decrease) in cash		(317)	(29)

WINGATE FOODS LTD

Net debt

	£'000	£'000
	Year 5	Year 4
Reconciliation of net cash flow to movement in net debt		
Increase/(decrease) in cash	(317)	(29)
(Increase)/decrease in loans	(1,150)	(550)
(Increase)/decrease in finance leases	152	(453)
(Increase)/decrease in net debt	(1,315)	(1,032)
Net debt at start of year	(3,357)	(2,325)
Net debt at end of year	(4,672)	(3,357)

Analysis of changes in net debt

	Balance at start of Year 5 £'000	Cash flows £'000	Balance at end of Year 5 £'000
Cash	17	(5)	12
Bank overdraft	(621)	(312)	(933)
Net cash/(overdraft)	(604)	(317)	(921)
Bank loans	(2,000)	(1,150)	(3,150)
Finance leases	(753)	152	(601)
Net total debt	(3,357)	(1,315)	(4,672)

WINGATE FOODS LTD

Notes to the accounts for year five

1 ACCOUNTING POLICIES

(a) Basis of accounting

The accounts have been prepared under the historical cost convention. The directors are of the opinion that the company has access to sufficient funds to meet its day-to-day working capital requirements for a period of at least 12 months from the approval of these accounts. On this basis, the directors consider it appropriate to prepare the financial statements on the going concern basis.

(b) Turnover

Turnover represents the invoiced value of goods sold net of value added tax. Turnover is recognised as income in the profit and loss account on the date the goods are delivered or otherwise made available to the company's customers.

(c) Tangible fixed assets

Depreciation is provided at rates calculated to write off the cost of each asset evenly over its expected useful life as follows:

Freehold buildings	2 per cent straight line basis
Plant and equipment	10 per cent or 20 per cent straight line basis
Motor vehicles	25 per cent straight line basis

Land is not depreciated.

(d) Stocks

Manufactured goods include the costs of production. Stock and work in progress are valued at the lower of cost and net realisable value. Bought in goods are valued at purchase cost on a **first in first out** basis.

(e) Leasing

Where an asset is acquired under a finance lease, it is capitalised and the liability to the leasing company included in creditors. Payments are treated as consisting of capital and interest elements. The interest is charged to the P&L over the term of the lease.

All leases that are not finance leases are operating leases. Rentals payable under operating leases are charged against income on a straight line basis over the lease term.

---

2 TURNOVER AND PROFIT

Turnover is stated net of value added tax. Turnover and profit before taxation are attributable to the one principal activity.

	£'000	£'000
3 OPERATING PROFIT	**Year 5**	**Year 4**
Operating profit is stated after crediting/(charging):		
Depreciation of tangible fixed assets	(495)	(402)
Auditors' remuneration	(22)	(19)
Profit on sale of fixed assets	8	–
Hire of plant and machinery	(17)	(12)
Total	(526)	(433)

4 EMPLOYEES

The average number of employees during the year was as follows:		
Office and management	34	28
Manufacturing	47	41
Total	81	69
Staff costs during the year amounted to:		
Wages and salaries	1,211	983
Social security	110	72
Pension costs	32	28
Total	1,353	1,083
Directors' remuneration		
Emoluments – all directors (excluding pension contributions)	199	174
Pension contributions – all directors	22	20
Emoluments of highest paid director (excluding pension contributions)	65	59
Highest paid director – pension contributions	7	6

5 INTEREST PAYABLE

Overdraft and bank loans	243	196
Interest element of finance leases	82	65
Total	325	261

6 TAXATION

The tax charge on the profit on ordinary activities for the year was as follows:		
Corporation tax on the results for the year	131	130

	£'000	£'000
7 DIVIDENDS	Year 5	Year 4

Dividends paid during the year in respect of the
previous financial year   184   153

The directors propose a dividend of £215,000 (21.5p per share) in respect of Year 5 (Year 4 : £184k). This dividend is subject to the approval of the shareholders and has not, therefore, been included in the Company's balance sheet as a liability at 31 December, Year 5.

8 TANGIBLE FIXED ASSETS

	Land and Buildings £'000	Plant and Equipment £'000	Motor Vehicles £'000	Total £'000
Cost				
At start of Year 5	3,401	2,503	588	6,492
Additions	570	656	165	1,391
Disposals	–	(35)	–	(35)
At end of Year 5	3,971	3,124	753	7,848
Depreciation				
At start of Year 5	269	1,430	348	2,047
On disposals	–	(20)	–	(20)
Charge for the year	46	345	104	495
At end of Year 5	315	1,755	452	2,522
Net book value				
At start of Year 5	3,132	1,073	240	4,445
At end of Year 5	3,656	1,369	301	5,326

	£'000	£'000
9 STOCKS AND WORK IN PROGRESS	Year 5	Year 4
Raw materials	352	287
Work in progress	17	12
Finished goods	862	654
Total	1,231	953

	£'000 Year 5	£'000 Year 4
10 DEBTORS		
Trade debtors less provision for doubtful debts	2,125	1,502
Prepayments	78	66
Other debtors	36	28
Total	2,239	1,596
11 CURRENT LIABILITIES		
Trade creditors	863	721
Social security and other taxes	150	115
Accruals	113	93
Cash in advance	20	10
Sub-total	1,146	939
Bank overdraft	933	621
Current portion of bank loans	525	350
Current portion of finance lease liability	171	152
Taxation	131	130
Total	2,906	2,192
12 LONG-TERM LIABILITIES		
Bank loans	2,625	1,650
Finance lease liability	430	601
Total	3,055	2,251

The bank loans are secured by a charge over the company's assets

13 CAPITAL AND RESERVES £'000

	Share capital	Share premium	Retained profit	Total
As at 1 January, Year 5	50	275	2,243	2,568
Profit for the year	–	–	463	463
Dividends paid	–	–	(184)	(184)
As at 31 December, Year 5	50	275	2,522	2,847

	£'000	£'000
	Year 5	Year 4
14 RECONCILIATION OF MOVEMENTS IN SHAREHOLDERS' EQUITY		
Shareholders' equity at 1 January, Year 5	2,568	2,294
Profit for the year	463	427
Dividends paid	(184)	(153)
Shareholders' equity at 31 December, Year 5	2,847	2,568

15 CALLED UP SHARE CAPITAL

Authorised		
1,500,000 ordinary shares of 5p each	75	75
Issued and fully paid		
1,000,000 ordinary shares of 5p each	50	50

16 FINANCIAL COMMITMENTS

At 31 December, Year 5, the company was committed to making the following payments under non-cancellable operating leases in the year to 31 December, Year 6:

	Plant and machinery	
	£'000	£'000
	Year 5	Year 4
Operating leases which expire:		
Between two and five years	19	21
Future liabilities under finance leases are as follows :		
Leases expiring within two to five years	727	961

At 31 December, Year 5, the company was committed to the future purchase of plant and equipment at a total cost of £126,300 (Year 4: £287,800).

Appendix 2: **Listco's accounts**

Listco plc: Consolidated income statement

£'m		52 weeks ended 31 Dec Year 5	52 weeks ended 31 Dec Year 4
1	**Continuing operations**		
2	Revenue	784.2	718.6
3	Cost of sales	(461.6)	(425.8)
4	Gross profit	322.6	292.8
5	Distribution expenses	(85.2)	(78.8)
6	Administration expenses	(147.2)	(132.4)
7	Exceptional items	(14.5)	(2.4)
8	Operating profit	75.7	79.2
9	Finance income	10.2	4.7
10	Finance costs	(6.0)	(9.2)
11	Share of profit of associated undertakings	4.6	3.9
12	Profit before tax	84.5	78.6
13	Taxation	(18.1)	(17.8)
14	Profit from continuing operations	66.4	60.8
15	Profit/(loss) from discontinued operations	(7.9)	(1.8)
16	**Group profit for the year**	**58.5**	**59.0**
17			
18	**Profit for the period attributable to ...**		
19	Parent's shareholders	53.3	54.6
20	Non-controlling interests	5.2	4.4
21	Total	58.5	59.0
22			
23	**Earnings per share attributable to the equity shareholders**		
24	Basic earnings per share – pence		
25	Continuing operations	21.5	19.5
26	Discontinued operations	(2.3)	(0.5)
27	Group total	19.2	19.0
28	Diluted earnings per share – pence		
29	Continuing operations	20.9	19.1
30	Discontinued operations	(2.2)	(0.5)
31	Group total	18.7	18.6
32			
33	Adjusted earnings per share – pence		
34	Basic EPS	28.1	23.3
35	Diluted EPS	27.3	22.7

Listco plc: Consolidated statement of comprehensive income

£'m	52 weeks ended 31 Dec Year 5	52 weeks ended 31 Dec Year 4
1 **Profit for the year**	58.5	59.0
2		
3 **Other comprehensive income**		
4 Items that will not be reclassifed to the P&L in future periods		
5 Actuarial gains/(losses) on defined benefit pension scheme	(2.8)	(3.5)
6 Deferred tax on the above	0.2	1.1
7 Total	(2.6)	(2.4)
8 Items that may be reclassified to the P&L in future periods		
9 Exchange differences on translation of foreign operations	0.8	(1.4)
10 Cashflow hedges	(0.3)	(1.8)
11 Cashflow hedges recycled to P&L	(2.4)	(0.8)
12 Deferred tax in respect of cashflow hedge movements	0.5	0.2
13 Revaluation of property	10.2	0.0
14 Tax on the above	(2.2)	0.0
15 Total	6.6	(3.8)
16		
17 Total other comprehensive income	4.0	(6.2)
18		
19 **Total comprehensive income for the year**	62.5	52.8
20		
21 **Attributable to ...**		
22 Equity holders of the group	57.3	48.4
23 Non-controlling interests	5.2	4.4
24 Total	62.5	52.8

Listco plc: Consolidated statement of financial position

	£'m	52 weeks ended 31 Dec Year 5	52 weeks ended 31 Dec Year 4
1	**Assets**		
2	Non-current assets		
3	Goodwill	135.6	149.6
4	Other Intangible assets	92.6	91.2
5	Property, plant and equipment	135.4	108.1
6	Investments in associates and joint ventures	32.3	27.7
7	Deferred tax asset	4.0	1.4
8	Non-current assets held for sale	15.4	0.0
9	Total	415.3	378.0
10	Current assets		
11	Inventory	101.1	92.6
12	Trade and other receivables	184.4	163.4
13	Other financial assets	5.5	5.5
14	Cash and cash equivalents	34.5	13.4
15	Total	325.5	274.9
16			
17	**Total assets**	**740.8**	**652.9**
18			
19	**Liabilities**		
20	Current liabilities		
21	Borrowings	45.6	36.4
22	Trade and other payables	117.8	134.9
23	Other financial liabilities	4.3	6.0
24	Corporation tax payable	10.4	8.7
25	Total	178.1	186.0
26	Non-current liabilities		
27	Borrowings	64.2	63.2
28	Provisions	2.4	1.9
29	Deferred tax liability	3.5	0.8
30	Pension liabilities	25.1	23.4
31	Total	95.2	89.3
32			
33	**Total liabilities**	**273.3**	**275.3**
34			
35	**NET ASSETS**	**467.5**	**377.6**

£'m		52 weeks ended 31 Dec Year 5	52 weeks ended 31 Dec Year 4
36			
37	**Equity**		
38	Shareholders' equity		
39	'Share' related		
40	Ordinary share capital	31.2	29.3
41	Share premium	206.2	176.5
42	Capital redemption reserve	5.3	4.8
43	Own shares reserve	(20.3)	(22.3)
44	Share-based payment reserve	14.1	10.4
45	'Profit' related		
46	Translation reserve	(2.6)	(3.4)
47	Hedging reserve	(2.5)	(0.3)
48	Revaluation reserve	11.4	3.4
49	Retained profits	197.9	157.0
50	Total shareholders' equity	440.7	355.4
51	Non-controlling interests	26.8	22.2
52	**Total equity**	**467.5**	**377.6**

Listco plc: Consolidated cash flow statement

£'m	52 weeks ended 31 Dec Year 5	52 weeks ended 31 Dec Year 4
1 **Cash flow from operating activities**		
2 Profit before tax	84.5	78.6
3 Share of post tax profit of associates	(4.6)	(3.9)
4 Finance income and expense	(4.2)	4.5
5 Operating profit	75.7	79.2
6 Add back non-cash items that are in profit figure above		
7 Depreciation	16.9	13.9
8 Amortisation	5.8	5.5
9 Impairment of goodwill	14.0	0.0
10 Loss/(profit) on disposal of PP&E	1.1	0.0
11 Share-based payments in the period	6.0	5.4
12 Operating cashflow before changes in working capital	119.5	104.0
13 Adjustments for working capital		
14 (Increase)/decrease in inventories	(13.6)	(4.1)
15 (Increase)/decrease in trade receivables	(26.1)	(7.2)
16 (Increase)/decrease in other receivables	(7.3)	(6.0)
17 Increase/(decrease) in trade payables	4.0	1.6
18 Increase/(decrease) in social security and other taxes	(2.1)	2.0
19 Increase/(decrease) in accruals and deferred income	(5.5)	10.2
20 Increase/(decrease) in provisions	0.5	(1.2)
21 Movement in retirement benefit liabilities	(1.1)	(2.5)
22 Net cash flow from continuing operations	68.3	96.8
23 Discontinued operations	(6.3)	(0.1)
24 Net cash flow from all operations	62.0	96.7
25 Income tax paid	(19.1)	(18.0)
26 Net cash flow from operating activities	42.9	78.7
27		
28 **Cash flow from investing activities**		
29 Proceeds on disposal of PP&E	0.7	0.0
30 Purchase of intangible assets	(7.2)	(6.9)
31 Purchase of PP&E	(45.5)	(42.2)
32 Purchase of financial assets	(1.0)	1.0

£'m		52 weeks ended 31 Dec Year 5	52 weeks ended 31 Dec Year 4
33	Sale/settlement of financial assets/liabilities	2.0	(1.0)
34	Finance income received	4.4	3.5
35	Investment income received	0.4	0.2
36	Net cashflow from investing activities	(46.2)	(45.4)
37			
38	**Cash flow from financing activities**		
39	Finance costs paid	(6.0)	(6.6)
40	Borrowings drawn down	21.8	15.2
41	Borrowings repaid (inc finance leases)	(16.4)	(17.2)
42	Proceeds from issue of shares	35.5	3.0
43	Proceeds from re-issue of Treasury shares	2.0	1.0
44	Purchase of own shares	(10.6)	(12.7)
45	Dividends paid to parent's shareholders	(3.6)	(3.2)
46	Dividends paid to NCI's	(0.6)	(0.5)
47	Net cashflow from financing activities	22.1	(21.0)
48			
49	**Net increase in cash and cash equivalents**	**18.8**	**12.3**
50			
51	**Cash and cash equivalents at start of period**	**0.6**	**(14.4)**
52	Net increase in cash and cash equivalents	18.8	12.3
53	Effect of currency translation	(2.5)	2.7
54	**Cash and cash equivalents at end of period**	**16.9**	**0.6**

Note: Cash and cash equivalents includes overdrafts

Listco plc: Consolidated statement of changes in equity, Year 5

£m		Ordinary share capital	Share premium	Capital redemption reserve	Own shares reserve	Share-based payment reserve	Translation reserve	Hedging reserve	Revaluation reserve	Retained profits	Total equity holders interests	Non-controlling interests	Total
1	Balance at end of Year 4	29.3	176.5	4.8	(22.3)	10.4	(3.4)	(0.3)	3.4	157.0	355.4	22.2	377.6
2													
3	**Changes during year 5**												
4	Total comprehensive income												
5	Profit for the period	A									53.3	53.3	5.2	58.5
6	Other comprehensive income	B												
7	Exchange differences arising on translation							0.8				0.8	–	0.8
8	Revaluation of land and buildings									10.2		10.2	–	10.2
9	Cashflow hedges								(0.3)			(0.3)	–	(0.3)
10	Cashflow hedges recycled to P&L								(2.4)			(2.4)	–	(2.4)
11	Remeasurement of pension liabilities										(2.8)	(2.8)	–	(2.8)
12	Deferred tax on all the above								0.5	(2.2)	0.2	(1.5)	–	(1.5)
13	Total comprehensive income (A+B)		0.0	0.0	0.0	0.0	0.0	0.8	(2.2)	8.0	50.7	57.3	5.2	62.5
14	Transactions with owners	C												
15	Issue of share capital for cash		2.2	32.5								34.7	–	34.7
16	Issue of shares for share options exercised		0.2	0.6								0.8	–	0.8
17	Treasury shares purchased					(10.6)						(10.6)	–	(10.6)
18	Cancellation of own shares held as treasury shares		(0.5)	(3.4)	0.5	6.8					(3.4)	0.0	–	0.0
19	Treasury shares used for share schemes					5.8	(1.0)				(2.8)	2.0	–	2.0
20	Cost of share-based payments in the period						6.0					6.0	–	6.0
21	Tax on the above						(1.3)					(1.3)	–	(1.3)
22	Payment of dividends										(3.6)	(3.6)	(0.6)	(4.2)
23	Total transactions with owners		1.9	29.7	0.5	2.0	3.7	0.0	0.0	0.0	(9.8)	28.0	(0.6)	27.4
24														
25	**Total changes in the period**		1.9	29.7	0.5	2.0	3.7	0.8	(2.2)	8.0	40.9	85.3	4.6	89.9
26														
27	**Balance at end of year 5**		31.2	206.2	5.3	(20.3)	14.1	(2.6)	(2.5)	11.4	197.9	440.7	26.8	467.5

Index

Note: Reference should also be made to the Glossary on pages 239-263.